M O D U L A R
W E B   D E S I G N

Creating Reusable Components for User Experience Design

Nathan Curtis

Peachpit
Press

Modular Web Design: Creating Reusable Components for User Experience Design and Documentation

Nathan Curtis

New Riders
1249 Eighth Street
Berkeley, CA 94710
510/524-2178
510/524-2221 (fax)

Find us on the Web at www.newriders.com
To report errors, please send a note to errata@peachpit.com
New Riders is an imprint of Peachpit, a division of Pearson Education

Acquisitions Editor: MICHAEL NOLAN
Project Editor: VALERIE WITTE
Technical Editor: AUSTIN GOVELLA
Copyeditor: DOUG ADRIANSON
Proofreader: SCOUT FESTA
Production Editor: CORY BORMAN
Composition and Interior Design: MAUREEN FORYS
Indexer: VALERIE HAYNES PERRY
Cover Design: TERRI BOGAARDS

ISBN-13: 978-0-321-60135-3

ISBN-10: 0-321-60135-1

9 8 7 6 5 4 3 2 1

Printed and bound in the United States of America

To my son Liam,
with whom I build.

To my daughter Caroline,
who tears down with glee.

And to my wife Tina,
who makes it so we can all play.

Foreword

THE OTHER MORNING I got called into an emergency online meeting to look at a new design that one of our marketing groups had created and needed to roll out worldwide on a one-day deadline. Frankly, I feared the worst. Cisco is a pretty big company, and in a typical week I may see between 10 and 20 different designs, some of which in their first incarnations start with visual comps of things our Web team can't quickly implement, or otherwise take liberties with the brand identity or style and therefore require a course correction. (If you work in a design group anywhere, I am sure you will empathize.)

As I opened the PDF from the marketing group, I had a delightful surprise: The group had recently adopted our standard wireframing templates, pioneered by Nathan Curtis, and everything they had put together on this fast-turn project was completely standard. In discussing the design with them, I made one note on a component that they'd placed in an unusual location, and that was that. Design approved, deadline met. And I knew that there would be a good-looking, user-tested visual design and HTML code and style sheets available from our off-the-shelf library to back up what they had designed.

At Cisco, we have a component system that includes all of the commonly used capabilities on our sites. Increasingly, this system extends down to the level of HTML code and CSS. We put this system in place not because a central group has tight control of every page, but because we don't. Our Web teams are distributed and work collaboratively, and need to work from standard templates and documentation so that all of the pieces on our millions of Web pages work together.

Our employees who support our designs across our many Web areas are distributed worldwide, and in addition we have dozens of vendors worldwide who produce new creative. The fact that we have templates—that work down to the component level—is a big win for global consistency.

In the years I have worked with him, Nathan Curtis has been a passionate and tireless advocate for the component-driven design approach to design and design systems that ultimately made the above possible, including that pleasant interaction with that marketing group's design. Nathan's natural, module-driven philosophy can benefit almost any size of Web or mobile experience, and is essential for large sites that often manage hundreds of key experiences and present them via millions of pages that need to stay consistent and clear.

I am looking forward to having this book within easy reach at work and at home.

—*Martin Hardee*
Director, Web Experience Design, Cisco

Preface

BY THE FALL OF 2007, I'd been working on—and become fascinated by—the component libraries that teams use to efficiently and consistently create user experience. I'd been "thinking components" for much longer. So when my family traveled back to my boyhood home in northeastern Ohio for Thanksgiving, I wasn't prepared for the giant revelation that awaited me.

On the holiday morning, we were all sitting around the living room, and my mom dumped out a huge container of LEGO bricks in front of my 2-year-old son. He was awestruck and dove right in, putting all sorts of pieces together. As he built "ships" and other things, I uncovered the directions for building an actual, formal spaceship. He was intrigued, so I took advantage of a "teachable moment" to show him how to build LEGO constructions.

Whoa. As I slowly sifted through the massive LEGO pile, retrieving each individual piece, my son quickly lost interest and began building his own stuff again. So I set about finding all the pieces we needed, one by one, for over an hour. The set wasn't that big, but it took forever to source the collection. As I did so, I laid them out on the floor in an organized way, arranging pieces in rows and columns based on shape, size, color, and other facets. When done, my son and I launched into building the ship, and got it done in no time at all. And he was ecstatic.

Partway through that process, I realized that "this is what I do for my job."

As a designer, each project begins with stakeholders requesting that we design and build something for them, much like some sort of spaceship. They may even bring a picture of what they want: a shiny fighter with all the latest bells and whistles.

Our initial reaction, knowing that we've built lots of ships before, is to respond with, "Well, here's how we build ships. It's not exactly like your picture, but it flies, goes really fast, has adjustable wings, engines, a cockpit, missiles, landing gear—the works." Collaborative discussions yield a common understanding of what they'll get, and then we go to the proverbial big bucket of LEGO to get started.

What do we find? An unorganized morass of all sorts of pieces. We start with the best intentions, but we must build it fast. We dump out all the LEGO on the floor. We grab pieces fast, and assemble a design. We have the best intentions, but we make compromises and uninformed decisions. Over many projects, we end up with a fleet of ships that sorta, kinda, look and feel the same. Or, more likely, they don't.

LEGO even goes so far as to clearly instruct us to start with two critical steps before putting any pieces together. First, make sure that you've got the right environment set up so that it's easy to snap each piece into place. For designers, that means using templates with grids, asset libraries, and more. Second, organize your pieces into piles, first by color but then those other "special" and miscellaneous piles. For designers, that means creating categorized, reusable chunks that are easy to find and use.

But what if, by sheer magic, when you dumped out your box, pieces magically aligned into helpful rows and columns based on color, shape, size, and special use? You could just glance at the table and grab the piece you need for each step. That's LEGO nirvana!

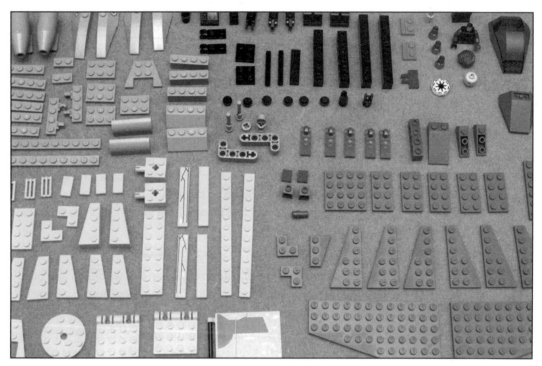

A table of near-perfectly organized LEGO pieces, arranged so that you can scan, choose, and use each piece to quickly build your ship.

That's usually how I feel when I'm assembling layouts based on reusable page components, even if they only solve 70 percent or 80 percent of the overall page design I need. I'm excited about creating the custom work needed for the last, focused innovation that's needed. But I get off to a great start, don't have to reinvent any wheels, and have a framework that's consistent with the overall design system. Your teammates, your engineers, and—most importantly—your users appreciate this.

This book covers two concepts: designing with components and standardizing an experience with a component library.

Part I explores design principles and techniques for chunking your design into components, and using those components to effectively design rich interactions and communicate them to others. Over the first six chapters, we'll cover the following:

1. **Define.** Understand components and how they fit in the design process.

2. **Divide.** Break down your page designs into meaningful chunks.

3. **Vary.** Communicate how a component changes under different conditions.

4. **Combine.** Assemble components together to form page designs.

5. **Reuse.** Apply principles for embedding and linking component instances in your artwork.

6. **Document.** Create useful deliverables to illustrate component-based designs.

With a solid foundation in component-based design principles and reuse, Part II teaches you how to build (chapters 7 through 11) and manage (chapters 12 through 15) a library of reusable component assets:

7. **Appraise.** Ask all the right questions to make sure you're ready to invest in a library.

8. **Discover.** Figure out what goes in—and what stays out of—your library.

9. **Organize.** Define categories, variations, names, keywords, and more.

10. **Setup.** Select your software tools, create templates, and decide conventions.

11. **Build.** Create each reusable chunk and package them up for everyone else.

12. **Administer.** Know your role as librarian, and be ready to curate the collection.

13. **Guide.** Document the role each component plays in your experience.

14. **Adopt.** Execute a planned series of activities so that your library takes hold.

15. **Integrate.** Transform how your team gets work done using components.

With that in mind, let's break it down.

Acknowledgments

WITH THE TRUST OF MICHAEL NOLAN and the team at Peachpit Press, this project got started down the right path. As for my lead editors Valerie Witte (project editing) and Jeff Riley (development), you kept me organized, the work flowing, and the mood as light as it needed to be. To Maureen Forys, Charlene Will, and the rest of the Peachpit team, I offer a hearty—if also a bit meek—thanks for sharing your keen sense, creating a polished design, and putting up with me and my pesky "details." This book is immeasurably better—less wordy, less one-sided, and more accessible to those who think about components less than I do—based on the feedback of my technical editor Austin Govella.

Through my work over the past five years, I've been exposed to design and library efforts across many, many organizations. I'm deeply appreciative to those who have given me the opportunity to learn, explore, and apply modular principles in ways that led to this book, including (in alphabetical order): Melinda Baker, Gordon Baty, Holly Beaver, Randall Blair, Carrie Garzich, David Hewitt, Barney Kirby, Crystal Kubitsky, Lee Fuhr, Livia Labate, Paula Lawley, Elijah Lovejoy, Tim McLaughlin, James Melzer, Francis Rupert, Marilyn Salzman, Yann Schwermer, Julia Stewart, Deanne Stock, Janet Wallin, Jim Webb, and so many others. Certainly not the least, Robert Fabricant and those with him at Frog Design have influenced me significantly through their inspiringly creative yet structured design delivery.

To my guest contributors, I send a hearty thanks for your effort. To Todd Warfel, keep it real. To Joe Lamantia, keep it modular. To Nate Koechley, keep it standard. To Keith Dufresne, keep rounding corners in wireframes! And to Christian Crumlish, my pattern foil who provided timely feedback and turned in twice the number of guest contributions I asked for, keep sharing the faith!

Jennifer Bohmbach, an information architect on Sun.com at the time, approached me after a conference talk and told me about this "component library" her team built. Through my work with the incomparable Sun.com and Cisco.com design teams, my belief in the potential of design systems is forever changed. Andrew Payne, you're the quintessential maverick we can't do without—never let us designers tell you how it's done! Chris Haaga, your colorful quips are exceeded by how you masterfully tune the dials of standards and creativity to keep the train moving. Martin Hardee, you are *the* master evangelist and design director, getting everything—and everyone—to gel in just the right way. This book would never have happened without my own "Gang of Four." Thanks for giving me a ticket to ride your train.

To be a good designer requires you to be a good communicator, including both pictures and words. Writing is hard. It takes time. It takes practice. I've got a long way to go. That said, thanks to Maura Stokes, the first manager of my career, who instilled in me the importance of writing.

To my crew at EightShapes—Dimple, Andy, Jason, and Chris—thanks for your patience and understanding the many times I had to say "no" to other things to get this book done.

To my business partner and friend Dan Brown, I offer continuous gratitude for our relationship. I couldn't have asked for a better, smarter, more patient, and more supportive colleague, and I appreciate how we drive to make each other better. Thanks for giving me the room to explore this diversion.

To my mom and dad, thanks for the gifts of education, love, and life.

To my 4-year-old son Liam and 1-year-old daughter Caroline, you bring me bountiful joy by building up and tearing down LEGO creations, respectively. You remind me that we don't *always* have to follow the directions.

Tina Curtis, my wife, is amazing. Not only did she patiently give me the extra time to focus on completing this project, but she did so without complaint. She shared my excitement during the peaks and held my hand during the valleys. I can't wait for you to read it!

Contents

I

COMPONENT DESIGN

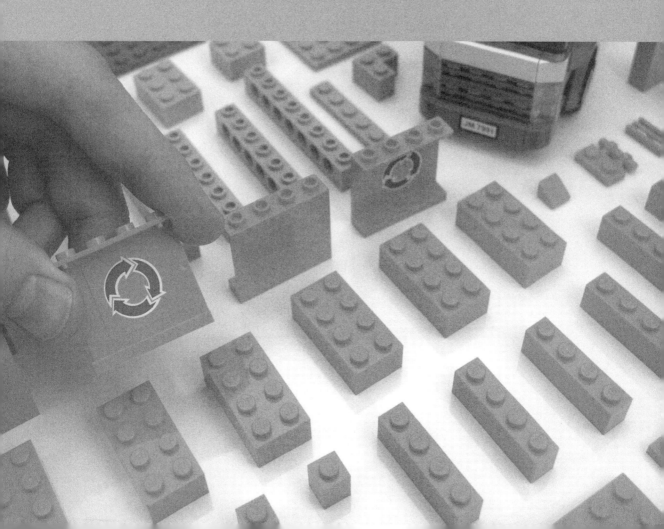

1

D E F I N E

A *component* is a chunk of a page design.

A component contains generic, atomic elements (like text, links, buttons, checkboxes, and images) combined into a meaningful building block used—and reused—in the interface design of an entire page. Other common terms you may have heard to describe a page chunk include *module, portlet, widget,* or even *molecule* (a term used in Robert Fabricant's guest contribution later in this chapter).

The word *component* can mean different things to different people. For example, if you want to be more precise, you could refer to the components of this book as *Web page components* to formally distinguish them from the broader and more technical concepts of *software components* that engineers think so deeply about.

You can use component-based techniques to break complex problems (a page or even an entire site design) into parts that are easier to conceive, understand, and communicate. Breaking down the design enables you to separate it into different areas and focus attention on smaller self-contained problems, one at a time. For instance, consider a sport-specific homepage within the Yahoo Sports experience (**Figure 1.1**). Here, an NBA fan can glean a wide array of sports information with a quick glance at the content spread across the page. In fact, the page is made up of approximately 22 components, each one serving a distinct purpose.

http://sports.yahoo.com/nba
Page Design

http://sports.yahoo.com/nba
Component by Component

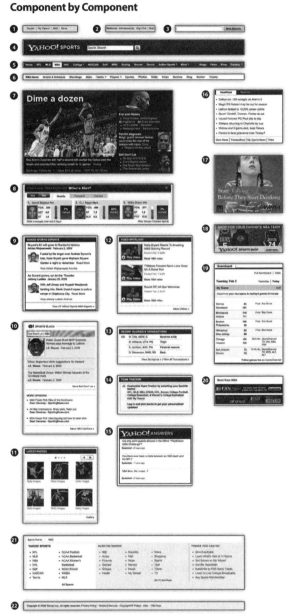

Figure 1.1 The Yahoo Sports NBA page, on the left displayed as a complete page design and on the right broken down into 22 separate component parts. (*Reproduced with permission of Yahoo! Inc. © 2009 Yahoo! Inc. YAHOO! and the YAHOO! Logo are registered trademarks of Yahoo! Inc. This book is neither endorsed, affiliated nor sponsored by Yahoo! Inc.*)

Once you've broken a page into components, you can do all sorts of things with these smaller bits: define something; vary how it looks in different scenarios; and annotate, prioritize, phase, build, maintain, and reuse it.

By dividing the page into components, a designer, an engineer, and other project participants can understand an entire solution but also focus on each part separately: a header and footer navigation system; photo galleries; or even the tone, quantity, and length of each headline in a list.

Components are essential for reusing a design in multiple places across a user experience. By breaking down a design into components, you increase the likelihood that you can reuse individual pieces again in other places with little or no modification.

Reusable components increase consistency, improve design productivity, reduce (or even eliminate) subsequent implementation time, and let you minimize the impacts of updates since many page designs rely on the same part. You can establish a modular design by creating sensible boundaries between each component, and then recombining them over and over in systematic ways.

In the Yahoo Sports experience, you'll find header components like a logo, primary navigation, and secondary navigation bars repeated together, virtually unchanged, across nearly every page of the experience. However, there are components on sports homepages (such as for football, baseball, and tennis) that can be reused on other page types. For example, you could reuse "Recent Injuries & Transactions" and "Latest Photos" components on sports pages, team pages, player pages, game recaps, box scores, scoreboards, and many, many other pages, too. Each instance may be used in different locations with different content for different purposes, but the underlying component structure remains the same.

I've never worked with Yahoo staff on any projects—including Yahoo Sports pages—and I break down this page only for the sake of an example. But I'm guessing that the boundaries I drew are pretty consistent with their understanding, too. Why's that? Components are usually all the same shape.

Rectangles!

Components are almost always rectangular.

In fact, every component in the Yahoo Sports NBA page is rectangular (**Figure 1.2**). In the page's body area (below the header and above the footer), a three-column layout emerges. Within each column, each component is stacked one on top of another, except for two components (#5 and #6) that span across left and center column.

http://sports.yahoo.com/nba
Page Design

http://sports.yahoo.com/nba
By Component Rectangles

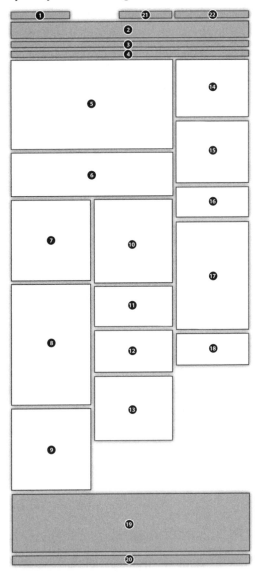

Figure 1.2 The same Yahoo Sports NBA page layout, rendered as component rectangles corresponding to the final layout, but with all other interface detail removed. Header (top of page) and footer (bottom of page) components are displayed as gray boxes, whereas remaining components in the body of the page are white boxes. (*Reproduced with permission of Yahoo! Inc. © 2009 Yahoo! Inc.*)

In fact, a component is almost always visually bound by a rectangle, even if the visual style includes properties like rounded corners and drop shadows. And there's a reason for this: The very nature of HTML—and the content within containers such as <div> tags—forces page designs to be defined by arrangements of rectangular blocks in which each chunk is displayed. That's not such a bad thing, actually.

Since page chunks are rectangular, we can establish a modular, grid-based framework in which we place, align, and maneuver components to assemble a page. It's easy to imagine yourself snapping different components into place within columns of standard widths and other well-defined areas of a layout. By contrast, it's pretty hard to imagine how you'd efficiently arrange chunks of nonstandard sizes and shapes. In fact, modular reuse could be difficult if not impossible under such circumstances. Rectangles easily fit into other rectangles.

Of course, not all authoring environments require page components to be rectangular. Flash is a great example, in which you can arrange, overlay, and publish against components of almost any shape you can imagine. Plus, technology promises to evolve and our publishing environments may support more frameworks for us to lay out content in rich, interesting, and still systematic and modular ways—beyond just rectangles. But today, and for the foreseeable future, we'll be working in environments that generally rely on markup to arrange rectangular blocks within a page layout.

Create a Common Language

AUTHOR: **Robert Fabricant**

ROLE: **Vice President of Creative, Frog Design**

It starts with a glimmer. You are talking to a designer, generally someone who works on a small team for your client. Marketing and product managers are constantly pushing new features and enhancements into the pipeline to meet their business goals, and your designer never seems to have the time to think these additions through. He/she is often on the defensive, debating the merits of specific ways to integrate these new features onto the page with the business lead—without any real user input to back him/her up. There doesn't seem to be any way to get ahead of the curve in an engineering-driven culture.

So you introduce the basic principles of a design system approach: a modular set of components and guidelines to improve consistency (which the designer cares about) and efficiency (which the business side cares about). And the light goes on! For the first time, the designer sees an opportunity to change this dynamic and get out of the weeds, maybe. Unfortunately, the biggest challenge to achieving this goal is not creative (ie., the creation of the assets and guidelines); it is cultural.

The general concept of a design system will have immediate appeal to a number of stakeholders, particularly in an engineering-centric organization.

Good software development relies on modularity and reuse of both back-end and front-end libraries. So your development team will seem like a good partner. Standard assets, such as UI widgets or layout templates, have obvious benefits for developers. But be careful: While modularity is at the core of software development, chances are that developers define the components a bit differently than you do.

This problem can quickly become a morass as you debate the definition of a component or a template. Language becomes very slippery when dealing with abstractions. And chances are that the development team has already baked their definitions into the code in some way. So don't try to convince them that you are right and they are wrong about whether search is a single component or multiple, separate components. It can be hard to move the effort forward and not get bogged down in very abstract debates.

If you can't quickly agree on a glossary of terms and a notation system for referring to various elements of the design system, such as "Controls" (e.g., a "submit" button), "Components" (e.g., a login widget), and "Templates" (e.g., a product page), then you might consider introducing a new language on purpose to separate different uses. We created a modular Web design system for Dell Computer in the late 1990s that helped them scale from $14 million to $55 million in sales in two years. It was organized around "Atoms" and "Molecules." This may seem goofy, but it avoided a lot of potential confusion. Everyone knew what we meant by a molecule (the metaphor was easy to relate to). And a Product Display molecule was not confused with the underlying software component(s) that it might contain.

This worked for a time, long enough to get the system embedded in their organization, though I doubt anyone at Dell now would recognize these terms. Design systems require a certain religious fervor to drive adoption, particularly in the early stages. Language, both text and symbols, is an important part of the conversion process.

For Designers, Engineers, and Everyone Else, Too

Components can be used by anyone contributing to the creation of an experience.

That said, conversations about components usually start with one or both of the key players who use them: designers and engineers. **Designers** are responsible for defining the organization, interactions, layout, and visual style of a user experience, whether within a Web browser (which is the primary focus of this book) or across other devices (such as a phone, kiosk, or tablet). Thinking modularly and using concepts like components are vital for a design to create a cohesive, holistic experience for anything but the most basic or narrow solution.

In your organization, design may be created by one or more roles with titles like information architect, interaction designer, user interface designer, visual designer, graphic designer, or usability specialist. The remainder of this book refers to this role simply as designer, except for special cases where a more specific distinction is necessary.

Designers rely on a myriad of techniques to visualize screen designs, all the way from low-fidelity renderings like sketches and rough design concepts through annotated wireframes to high-fidelity, polished visual comps that depict a screen in a pixel-perfect way. **Figure 1.3** depicts these screen visualizations on a continuum, ending with the actual, formal HTML markup interpreted by a browser to render a component design.

Designers rely on **engineers** to build the applications, content management systems, and other technical frameworks on which an experience is built, published, and maintained. Engineers are just as often referred to as developers or programmers. They create code to build software, databases, and infrastructure to support a living, breathing, and evolving technical system. And, more often than not, thinking modularly is already a part of their psyche.

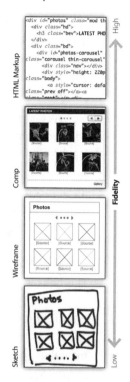

Figure 1.3 A photo gallery component rendered at different fidelities during a design and development process, perhaps from its first consideration within a sketch through wireframes and comps to its ultimate definition and publishing via final HTML markup and styles.

Intersecting Design and Code

Adopting component-based techniques helps designers and engineers become faster, more efficient, and more effective at building a design system for a user experience. We've seen considerable improvements even when we've taught teams limited to just one discipline—information architects or visual designers or even engineers. For sure, designers can leverage and benefit from components without deeply mapping their efforts to an engineer's vision. Likewise, engineers can improve reuse and reduce costs by using components that a design team need not even appreciate.

However, some seek a greater sort of "component nirvana" where components are adopted comprehensively across disciplines. Mostly, that hinges on your success at bridging design and development together at their point of intersection: the presentation layer where a design is transformed into the HTML, CSS, and JavaScript rendered in a browser.

It's during this transformation that the design and engineering can reach for a shared vision on what makes up each and every component of their design system.

Spreading Far and Wide

This book is written first for designers—and secondly for engineers and design technologists—so they can understand the principles of component-based, modular design and then use them to create design systems. But components can permeate the deliverables and discussion of almost anyone involved with the planning, design, development, implementation, publishing, and maintenance of an experience.

Other roles that can be directly impacted by and benefit from components include the following:

Content strategists (and their partners, copywriters) who plan for and create useful, usable content utilizing components as a framework of bite-size, focused chunks

Testers (also known as quality assurance, or QA) who break down an experience when creating test plans and can find that components provide a logical, well-organized foundation to work from

Stakeholders (such as product managers, brand specialists, and even executive sponsors) who commission an experience and increase their return on investment from component reuse and consistency

Producers (and their cousins, site strategists) who work with stakeholders to collect, organize, strategize, and even produce content in components that guide them toward consistent and informed application of a design system

Publishers who routinely assemble pages (whether through a content management system, cobbled together HTML of their own, or a mix of the two) using components that afford a plug-and-play model for building

Some of these partners may have been exposed to techniques for design reuse before, and may even jump to the conclusion that components are the same as design patterns.

Components and Patterns

Components aren't design patterns, exactly.

Invariably during design projects or at the outset of planning a component library, stakeholders will query, "Ah, so we are working with design patterns?" Actually, no.

The two concepts are similar in many ways. Both are built out into libraries. Both are motivated by reuse, consistency, and productivity. But they *are* different. Understanding how patterns and components are different will reinforce the nature and benefits of each and improve how effectively you apply them to your design problems. Consider the difference as principles versus prescriptions.

What Is a Pattern?

A pattern is a solution to a recurring design problem, such that you could use the solution many times and never use it the same way twice.

For example, there's no reason for you not to employ the common tenets of tabs (such as at least two tabs are required), video playback (that can be played or paused), or authentication (that, at a minimum, requires some form of username and password). Patterns are essential in interaction design, serving as a basis for designers to apply common, consistent, and usable principles.

How Are Components and Patterns Related?

Patterns and components can be complementary and coexist within design solutions.

Consider again the Yahoo Sports NBA page, broken down into components, many of which are reused on other pages in Yahoo Sports. The page also uses many patterns, indicated by the labeled callouts in **Figure 1.4**.

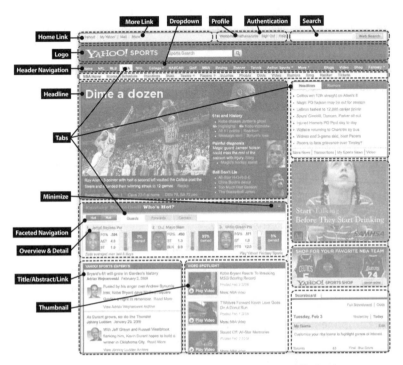

Figure 1.4 Yahoo Sports NBA page annotated for both component chunks (as dashed outlines) and patterns (as labeled callouts). (*Reproduced with permission of Yahoo! Inc. © 2009 Yahoo! Inc.*)

Are the components and patterns the same? Not at all. The components represent chunks of visual design and HTML/CSS code that are combined into a composite Web page. Patterns are sprinkled within and across components. Do they overlap? Sometimes. A few components are simple enough to map to a specific pattern, such as search and tabbed navigation. Other components combine several patterns, such as the Who's Hot component that combines patterns for tabs, faceted navigation, and overview and detail content. A pattern is a theory about how a general design problem can be solved. A component is a specific way that your organization has decided to solve its specific design problems.

Used in concert, patterns and components blend to become parts of an effective, modular design solution.

Components Inspired by a Pattern

Often, many components in a library will utilize the same pattern. For example, consider the tab pattern that enables a designer to segment content into several sections, with all accessible but only one visible at a given time. On the Yahoo Sports NBA page, the tab pattern is used in three components (as shown in **Figure 1.5**) that organize the following:

1. Sports (NFL, MLB, NBA, NHL, and more)

2. Article types (Headlines as a default and Rumors as an alternative)

3. Players by performance (Hot or Not) and position (Guard, Forward, or Center).

Figure 1.5 Tab pattern used within multiple components on sports.yahoo.com/nba/ for sport-by-sport navigation (such as NBA and NHL), article types (Headlines and Rumors), and player attributes (Hot and Not as well as positions like Guards, Forwards, and Centers). (*Reproduced with permission of Yahoo! Inc. © 2009 Yahoo! Inc.*)

In every case, the design adheres to the fundamentals of a tab pattern, for example, distinguishing the active tab from other tabs. However, the use, page region, style, scale of reuse, and design details differ considerably for each component.

Reconciling a Pattern from Components

Similarly, differences across many components can be reconciled into a single pattern to establish a common baseline across teams and efforts.

For example, consider the countless video players proliferating across a Web site: embedded in a product spotlight, unique players in lightboxes and popups, new players for content from the training group, etc. Built by different teams at different times, the designs all play video with interfaces that have inconsistent behavior and appearances.

Teams can resolve component differences with a pattern for basic controls like play/pause, scrubber, timing (current and overall duration), and volume. With a pattern in place, consistency increases but teams still have the flexibility to include (or omit) additional controls and features—video size, full screen view, rating, commenting, and embedded code.

How Are Components and Patterns the Same?

Both patterns and components are reusable design solutions for specific problems. This reuse—and the consistency and cost-savings that result—is a key selling point. In addition, patterns and components can be

▶ Described via attributes like Use When, Rationale, and Solution Guidelines

▶ Managed in a library

▶ Rendered as reusable assets, whether HTML/CSS frameworks or design libraries used to produce wireframes and comps

▶ Utilized during projects by designers, design technologists, engineers, and other disciplines

▶ Authored and maintained via a (hopefully) well-defined workflow

▶ Based on the design needs of an organization

▶ Influenced and enhanced based on user research

How Are Components and Patterns Different?

Despite their similarities, components and patterns differ in important ways.

One should be able to define and assemble a page from top to bottom, left to right, using components. However, while a page may contain patterns, there are also many page areas that contain no patterns at all. Also, patterns are design baselines open to interpretation and subjective application, while components are quite specific to an established design and thus more prescriptive and fixed.

Additional distinctions are outlined in **Table 1.1**.

Table 1.1 Distinctions Between Patterns and Components

Distinction	Patterns	Components
Type(s)	Could be a page chunk (login module), flow (shopping from product to cart to checkout to receipt), behavior (e.g., autocomplete), or something else	Always a chunk of a page or screen design
Specificity	Globally applicable across a range of contexts	Specific to one design system, including layout, color, type, and behaviors
Location	Up to the designer to appropriately apply principles and locate within a screen design	Targeted to specific location(s) within a page layout, based on approved usage

Distinction	Patterns	Components
Style	Abstracted from any specific skin, and flexible to adapt to many visual treatments	Finished within one visual system, although variations may be defined
Editorial	Perhaps some basic editorial guidance	Specific data, formats, guideline, style/tone, and even defined feed
Markup & code	While starter code may be available, it needs to be tailored to fit the system	Ideally represented by formalized HTML, JavaScript, and CSS if the library is built
How it works	Represents how a design should work, under preferred conditions (but may suggest how to cope with tradeoffs)	Represents how a design does work, inclusive of the tradeoffs and constraints established during the design process

It Started With Patterns

AUTHOR: **Christian Crumlish**

ROLE: **Curator, Yahoo! Design Pattern Library**

While the Yahoo! Design Pattern Library emerges from our community of designers, our set of universal network components (which we call ONE, for One Network Excellence or One Network Experience, depending on the day you ask us) are prioritized by a central committee called the Design Council, which includes representative user experience design leadership from all of our major lines of business and contexts. This group collaborates on developing a short list of components to develop.

The goals of ONE are to distribute our best thinking on user interface solutions as widely across our design community as possible, to provide our users with an experience that's as consistent as possible, and to promote rapid, efficient development through reuse of modular interface components.

Designers derive aspects of patterns and apply them to components using the interfaces they've tested and built as prototypes. A pattern isn't a full spec, of course, but it will point to representative specs on our intranet, and we will sometimes create a generic ("scrubbed") spec that a designer could use as a template when implementing the pattern. We'll also include stencils or other creative assets when appropriate to make it easier for designers to add the component as a module to their wireframes and to improve the communication process between designers and developers by being able to point to a consistent "symbol," as it were, of each component.

In the ONE collection, the patterns are complemented with code samples, engineering implementation guides, prototypes, and even reference implementations. We don't really consider the pattern by itself to be a component, because without assets for designers to aid sketching and composition or reference code for developers to play with, it's just a set of recommendations. If you put tools into the hands of your makers (designers and engineers) and thereby make their lives easier, they have no reason not to build with components. If all you have to offer is "something to read," the benefit will be much more subtle and thus much less compelling.

We're working on pulling together a single universal interface for our internal patterns and component libraries, but we do have some distinctions we want to maintain. The general, all-purpose interaction patterns (such as most of those available in the public Yahoo! Design Pattern Library) provide a baseline of current best thinking about interaction design. We use them to share what we've learned with our entire distributed design community, but individual designers are relatively free to ignore them if they wish. The ONE components are modules that we want to see eventually implemented with 80 – 90 percent consistency across Yahoo! (making exceptions for unique contexts). The interaction patterns don't ordinarily turn into ONE components, although they can be seen as a sort of bedrock on which the components stand, as many of the components refer to the interaction patterns that underlie them.

Divide and Conquer

User experience design teams can suffer from a decentralized, blank canvas approach to creating and documenting a design solution for each new project. Screen designs are reinvented over and over again, inconsistency quickly expands, and IT teams scramble to pick up the pieces. Pattern libraries only go so far, suggesting general solutions to common problems instead of offering concrete, specific design treatments. At times, documented solutions turn into a costly mess of unclear expectations, unrealistic goals, and abandoned work.

As your user experience grows into a vast, interconnected system of pages, you can establish a component library to improve efficiency, consistency, and reuse. This library can be a shared venture of many teams, used across many projects, and applicable to many areas of an experience. Designers can produce wireframes, comps, and markup far more quickly reusing components from a library rather than creating everything from scratch. And your development team can begin to build for the long haul by creating similar, reusable chunks.

A component library isn't about limiting innovation. Instead, it empowers designers to reuse solutions to problems that have already been solved so they can focus more on the problems that don't have solutions. When individuals no longer reinvent vast portions of a design with every project, productivity increases and headaches diminish. In addition, a library provides a platform for improved governance, a deeper baseline for collaboration, and a structure for useful and predictable documentation.

A component library can serve as a centerpiece for integrating component-based thinking, efficiencies, and standards into your process and culture. However, creating a library is no small task. It takes time, planning, adapting to change, and commitment—both financially and organizationally. And libraries aren't appropriate for every team. So let's not get ahead of ourselves. That's why Part 2 of this book details when to build a library, how to build it, and how to adopt and manage it once it's ready for prime time.

Instead, start with the remainder of Part 1 that introduces you to the mindset of designing and communicating modular solutions using components. You create designs, you modularly divide those designs into smaller parts, vary each part, combine them back together in interesting ways, and communicate your design with those you collaborate with.

Let's get started by dividing and conquering our page designs.

2

DIVIDE

Dividing a page design into chunks is fundamental to taking a modular approach to your design process. This chapter explores the chunking process, beginning with why we must move past designing pages to an approach where we can communicate design at multiple levels: pages, components, and even individual elements.

Beyond Pages

The user experience field has come a long way, providing a range of specializations from information architecture to interaction design and visual design to engineering HTML and cascading style sheets.

However, when a friend or family member asks me what I do, I often begin with "I design Web pages." From there, one can get more specific via comparisons (like an information architect comparing his role to an architect of buildings), concrete explanations (like a visual designer talking about layout, color, and Adobe Photoshop), or even mystifying terms like "AJAX!" But to those unfamiliar with our industry, a general and basic answer may be all you need. And in that simple answer—I design Web pages—is the core unit of design: the page.

Pages are what everyone experiences when navigating the Web. A page represents a user's view at any point in time. Pages are the fundamental unit of the experience. A page has purpose. Everyone knows what a page is.

But thinking only of pages limits our potential to address design challenges at a lower level. Sure, starting with a page design may make sense. But by the time you start on the second page, the mindset should shift to looking for reusable chunks. By the third, fourth, and fifth page designs, reusable components become increasingly obvious.

So, for any given online experience, I start with the design of a page—a full page—from the ground up. For every page after that, design becomes a balancing act between creating new, custom, specific solutions and reusing parts of other pages, all the while being mindful of how pages combine to create a fluid, meaningful experience.

A Design's Hierarchy

But where does the page fit in the overall experience? Not the experience from a user's perspective—but where does the page fit within the complex system of flows, areas, pages, elements, and other things you design? If you think of your design system hierarchically, *Pages* actually fit right in the middle.

At the top of the hierarchy displayed in **Figure 2.1**, an entire *Experience* solution captures every flow, every page—every part of a design system that would be presented.

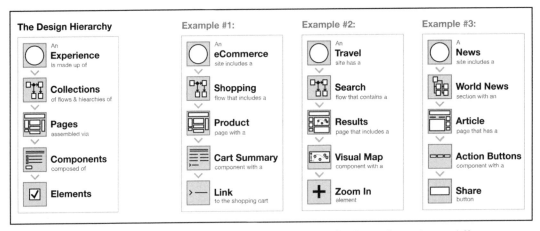

Figure 2.1 The design hierarchy, along with three examples of how that hierarchy applies to different types of sites.

A holistic experience usually contains many different page types, often organized into *Collections* of pages like the following:

- ► Page suites, such as a product's overview, features, gallery, and tech specs
- ► Flows, such as a wizard installation or ecommerce sequence through the shopping cart, billing and shipping information, order review, and receipt
- ► Sections and hierarchies, such as a catalog of products browsed in increasingly narrow categories
- ► Content types, such as collections of videos or photographs found via search

Just as pages can be grouped together, they can also be divided into pieces. Instinctually, a designer first tends to break down pages into *Elements* such as the following:

- ► Page title
- ► Headers
- ► Paragraphs
- ► Buttons
- ► Checkboxes

Each element is atomic, incapable of being further divided or described as multiple parts. As a designer, you should remain ever mindful of how each element fits in and contributes to the mission of an entire, cohesive page.

However, designing a page as a combination of elements doesn't get you very far in creating a modular design system. The level in between a page and an element—referred to as page chunks, or *Components*—is invaluable in creating a modular page design. Components combine one or more elements that can be assembled, reused, and documented to solve a specific design problem, with the potential of reusing that solution again in the future.

Sure, there are many examples of atomic elements that are reusable, documented, and useful in solving a specific design problem, which belong in a library of reusable items. Generic elements like a site logo (that links to a homepage), page title, section header, paragraph, and button all warrant standardization and reuse. No doubt about it. However, generic elements address only the most basic baseline of standards.

In designing and documenting pages with a bevy of sophisticated states, behaviors, and content structures, most components are combinations of many elements organized together in a meaningful, specific way.

Page Chunks

How do you find the components in a page? Divide the page into chunks.

Chunking a page design is a process of decomposing a page into a set of building blocks. Each component chunk is a cohesive but smaller portion of the page, both reusable and independent of other chunks. Once identified, the chunk is a concrete unit of design that you can focus on, add more details to, vary, and reuse. Such a process is also referred to as "modularizing" or "factoring" a page design. Chunking a page into components is a great way to break down a design into sub-problems so that each one is simple enough to be solved directly and independently. For a page designed from scratch, chunking identifies all the parts, considering each as a cohesive whole, but also homing in on relevant details of each part. For a page built upon an existing design system, the process of chunking enables you to frame and focus innovation on what makes that design solution unique.

For information architects, chunking feels entirely natural, as it focuses on the structure of an experience. However, visual designers may feel a bit more challenged by chunking since the overall page aesthetic and composition are vital. But such challenges don't diminish the need for all designers to deconstruct a design and consider the scale, flexibility, and independent impact of each component.

The Chunking Process

Chunking is rather easy, actually.

The process is as simple as drawing rectangles on page layouts to identify and distinguish each chunk. In fact, these rectangles are often the first, lowest-fidelity rendering of a page via a sketch or crude wireframe. Or, perhaps it's a printed screenshot that peers draw on to annotate.

The concept of annotating component chunks can be applied to any screen visualization, from a sketch to a prototype, from a comp to a rendered snippet of code. You can use rectangles or outlines of a page design to identify chunks, and then add markers that map each chunk to a component list adjacent to the layout (**Figure 2.2**). Alternatively, you can add callouts to identify each chunk, more directly tying together the component design and name (**Figure 2.3**).

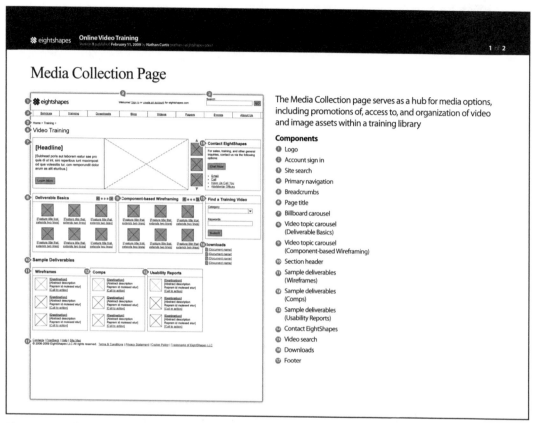

Figure 2.2 A chunked wireframe page, annotated using markers and a component list.

Although seemingly trivial, the investment in annotating page chunks pays off many times over. Annotated chunks enable designers and stakeholders to do the following:

▶ Understand an entire page simply by walking through enumerated component parts.

▶ Refer to specific components without ambiguity, and even establish a shared vocabulary to refer to it over time.

▶ Relate one component to another on the same or different page layout.

▶ Extend or mark up components with additional properties, such as priority.

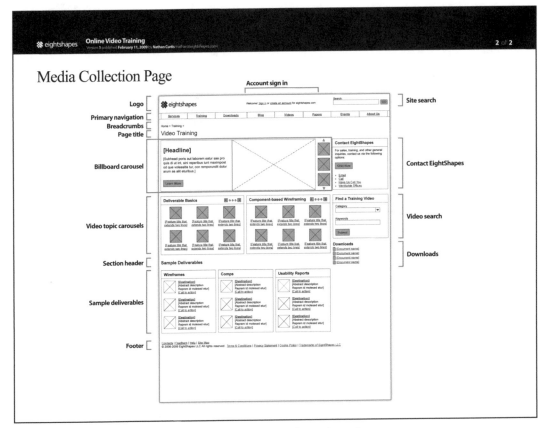

Figure 2.3 A chunked wireframe page, annotated using callouts for each component.

Without clearly identified page chunks, early reviews of basic page layouts can go awry, or at least take far too long. Who hasn't replied to a five-minute nonstop diatribe with a meek "Which part are you referring to?" Remote collaboration intensifies such challenges, as voices on the phone begin to refer to items by different names in different locations in different contexts, while maybe even looking at a different page! Chunks remove this challenge by enabling a clear basis for efficient, predictable design communication.

While annotating component chunks with callouts or markers can have the same initial benefits, using markers is a more scalable solution. If the screen design will evolve over time (adding, removing, shifting components in the page layout) and details are recorded over time (specs like behaviors, states, and content), then markers are easier to reorient to accommodate change and growth. However, if the document is a one-off, never to be updated again, then callouts can provide a more direct, effective form of annotation.

Right-Sizing the Rectangles

The challenge of chunking isn't drawing rectangles, or even drawing meaningful rectangles; it's drawing the *right* rectangles. Carving out every textbox, paragraph, link, header, button, and other page element won't yield as much reuse, scale, and context. Instead, annotating every element on a page will limit reuse, miss relationships that tie elements together, and diminish your capability to quickly describe a page by its component parts.

Even when you've combined elements that naturally fit together, the chunk may still be too small to effectively document, vary, or reuse. A video player's toolbar for play, pause, and sliding across a timeline is useless without including the player's viewing area, too (**Figure 2.4**).

Similarly, an interactive map's toolbar for choosing zoom levels has neither context nor reuse value outside of the map itself. In that case, the better rectangle is drawn around the entire map, not the zoom toolbar it includes.

Chunks can be too large, too. **Figure 2.5** shows a sidebar with blocks for contact us, search, and downloads that are used together throughout the experience. Intuition may suggest that you combine all three into a single reusable chunk, but that's a poor choice. In fact, each block has a range of independent states: contact us options that vary per page and time of day, search with various fields shown or hidden based on page context, and downloads rotated with another component or hidden based

Figure 2.4 A video player component should not be limited to just the player's toolbar (buttons for play and pause, a timeline scrubber, and volume), but should instead be the entire, reusable chunk that includes the viewer as well.

Contact EightShapes

For sales, training, and other general inquiries, contact us via the following options:

Chat Now

» Email
» Call
» Have Us Call You
» Worldwide Offices

Find a Training Video

Category

Keywords

Submit

Downloads
[Document name]
[Document name]
[Document name]
[Document name]

Figure 2.5 A sidebar with three distinct components.

on page needs. Since the blocks have distinct purposes and vary independently, separate them into different chunks.

Getting chunks just right takes practice, collaboration, experience, and learning when you need to go larger or smaller to vary, document, and reuse it over time.

Chunks Matter

Chunking a page design enables you to break down what can be a very complex page design into a collection of easier-to-understand, bite-size portions. A designer must solve problems—and discuss those solutions with peers and stakeholders—in ways that can be communicated succinctly and clearly. Component chunks provide a simple structure that can focus conversation while sustaining the context of a broader page or experience.

Sure, some pages may be so simple that chunking seems like overkill. Other times, design reviews drill deeper past components to focus on nitpicky states and behaviors of a single element. But more often than not, a chunked page provides an effective way to set the stage for detailed conversations about important parts while setting aside other parts that are already well-defined or less important.

It's important to think about component chunks early. Sooner or later, those component chunks will be the basis for variations based on relevant states, behaviors, and content (see Chapter 3, "Vary"), as well as illuminate opportunities for reuse across design files, in documentation, and throughout a solution (see Chapter 5, "Reuse").

Additionally, breaking down a page into components suggests a structure for document-ing a solution. As you chunk a page, you'll begin to refer to each item by name, use these names in discussions with stakeholders, and even start to number each chunk per page, site area, project, or whatever organizational model you create with your document(s).

Such names and reference numbers provide a roadmap for you—and your colleagues—to use across project artifacts, whether the work is done in parallel or one project after another. An interaction designer creates detailed, well-organized design specifications. A visual designer modularizes comp artwork with similar boundaries. Engineers and quality assurance analysts use component chunks as a roadmap for creating systems documents and test plans. The thoughtful organization of components can create efficiencies in com-munication and delivery that ripple across a team. Chapter 6, "Document," provides more information on documenting components during a project.

Just as well, chunked page designs create a more fluid discourse between designers and whoever is tasked with monitoring emerging designs in the context of a holistic experi-ence—or even an ongoing library. Instead of having to decipher and compare many unorga-nized pages, reviewers can quickly scan designs and understand how an experience is—or could be—organized. Such collaboration can trigger critical discussions of standards, constraints, scale of reuse, and ultimately, a design system's return on investment.

Relating Components

Component chunks also provoke discussions about the relationships of components to one another and to the overall experience. Which chunks are going to be reused frequently on many pages, sections, or an entire experience? What components are often—or always—displayed together? Is one component dependent on another?

Designers grapple with questions like these during a design process, and also when identifying components to add to a library over time. Many decisive themes bubble up during project conversations, and it's up to the designers to balance project needs against the evolving, holistic experience. For more information on component themes to consider during a project and when creating a library, refer to Chapter 8, "Discover."

From Sketching to Code

So you may think "OK, I get it. So where does chunking fit into my process?" Actually, there's not a well-defined time during a project where chunking is always done, such as during the first round of wireframes (although that is certainly a great time to do it!). Rather, designers deconstruct design across many different activities. Even when sketching or brainstorming a solution, a designer may be considering what different chunks should be included in a page.

Early in a project, a designer could even aggregate elements into chunks *without* the priorities, groups, and categories implied by a page layout (Singer, 2004). To start, a designer lists every element—or "bit"—to be considered, such as company contact information, current account plan, or a link to change passwords. Once the list is complete, the bits are grouped into chunks, which are then prioritized and designed independently. Only then are chunks assembled into a page layout based on those newfound assumptions.

The technique of using page description diagrams (Brown, 2002) takes a similar approach. A page description diagram consists of prose descriptions of content and functional areas (chunks in prose) that are arranged to communicate priority (**Figure 2.6**). Once the areas are prioritized, the designer creates "mini-layouts" (visualized chunks) of each area independently and positions the mini-layout adjacent to the description.

What is the advantage of these two approaches? Stakeholders and peers use chunks to interpret priorities, content, and relationships early in a project. These considerations are made absent a predetermined layout, which can bias perceptions of reviewers steeped in the status quo. After such discussions clarify design objectives, many early chunks may persist as structures within subsequent, more formal page layouts.

Home Page Contents

Higher visual priority → Lower visual priority

1

Knowledge Base

The primary focus of the Extranet's home page is the list of categories that constitute the knowledge base. It is through this list that users access all of the knowledge resources. The list could look like this:

- Athletes and Athlete Health
- Coaches, Skills, and Sports Training
- Competition and Sports Rules
- Event Planning
- Families and Schools
- Finance and Operations
- Fundraising
- Governance and Boards
- Information Technology
- Organizational Development
- Outreach and Involvement
- Public Relations and Communications
- Research
- Stories of Special Olympics
- Strategic Planning
- Volunteers

The knowledge categories will include Best Practices, FAQs, the Glossary, the Dictionary, and Testimonials. In the future the collaborative applications like the bulletin board and expert directory will be accessed through the knowledge base.

Special Olympics Around the World

The home page will include an area that highlights information specific to particular regions. Includes messages from the Regional Manager Directors.

- Messages from the Regional Managing Directors
- Regional Calendars
- Regional and Program Profiles
- Regional News, Announcements, and Accomplishments

Navigation on Every Page

Certain items appear throughout the site. A global "navigation bar" includes five items on the home page: Contacts, Around the World, Knowledge Base, User Guide, and Search. On internal pages, there is always a link to "home." Global items could be rendered:

User Guide • Contacts • Around the World • Knowledge Base • Search: [____] (go)

2

How to Add Documents

Posting instructions appear on the home page to facilitate community participation.

You can contribute to any page by clicking on the "Switch to Edit Mode" link at the top. If you do not see this link and would like to contribute, please contact your system administrator.

for more information, check the user guide.

Recently Added

The home page includes a link to items recently added to the knowledge base.

Language Selection

With Programs all over the world, Special Olympics needs an extranet that appears in multiple languages. The home page will have a language selection menu, which might look like this:

language - language - 语言: [English ▼]

Announcements

Announcements are internal messages, directed toward the field from Regions and HQ. The home page shows the three latest announcements with a link to more, looking possibly like this:

- Special Olympics launches multi-lingual extranet to address needs of Programs
- Contribute your best practices to our new knowledge management system
- Quarterly reports due to regional managing directors by April 7, 2003

more...

3

Mission and Vision

The home page includes links to organizational mission and vision. It could look like this:

"...to develop physical fitness, demonstrate courage, experience joy ..."

our mission • our vision • message from our CEO

Essentials

The small "essentials" area includes 3-5 links to topics or documents within the knowledge categories. It could look like this:

essential tools from the knowledge base
- Branding Guidelines
- Volunteer Registration Form
- Budget Template
- Sports Guides (Winter, Summer)
- Coaching Guides

Applications

The home page includes a menu of Special Olympics applications. The applications menu could look like this:

applications
[Program Development System ▼] (go)

Switch to Edit Mode

So long as the user has security privileges, the system will expose a link allowing him to enter the edit mode.

[switch to edit mode]

Items italicized must appear above the fold

TISANI | The layout and design depicted herein represents content priorities only and should not be construed as actual layout and design. Final product may vary. | home page contents | Dan Brown / dan.brown@tisani.com / Special Olympics Extranet / 7 March 2002 / Version 1.1 / Tisani Consulting, LLC / 9485 Suitsboro Rd / Bethesda, MD 20817

Figure 2.6 A page description diagram. *(Courtesy of Dan Brown)*

Just as chunks can influence our early discovery and design, they also permeate our design documentation, code snippets, test plans, and myriad other aspects of a project. Component-based documentation is addressed in more detail in Chapter 7, "Appraise."

You're Soaking in It... Relax

AUTHOR: **Chris Haaga**

ROLE: **Director of Web Experience Design, Sun.com**

Thinking in terms of styles and objects isn't new in the world of design and publishing. In fact, applying styles to common, repeating elements is not only efficient, it's fundamental to delivering a consistent, dependable (read: usable), branded experience. Look at the tools of the trade for creating page layout. They are primed to support the styles and objects that form the support structure for component-based design.

So if you've been toiling away at designs for large-scale Web sites, and you aspire to work smart, it's well worth your while to consider the benefits of a component-based approach. If terms like *consistency* and *system* or *repeatable* and *re-usable* frequently pop up in your discussions with designers, business people, and those on the build and deploy side, then you're already making the case for using components.

I got into the Web design space as part of a tiny visual design team tasked with applying basic brand/experience design principles to a very "dynamic," distributed design space. It was 1997, and our Sun.com site already had several thousand pages in play. Our brand design team was coming into the publishing community from the outside, and we needed to work our way in carefully ... and we literally took that approach as we conducted our initial design plan: normalize the header and footer across all pages, then start to standardize common elements in the body of each page. As we expanded our influence and gained ground bit by bit, we wondered how we would be able to keep the doors on the beast.

Fast forward a few years. The site had grown to tens of thousands of pages. Our tiny team had kept moving on the battlefield of design by creating page templates, developing a common style sheet, and drifting toward a component-oriented design strategy. But a site-wide redesign provided us with our big opportunity. We met with a design agency that strung these practical, near-mystical words together in their RFP in the "design deliverables" section:

"A system of modular design components to comprise a design toolkit and framework demonstrating a cohesive identity throughout the site."

Ding, ding, ding. (Or "duh," I guess you could say.) The words put everything into focus and started us down a path toward a site design methodology that we're still exploring, evolving, and exploiting years later.

What is remarkable and cool about a component-based approach to Web site development is the degree to which it can be bred into describing, designing, building, documenting, deploying, and evolving a design system. Our information architects use page layout templates pre-loaded with styles and objects that correspond to our component specs. Our technologists have documented component samples and code snippets to expedite publishing. And when we need to extend or improve, we have a design baseline to work from and, by controlling the style sheet and global assets, we deploy upgrades across Web properties that span over two million pages.

Components aren't the complete solution, but they provide a platform to cover the basics. They also pay big dividends, saving money and time—time that can be used to think of interesting ways to evolve your design system.

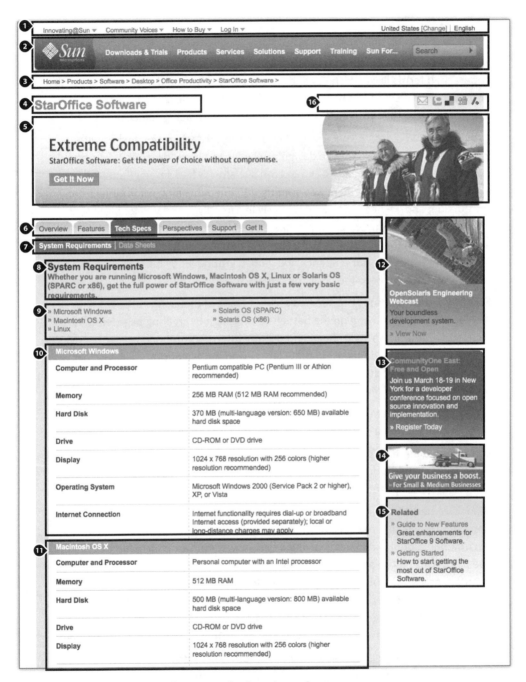

Figure 2.7 A Sun.com product page of technical specifications.

Example: Product

Product-oriented sites must present a catalog of offerings that supports the overall company brand but also communicates the unique characteristics of each product. The Sun.com product page shown in **Figure 2.7** displays product specifications such as memory, processor, and operating system requirements. At the same time, the overall page composition surrounds such detail with navigation to other product information (such as Features and Perspectives), branded photography, and promotions and community events in the sidebar. All the while, the entire page design is wrapped in a consistent, modular header and footer to sustain a sense of place and to guide users around the site's architecture.

Components

1. Global and utility navigation
2. Masthead (primary navigation)
3. Breadcrumbs
4. Page title
5. Billboard
6. Primary tabs
7. Secondary tabs
8. Introduction
9. Anchor links
10. Spec table
11. Spec table (repeated)
12. Banner with image
13. Banner without image
14. Small banner
15. Related links
16. Page tasks

Spotlight: Sidebar Banners

Not every sidebar is the same, and creating a modular system of reusable banners, link collections, and other sidebar content can prove very effective. In **Figure 2.8**, the page uses three different banner types. The banners are similar, sure, but content varies: image or no image; HTML text or text embedded in the image? By including a set of different variations, designers can define standards such as overall quantity, quantity per type, order, and other editorial guidelines. And by addressing each banner as a separate component (rather than a standard stack that is always placed on every page), designers and publishers establish a more flexible system.

Figure 2.8 Sun.com banner components.

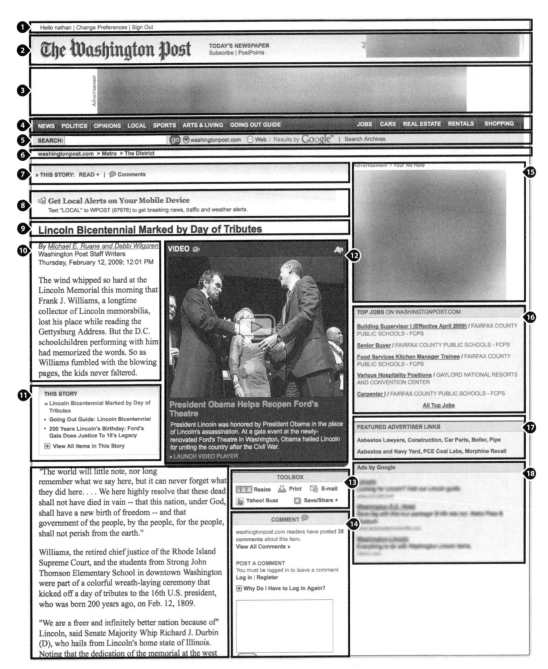

Figure 2.9 A Washingtonpost.com article page. (© Copyright 2009, Washingtonpost.Newsweek Interactive LLC. All rights reserved.)

Example: Article

Informational sites, particularly those like news site Washingtonpost.com, can include innumerable articles. An article template may be thought of as fairly straightforward: a title, an author, a date, article copy, and perhaps a few photographs sprinkled in. Not so simple in today's world of online publishing, where one article can include a range of content types (like videos and photo galleries), tasks to share and comment on content, and links to related articles and advertisements. The Washingtonpost.com article template includes many such modular components (**Figure 2.9**).

Components

1. Personalized utility bar
2. Header (with advertisement)
3. Leaderboard advertisement
4. Global navigation
5. Search
6. Breadcrumbs
7. Read and comment bar
8. Mobile promotion
9. Page title
10. Article body copy
11. Related articles
12. Video highlight and launch
13. Toolbox
14. Comment box
15. Medium rectangle advertisement
16. Top jobs
17. Featured advertiser links
18. Ads by Google

Spotlight: Article Content Types

Washingtonpost.com positions an article's related content inline with body copy, as well as a highlight in the top right of the article area. Depending on the article, the highlight may be a single photograph, a photograph slideshow you can page through using previous and next buttons, or even a photograph that launches a video player (as shown in **Figure 2.9**). If no supplemental article content is available, the highlight area is replaced by a poll or omitted such that the body copy fills that space.

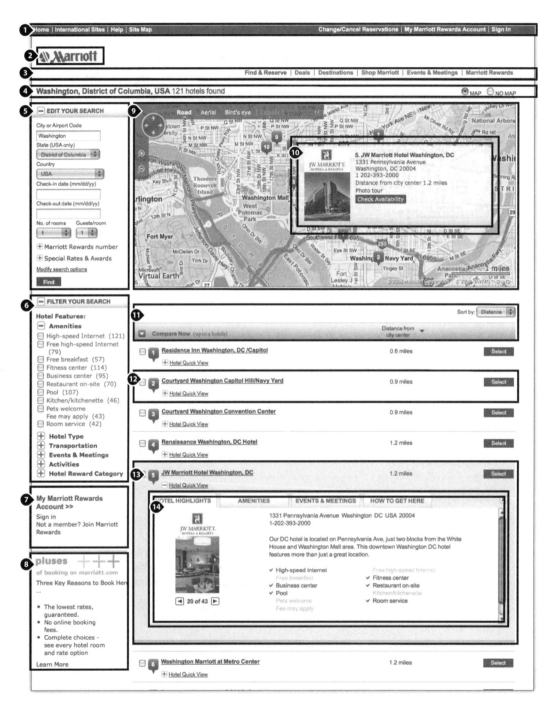

Figure 2.10 Marriott.com location search results and map. *(Courtesy of Marriott.com)*

Example: Search Results

Travel Web sites provide a rich array of features to help customers locate, filter, and ultimately select a destination of interest. On Marriott.com (**Figure 2.10**), a graphical map enables visual exploration of hotels displayed via a search tool, and hovering over a location triggers a panel with a photograph and other location details. The map is positioned above a table of locations—connected to the map via numbered markers—that includes even more location information in an embedded tab module. If the results don't match what you were looking for, other components let you edit and filter locations based on a range of criteria.

Components

1. Utility navigation
2. Site logo
3. Primary navigation
4. Search location & result quantity
5. Edit search
6. Filter search
7. Account sign-in

8. Promotion
9. Map
10. Map detail panel
11. Results table header
12. Results table row (collapsed)
13. Results table row (expanded)
14. Results inline tabs

Spotlight: Maps

Discerning the right chunks for a mapping interface—or any sophisticated interface, for that matter—can feel challenging at first. The key theme in identifying components in this context is reuse: what is reused; what is reused together; and are various parts shown or hidden without impacting the rest of the interface. In this case, the mapping controls (zooming in and out, toggling across type, moving in different directions) would *always* be displayed as a part of this mapping component. Therefore, it doesn't make sense to treat these controls as separate components from the map underneath, but rather, all as part of one reusable chunk. However, the panel triggered by hovering a location marker appears independently and would likely have its own range of variations, so it's treated as a separate chunk.

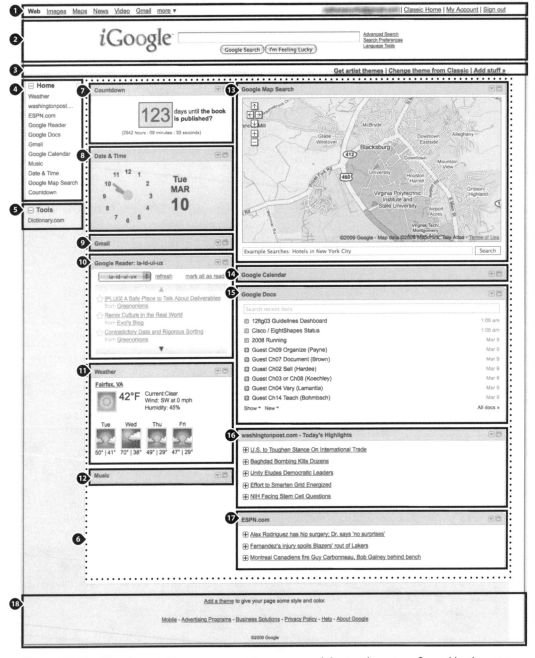

Figure 2.11 The iGoogle portal homepage contains many modules in a layout configured by the user.

Example: Portal

Customizable portal pages are a great place to start teaching someone about the benefits of modularity. The layout of the iGoogle portal homepage (shown in **Figure 2.11**) can be configured to have one, two, or three columns; in this case, the setup includes a narrow left column and wide right column. The layout is contained with a side tab component that enables you to toggle between *home* (currently displayed) and *tools*. The dotted line surrounding the content modules reflects the tab's container, a nearly invisible component that nonetheless controls the layout.

Each module is standardized to include two parts: a content area and a labeled header with options buttons. Standard layouts and typography are critical for flexible reuse and configuration; without them, the page's rhythm and appearance would be compromised. With the standard construction, each module remains a separate concern, with well understood, logical boundaries.

Components

1. Google global navigation
2. iGoogle header and search
3. Configuration bar
4. Tab 1: Home
5. Tab 2: Tools
6. Tab container
7. Countdown
8. Date and time
9. Gmail

10. Google Reader
11. Weather
12. Music
13. Maps
14. Google Calendar
15. Google Docs
16. Washingtonpost.com feed
17. ESPN.com feed
18. Footer

Spotlight: Content Lists

Many iGoogle modules contain a list of links, and link list displays appear to be quite standardized across modules from different content providers. The modules for Google Docs, Washingtonpost .com, and ESPN.com each include a set of links, each of which is left aligned, the same size (and color), customizable for link quantity, and inclusive of an icon to reveal the content type (such as a Google Docs spreadsheet) or expand to show a document abstract. The Google Docs module also includes functional rows for search and customizing the list drop-downs for Show and New. However, this doesn't violate the tenets employed consistently across each module variation.

Notes

Singer, R. 2004. An Introduction to Using Patterns in Web Design. 37 Signals: http://www.37signals.com/papers/introtopatterns/.

Brown, D. 2002. Where the Wireframes Are: Special Deliverable #3. Boxes and Arrows: http://www.boxesandarrows.com/view/where_the_wireframes_are_special_deliverable_3.

3

VARY

"Plus ça change, plus c'est la même chose" (loosely translated as *"The more things change, the more they stay the same."*)—Jean-Baptiste Alphonse Karr

One thing we can be sure about is that nearly everything we design online needs to adapt to change. While a few components may end up having a static, fixed state, so many more require a designer to identify, visualize, and communicate a design's range and flexibility.

This chapter focuses on how to communicate component variation by doing the following:

- ▶ Documenting different component instances
- ▶ Understanding and communicating states
- ▶ Choosing the right techniques to display visualizations
- ▶ Composing precise and effective descriptions
- ▶ Thinking about how to best combine visualizations and descriptions

Varying Components

A component needn't—and, in many cases, *shouldn't*—always be the same. In fact, components can vary in many ways due to the following:

▶ Personalized content and functionality based on business rules

▶ Customized presentations based on user preference

▶ Dynamic navigation and content driven by taxonomy

▶ Behaviors, including interactions and transitions

▶ Diverse, editorialized copy

▶ Features available or limited due to platform considerations

▶ Computed data such as price and discount

▶ Content quantity and scale, such as a shopping cart's product quantity and diversity

As a designer, you must consider these varied circumstances to fully illustrate a component's flexibility and potential for reuse. But more importantly, thoughtfully considering such change should prompt you to tell a more complete story of how, when, why, and how much a component can be different.

During projects, the need to vary a component may be obvious from the outset. For example, the site header's secondary navigation bar has distinct options for each primary navigation option: Primary categories for Products and Support would each have a distinct set of secondary navigation options. Designing, documenting, and maintaining primary and secondary navigation options in a header can be helpful to all involved in a large-scale design project.

On the other hand, other components may not seem to require any variation until later in the project when teams drill into details to finalize a design. Initially you might think each pleat of an accordion need only include a basic paragraph with embedded links. However, later in the project, the team could agree that content may also include thumbnails and/or subheads. In that case, the accordion must be varied to address such cases.

You shouldn't be resistant to creating new variations per se. Each variation is an opportunity to communicate more thoroughly, whether to extend a component or clarify its current use. With variations, an entire project team—designers, engineers, and stakeholders alike—can accurately assess if, how, and to what extent something can change and adapt to different circumstances.

Exploring and documenting variations can also suggest to a librarian what items—at what range and flexibility—should be considered for a library or other set of standards. Project conversations may result in adding only a subset of variations to a library, and that's OK.

States

Variations are often considered as component states with distinct behaviors, content, style, and structure. States address how a component appears when a page is loaded and how its appearance shifts as interactions occur. Each state is a mode of being, where the user interface is rendered based on specific conditions. Under varying conditions, the interface may and often does render perceptibly different displays.

Granted, some components are entirely fixed. The site logo in most designs is positioned in the upper left of a page and may never, ever be changed, located elsewhere, or linked to anything other than the site's homepage.

But most components vary at least a little, either via a known set of discrete states or a more flexible, continuous range of states dependent on available content and events that occur. The site utility bar depicted in **Figure 3.1** has two states and only two states: not logged in (which includes a link to log in) and logged in (which displays the username as well as a link to log out).

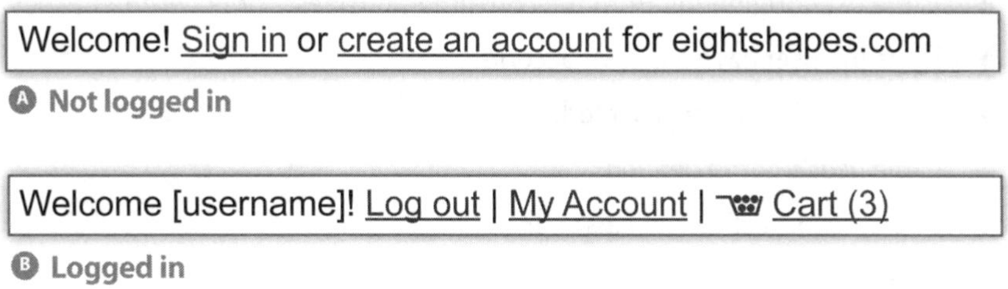

Welcome! Sign in or create an account for eightshapes.com

Ⓐ **Not logged in**

Welcome [username]! Log out | My Account | 🛒 Cart (3)

Ⓑ **Logged in**

Figure 3.1 A site's utility bar, with two states.

A homepage billboard of feature stories could have an innumerable array of states that address unique headlines, large product photographs, story snippets, links, and even embedded video, all of which depend on how the editorial team chooses and publishes content. The potential variation is infinite. However, the designer can create a handful of billboard variations to sufficiently convey component diversity and flexibility.

Stating the Question

When describing states, the designer's primary focus is the user's perception: usually, what can be seen on a screen. Ultimately, states serve as the answer to a fundamental question broken down into three key parts:

When can you see what?

Part #1: When

Stated first, "When" focuses on the conditions or circumstances of a state that set the context of what is shown. Here, you must describe conditions in terms of precise statements and unambiguous visualizations. Be as clear as possible as to when such a state does or does not occur. If a designer can't accurately describe conditions for "When" a state occurs, then any hope of expressing the "See" and "What" is fruitless.

There are a countless number of conditions that could impact a display, and all are predicated on the specifics of the experience and component in question. Example circumstances include the following:

- ▶ Is the user signed in?
- ▶ Is the user's age known, and is the user old enough?
- ▶ Is content for this field available for display?
- ▶ Is the user originating from the consumer, business, or government section?
- ▶ Does the user have a known account?
- ▶ Is a particular option selected?
- ▶ Is the user's name defined?
- ▶ Does the playlist contain a song?
- ▶ Is the inbox empty?
- ▶ Is the page set up for A/B tests, and if so, which example should be shown: A or B?

If the question is established clearly, then it can be answered in a way that cannot be misinterpreted. Yes, the user is signed in, or no, the user is NOT signed in. Yes, the user was born before a specific date, or no, either the user is too young or the system doesn't know the user's age.

Part #2: See

Next, "See." This is pretty simple. When taking the user's point of view, you define whether the system should show or hide a component or some portion thereof.

For example, the interface will hide content that is inappropriate for unauthenticated visitors. Similarly, if an ecommerce site recognizes that a customer is interested in government products, then the interface shows such promotions and purchase options.

Part #3: What

Finally, the "What," which isn't that complicated, either. Here, the designer is looking to define precisely how the user interface appears. Is the component revealed? And if so, what elements are displayed, what content appears in each element, what is each element's appearance, and so on.

How does a designer document the answer to "When do you see what?" One can communicate that answer via pictures (visualizations of a screen design), words (annotations, prose statements, lists, and tables), and often both pictures and words together when neither would suffice without the other.

Variation via Pictures

Edward Tufte's *Visual Display of Quantitative Information* provides a powerful starting point for how to visualize component variation through the related concept of small multiples: "Small multiples resemble the frames of a movie: a series of graphics, showing the same combination of variables, indexed by changes in another variable."

While visualizing interface variations does not map exactly to small multiples, each part of the question "When do you see what?" corresponds to a portion of his definition:

- ▶ Conditions and circumstances ("When") correspond to "indexed by changes in another variable" (or really, one *or more* other variables).

- ▶ Rendered displays ("See") correspond to "Showing."

- ▶ Component appearance ("What") corresponds to the "series of graphics, showing the same combination of variables."

Displaying component variations follows many of the same principles of small multiples, with goals like, as Tufte writes, "inevitably comparative" and "efficient in interpretation." You can more effectively communicate components by improving your ability to render, position, relate, and contrast variations in documentation. It's how you place variations side by side, as well as within a page context, that can make all the difference in telling a component's story.

#1. Compare

First and foremost, lay out component variations to facilitate easy comparison. A sufficiently diverse collection of variations enables readers to examine distinctions, whether straightforward or very sophisticated. Each alternative should inflect meaningful information, making it worthwhile and unique.

Consider the rich array of contact options that sites provide. **Figure 3.2** presents four variations of a prominent and reusable Contact Us component.

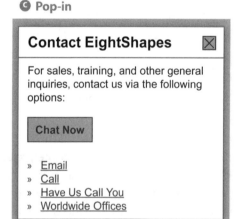

Figure 3.2 Comparing alternative Contact Us options.

The nearly ubiquitous default variation includes a button that initiates an interactive, real-time chat. Therefore, this primary version is positioned in the upper left. To its right, a scaled-down version omits the chat button for when the business is closed or support representatives aren't familiar with that page's content. On the lower left, the default variation is repurposed as a "pop-in" presented above page content after a prescribed period of time has elapsed. The final alternative depicts a static variation with basic contact information, appropriate for an "About Us" section of basic corporate content like press releases and governance.

By positioning all four options tightly together, stakeholders can compare the alternatives easily and ask more probing questions such as "Do I always have to display all four links under the Chat Now button?" and "When would I turn off real-time chat?"

#2. Order

You can communicate important context with the order in which you present alternatives. Avoid a jumbled layout of variations haphazardly placed in no particular sequence. Instead, use order to reveal aspects like status and priority, or to create a progressively more personalized collection of content.

For example, if variations include an archetype that is the basis for other alternatives or is used in the majority of cases, position that variation first in the upper left, as shown in **Figure 3.3**.

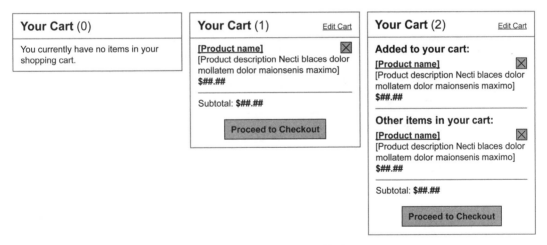

Figure 3.3 Ordered variations of a shopping cart as items are added.

Similarly, you can use order to reveal variation as more information is added over time. For example, one may progressively add items to a shopping cart. The first variation depicts an empty mini-cart (displayed in the site's sidebar), and additional variations as a user adds products over time. Notice how the implied order from left to right communicates growth from the default state to a progressively fuller cart.

#3. Attribute

You can use one or more features, traits, or attributes to vary components across a discrete set of values. These attributes enable stakeholders, engineers, and testers to tie variation to explicit conditions. Visualizations should cover sufficient attribute values to communicate component range and flexibility.

For example, **Figure 3.4** depicts three variations of a credit history check shown on a checkout page. If the system assumes the audience is a consumer, display common consumer fields such as Social Security Number and Date of Birth; otherwise, show business fields like Tax ID and Company Name. If the purchase is already preauthorized based on other known factors, then hide the credit history fields and show a message.

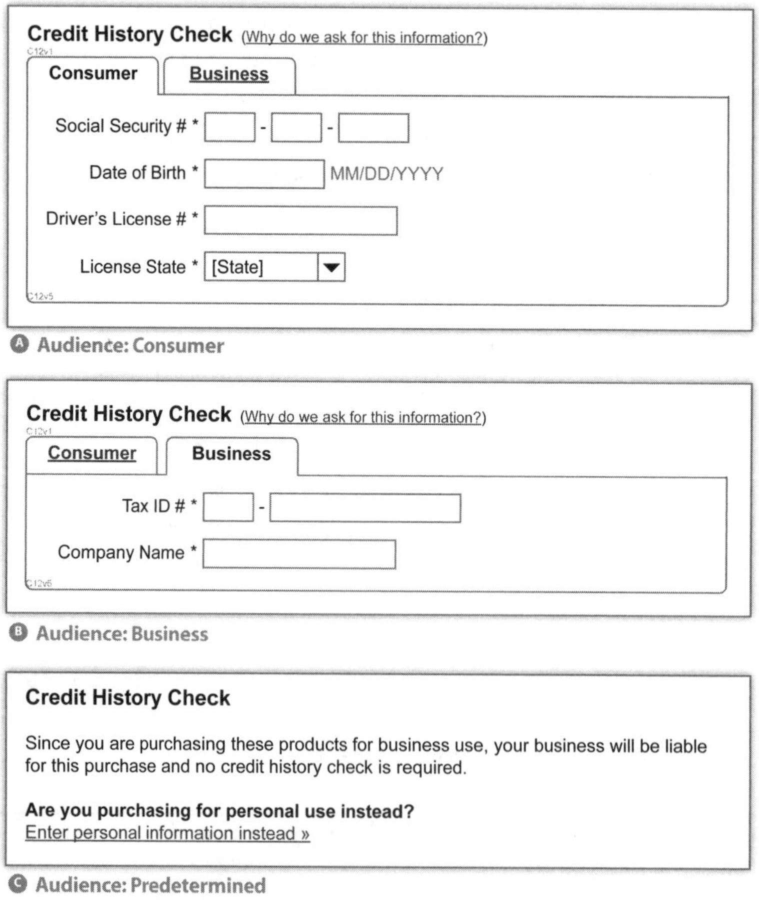

Credit History Check (Why do we ask for this information?)
C.12v1

| Consumer | Business |

Social Security # * [ ] - [ ] - [ ]

Date of Birth * [ ] MM/DD/YYYY

Driver's License # * [ ]

License State * [State] ▼

C.12v5

Ⓐ Audience: Consumer

Credit History Check (Why do we ask for this information?)
C.12v1

| Consumer | Business |

Tax ID # * [ ] - [ ]

Company Name * [ ]

C.12v6

Ⓑ Audience: Business

Credit History Check

Since you are purchasing these products for business use, your business will be liable for this purchase and no credit history check is required.

Are you purchasing for personal use instead?
Enter personal information instead »

Ⓒ Audience: Predetermined

Figure 3.4 Three variations of a credit history check, depending on audience type.

#4. Arrange

You can enrich component visualizations by arranging them in rows and columns that correspond to discrete attribute values (such as gender or age range) or more continuous spectrums (like quantity, age, or time).

For example, consider a mini–shopping cart that displays the current contents of your cart as you navigate through a shopping section (**Figure 3.5**). Here, the y-axis is used to communicate the quantity of items in the cart, and the x-axis reveals the distinct appearance based on whether a promotions code has been applied. In this format, readers can identify what combination of attributes fits their current scenario, and use the grid as a lookup table to find the right visualization.

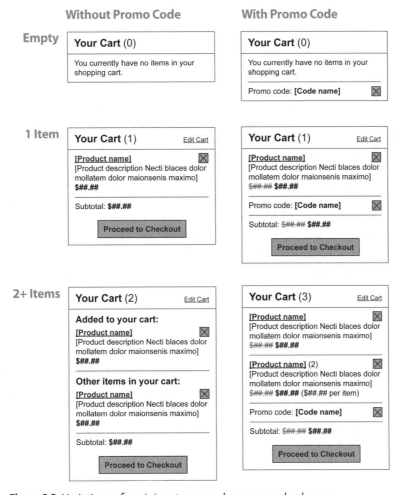

Figure 3.5 Variations of a mini-cart arranged as rows and columns.

#5. Concentrate

Sometimes designers feel compelled—or are asked—to visualize every single instance of a component, based on every combination of attribute values. Consider a checkout's shipping component that varies across five properties (each with two possible values) that independently impact the display, as shown in **Table 3.1**:

Table 3.1

Attribute	Possible Values
Customer type	New or existing customer
Shipping	Regular options or free shipping promotion
Segment	Consumer or business
Store type	Public or private affinity-based experience
Order contents	Shipped products and/or subscription-only plans

Does it make sense to visualize $2^5 = 32$ (or more) variations to cover every combination? Absolutely not. Can you imagine how long it would take to render each one? And then maintain all of them if and when updates are required? The range of variation can be established with far fewer alternatives.

Strategically choose a subset of combinations, avoid or remove the need to create the bulk of alternatives, and concentrate information in variations that are rich, easy to interpret, and sufficiently revealing. This technique enables you to better balance thoroughness versus available time. Instead of realizing every instance, you can pack in much information without wasting your precious time visualizing each one.

In the case of shipping options, four variations are sufficient to display all the possibilities (**Figure 3.6**), whereas many more may have been needed to visualize every possible combination. For shipping destination, combinations of business rules will result in one of three types: fixed destination (A), entry (B), or options (C). For shipping method, it's just as flexible with a radio button toggle (A), fixed (B), and free (or fixed discount) (C).

In this case, it's up to you to complement these visualizations with sufficient annotation and specs to clarify when destination and method options can be mixed and matched. Once a sufficient set of variations has been prepared, readers can compare and contrast variations to interpolate and construct a different alternative in their mind's eye. In that sense, reduce the amount of documentation—and the work required to prepare it—to visualize variations that pack the biggest punch.

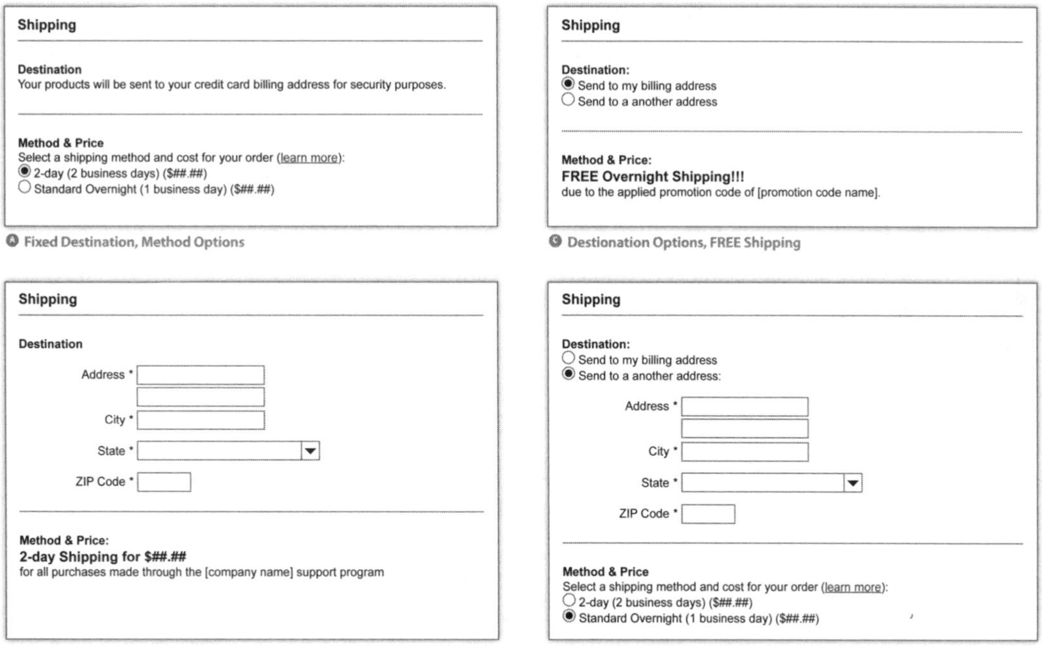

Shipping

Destination
Your products will be sent to your credit card billing address for security purposes.

Method & Price
Select a shipping method and cost for your order (learn more):
◉ 2-day (2 business days) ($##.##)
○ Standard Overnight (1 business day) ($##.##)

Ⓐ Fixed Destination, Method Options

Shipping

Destination:
◉ Send to my billing address
○ Send to a another address

Method & Price:
FREE Overnight Shipping!!!
due to the applied promotion code of [promotion code name].

Ⓑ Destionation Options, FREE Shipping

Shipping

Destination

Address *
City *
State *
ZIP Code *

Method & Price:
2-day Shipping for $##.##
for all purchases made through the [company name] support program

Ⓒ Destination Entry, Fixed Method

Shipping

Destination:
○ Send to my billing address
◉ Send to a another address:

Address *
City *
State *
ZIP Code *

Method & Price
Select a shipping method and cost for your order (learn more):
○ 2-day (2 business days) ($##.##)
◉ Standard Overnight (1 business day) ($##.##)

Ⓓ Destination Options, Method Options

Figure 3.6 Visualizations that vary across several dimensions concentrated into a few revealing alternatives.

#6. Bound

Some components vary significantly, and stakeholders may not know how much they can customize a chunk based on their own project settings. Content can scale (for example, lists), be personalized, and change after the design process concludes. That means readers must interpret a component's existing states to know if they can change it in other ways to suit their purposes.

Effective component variations imply or overtly communicate outliers on the fringe of acceptable use. However, collaborative discussions—and real-life application—will shed light on unacceptable deviation that is outside reasonable limits and that must be documented. Therefore, you can use variations to constrain component usage within acceptable boundaries and increase the likelihood that engineers, copywriters, and other designers use it correctly. Such boundaries communicate not just how a component should look, but also how a component should never look, and may take the form of Dos and Don'ts communicated visually.

For example, consider the rich interaction of an accordion of expandable and collapsible pleats. Stakeholders, designers, engineers, and publishers must work together to ensure consistent implementation and repeated use. The first row of variations in **Figure 3.7** displays two acceptable content variations in an accordion's pleat: a paragraph and link with or without a thumbnail and subtitle. The second row shows unacceptable diversions in structure (such as a table of links), state (such as having two pleats open at one time), and scale (such as having more than three pleats in one accordion).

Illustrating unacceptable variation is just as effective for matters of copy and visual style. Where copy is concerned, illustrations can efficiently highlight inappropriate length, tone, quantity, structure, hierarchy, and more. For visual style, boundaries can cover an incredibly diverse collection of aspects that include image size, photographic style, typography embedded in images, type family, type weight, and so much more.

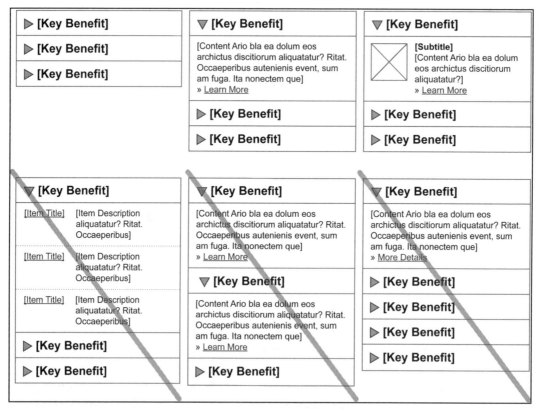

Figure 3.7 Two rows that contrast appropriate use against unacceptable structure, state, and scale.

#7. Narrate

Component variations can be powerful for changes in state over time. A storyboard may span significant time, or be representative of a quick and rich inline interaction. The primary axis of the illustration is time, over which the designer threads a story using static illustrations of key steps, transitions, and content.

Simple interactions, such as a product rating, can include many interesting moments to record (**Figure 3.8**). Here, time passes implicitly across variations. A product is initially not yet rated, but then the visualizations reveal hovered, clicked, saved, and applied states. The visualizations also enrich our understanding in other ways: labels for each of the rating levels (such as "Poor"), the distinct appearance of filled and empty stars, and applied ratings that include an average rating and allow for partially filled stars.

Don't disrupt changes in state across a timeline with obscure logic that isn't evident in the display. Instead, the progression across time should be smooth, meaningful, and evident as the timeline advances from one frame to another. Keep pictures simple if such logical details are better communicated with words.

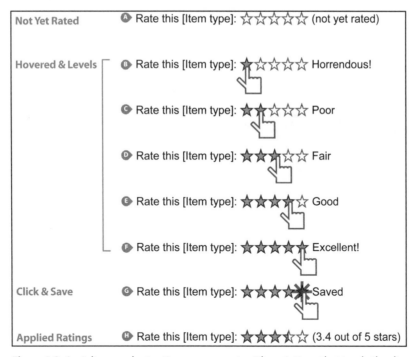

Figure 3.8 An inline product rating component, with variations that imply the dimension of time.

What about prototypes? Isn't it far more real to communicate behaviors with actual interactions? Absolutely. Interactive prototypes, references to internal and open source code libraries, and even sample code can be invaluable for getting behaviors right. However, supporting documentation provides a separate perspective, annotating illustrations of key moments and identifying an auditable track against which others can develop, test, or compare after features are launched.

Too often, designers think prototypes are sufficient. But a prototype may hide variations of states, behaviors, and content behind interactions that are not self-evident to an engineer or tester. While they develop and test a solution, they don't know to click on certain prototype elements, or fail to remember all the different states you've embedded and how to get to them. If they miss these important details and lack a way to audit each one, the final product could suffer.

Very sophisticated interactions can seem far simpler when illustrated via highly structured displays such as Bill Scott's matrix of sophisticated interactions (Scott, 2005). Common yet sophisticated interactions, such as drag and drop, can be fully documented by relating each element of an interaction (such as a cursor or dragged object) to an interaction's "interesting moments" (such as the page load, drag initiated, and drop accepted), as displayed in the table in **Figure 3.9**.

Drag and Drop Interaction Storyboard

Property: ___ ID: ___ Date: ___

	Page Load	Mouse Hover	Mouse Down	Drag Initiated	Drag Over Valid Target	Drag Over Invalid Target	Drag Over Parent Container	Drop Accepted	Drop Rejected	Drop On Parent Container
Page										
Cursor										
Tool Tip										
Drag Object										
Drag Object's Parent Container										
Drop Target										
	What does the page contain to indicate drag and drop?	What happens when the mouse hovers over the draggable object?	What happens when the mouse is pressed on the draggable object but dragging has not initiated?	What happens when drag starts?	What happens when I drag over a valid drop target?	What happens when I drag over an invalid drop target?	What happens when I drag back to my home area/container/slot?	What happens when the drop is accepted?	What happens when the drop is rejected?	What happens when dropped over the original position/container?

Figure 3.9 An interaction matrix for drag and drop, pitting each relevant UI element against "interesting moments."

Not all interactions or timelines can be so cleanly and comprehensively communicated. However, the matrix suggests how to identify interesting moments in an interaction and communicate states over time.

#8. Embed

As you visualize variation, it may be necessary to clarify its position within a page. You can choose from a variety of techniques to establish page location but still focus interest on a component, including those depicted in **Figure 3.10**:

Expanded Crop: Display the component within a portion of a page, where the page is cropped either via a fade into the remainder of the page or a more explicit jagged border.

Page Thumbnail: Reveal the component location within an adjacent, smaller page thumbnail.

Zoom: Connect a scaled-up component visualization to its location in a smaller page underneath.

Reverse: Overlay a semi-transparent layer on a page layout, but remove the portion of the overlay atop the component of interest.

Variation via Words

While variation illustrations are undoubtedly powerful and efficient to interpret, pictures may lack, obscure, or be incapable of illustrating every aspect of a design solution (or a designer's expectation of how something should be built). That's where words can prove supplementary or complementary.

Stated Structure

When describing variation via prose, lists, and tables, you can rely on the fundamental question ("When do you see what?") to structure a statement in a similar and consistent form:

If When, then See What.

This roughly translates to:

If [one or more conditions], then [show or hide] [elements of the user interface].

A Reverse

B Zoom

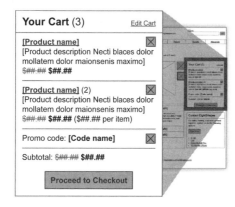

C Thumbnail

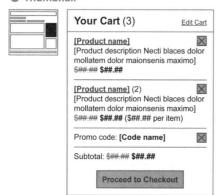

D Faded Crop

E Jagged Frame

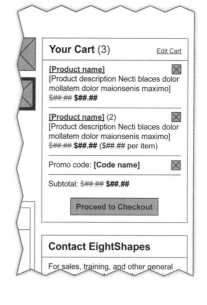

Figure 3.10 Various techniques for relating a component to a page location.

As described earlier, the "When" can be described as one or more conditions, the "See" as whether to show or hide elements or the component itself, and "What" corresponds to aspects of the component or a portion thereof. This form is effective for structuring your thoughts, accounting for a range of different conditions, and conveying details in a written, auditable way.

Crafting effective textual descriptions can borrow from programming, but don't let that scare you. When considering and communicating various states, it's good to think logically about the range of possible alternatives, and under what conditions each one occurs. The following techniques can help you organize your thoughts and communicate variation via words more clearly and accurately.

If/Then

The simplest structure is to start with the form shown previously: if and then. Describe the conditions, whether or not to show something, and then describe what is shown.

Consider a sidebar "Badge" component that reflects a user's profile information. The Badge is only displayed to a logged-in user. Such a scenario could be described as shown in **Figure 3.11**.

> # If the cart contains no items, then show the Empty Cart Message.

Figure 3.11 Variation if/then statement.

Component displays can be based on an either/or scenario: Either you see one thing or you see something else. In that case, extend the if/then form to include the "or else" too. An effective, natural language way to break up your statement is to begin a second sentence "Otherwise," followed by a description of the alternative presentation.

In the aforementioned Badge component scenario, suppose that if a user is not signed in, then the interface would expose a cue to log in and/or add profile information. In that case, perhaps the statement could be extended as shown in **Figure 3.12**.

> # If the cart contains no items, then show the Empty Cart Message; otherwise hide this message.

Figure 3.12 Variation if/then/else statement.

While the preceding sentence may seem relatively simple to compose, there are many problems that can obscure meaning and lead to an ineffective if/then statement. Therefore, when authoring descriptions of variation states, try to be the following:

Objective. Don't leave the condition or result up to the subjective interpretation of the reader.

Positive. Omit needless modifiers that create double negatives, such as "isn't logged out" instead of "is logged in" or "don't hide" instead of "show."

Specific. If a simpler but broader context raises doubt, clarify the context of your statements by including relevant details, such as expanding "logged in" to "logged into Acme.com" or even "logged into Acme.com's account management."

Concise. Omit needless words that are implied by the context, such as reducing "Acme.com online experience" to simply "Acme.com." Such words slow a reader down while adding no value.

Additionally, if your audience includes more technical readers such as developers and testers, you can improve the usability and effectiveness of deeper specifications with prose descriptions. For these audiences, work even harder to make your descriptions the following:

Scannable. If you are authoring numerous statements that have similar structure within a page or across a document, create visual structure with text to improve reading speed and comprehension. For if/then statements, this may mean including the "If **When**" on the first line, and the "then **See What**" on subsequent, indented lines, as shown in **Figure 3.13**.

If the cart contains no items,
    then show the Empty Cart Message;
    otherwise hide this message.

Figure 3.13 A scannable structure for more formal if/then statements.

Logical. Add delimiters (such as parentheses around conditions) and replace longer words with symbolic characters like = and > (**Figure 3.14**).

Designers knowledgeable of a programming language (such as JavaScript) can be particularly effective at authoring logical specifications, but be mindful of the risks and rewards of such pseudo-code. The eyes of less literate stakeholders may glaze over, teaching them to ignore words and rely only on visuals to understand an experience.

And, actually, maybe there's nothing wrong with that. On the other hand, developers and testers—if educated and influential in how specs are written—can strongly embrace logical statements as a way to understand design details and expectations.

> If (cart item quantity = 0),
>   then show the Empty Cart Message;
>   otherwise hide this message.

Figure 3.14 A logical structure that includes delimiters and symbols.

Citable. Empower others to connect their work to the documentation you compose through numbered references (**Figure 3.15**) by otherwise arranging your statements so others can trace back to them. Testers may appreciate this rigor the most by mapping test plans to design documentation to better audit functionality and concretely influence design details before a designer is off the project.

> 3.1.4 Cart Message Display
> If (cart item quantity = 0),
>   then show the message #41;
>   otherwise hide this message.

Figure 3.15 A citable structure that enables others to find and reference details.

Precise. If specific names, codes, or numeric references exist for an item you refer to, then use that reference in your statement(s). However, only be as precise as circumstances require. Don't go overboard and burden a reader with countless, disruptive references if they will never be used.

What is the bottom line? Know your audience! Collaborate with your readers early on to establish expectations of depth and formality.

You could even go so far as to usability test your documentation. This doesn't mean setting up a lab, writing a test plan, and facilitating hour-long tests with eight developers. Instead, this could mean informally visiting the desk of a collaborator, observing her or him interpret passages you composed, and then brainstorming approaches of how you can improve—and they can best use—your documentation. Borrow what works best for you from these techniques, and avoid techniques that burden you as a writer or your stakeholders as readers from understanding a solution at an appropriate level of detail and rigor.

Cases

In some situations, conditions may warrant three or more separate states. When this happens, codify states based on the range of alternative cases. For each state, follow the condition(s) with the resulting display structured as a list or table.

Consider a public version of a user's profile, in which the user can customize the display of personal details based on many levels. **Figure 3.16** displays a table that relates each level option with the details exposed to that user type.

State Matrix

When the display of more than one component and/or element is impacted by multiple criteria, you can use a more sophisticated tabular structure—referred to as a *state matrix*—to efficiently and compactly summarize what is displayed when, and how. A state matrix is formed as a table, with columns for conditional criteria (the **When**) displayed on the left, and resulting display descriptions (the **What**) on the right.

Logged in as...	Name	Profile Picture	Member Since	Email Address	Address	Phone Number	Work History	Places I've Lived	Status Updates	Photos
Self	✓	✓	✓	✓	✓	✓	✓	✓	✓	✓
Family	✓	✓	✓	✓			✓	✓	✓	✓
Friends	✓	✓	✓	✓				✓	✓	✓
Public	✓		✓							

Figure 3.16 A table of different conditions, each mapped to a variable interface display.

A state matrix is really a scaled-out case list, adding multiple dimensions to the conditional criteria and display descriptions. **Figure 3.17** displays a combination of two conditions: "Is a user logged in?" and "What test alternative is selected?" Based on the combined answer of both questions, a particular product is displayed.

Logged in	Test Alternative	Feature
True	A	[Product 1]
True	B	[Product 2]
True	C	[Product 3]
False	A	[Product 4]
False	B	[Product 5]
False	C	[Product 6]

Figure 3.17 A table that displays a state matrix in which rows reveal each state across different scenarios (columns on the left) and resulting displays (columns on the right).

While case lists and state matrices can improve scanability and condense information, they aren't a panacea for documenting all types of conditional displays. If you find that many cells of a state matrix remain blank since not all conditions impact all displays, it may make sense to simplify the matrix by removing columns for criteria or display, or even abandoning the tabular structure altogether.

Pictures and Words Together

Better visuals can compact more information into a data-rich display, and can be interpreted more quickly. Visualizations draw interest, provoke immediate conversation, and are always perceived and evaluated—at least skimmed—before prose descriptions. In fact, visuals enable others to respond immediately and do not require review and consideration before a meeting begins (although that always helps).

However, don't discount the value of descriptive prose, either. With at least one or two visuals at hand, words can be far more efficiently produced and scaled out to include a range of alternative variations (such as copy variations like branded or error messages).

In large part, balancing the two boils down to positioning pictures (for example, a wire-frame or comp page design) adjacent to words (for example, the annotations) to tell a story that neither could tell completely without the other. Annotations commonly describe behaviors, states, content, and other properties of a page or component, and generally the two are mapped together via callouts (lines connecting the pictures and words) or markers (number or letter references placed on top of the picture).

Just as you can concentrate information amid a set of visualizations, you can also more sufficiently document design by using pictures and words together. This is particularly relevant where one of a few visual variations must accommodate a plethora of distinct copy, such as headlines, announcements, product lists, or error messages.

What does a stakeholder do when context is clarified by seeing real copy in a wireframe or comp? That stakeholder asks for more variations to ensure that all copy is written and dis-played as desired. In such cases, don't visualize each and every variation of copy. Instead, augment no more than a few visualizations (pictures) with the full collection of variable copy documented in an adjacent list or table, such as that displayed in **Figure 3.18**.

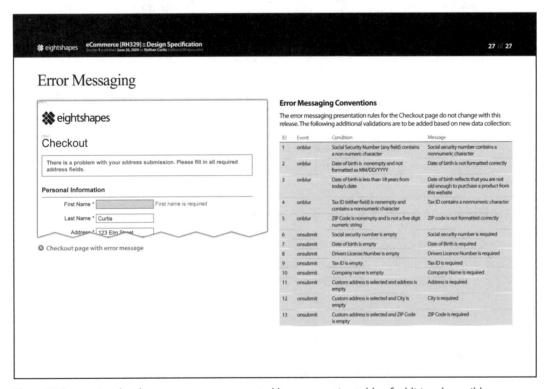

Figure 3.18 One visualized error message, augmented by a supporting table of additional possible errors.

Many designers are excellent writers, while others lament writing deficiencies and shirk opportunities to express design through words. This lack of writing proficiency can apply regardless of what specific discipline one ascribes to, be it information architecture, interaction design, visual design, or even usability engineering. That said, technical writing plays a significant role in a designer's capability to communicate design details.

Don't know where to start? Do you find yourself staring at a few component variations on one side of a page, but a blank canvas on the other side where words are supposed to go? Here's an idea: Describe the visualizations out loud. Listen to your own words verbalized. Then transcribe that description onto the page. Build the relationship between the picture(s) and words to tell a more complete story of how a component can change.

Always Look Both Ways When Componentizing the Street

AUTHOR: **Joe Lamantia**

ROLE: **Senior Strategist & Experience Architect, MediaCatalyst B.V.**

Working with components and variations is a smart way to take on tough design situations. Breaking difficult problems into smaller, more manageable pieces and then taking them on one at a time provides many benefits. In work settings that emphasize planning and process, the appearance of consistent measurable progress is sometimes addictive. Once you've begun to identify components and describe their variations, the temptation to define all the variations of every individual component separately and in advance is powerful, especially in the earlier conceptual stages of the design cycle. Savvy design teams know to balance the powerful inertia of serialized divide-and-conquer style approaches with awareness of the user experience as a whole.

I witnessed one example of what happens when designers neglect the holistic view of user experience while working briefly with a team designing a complex business information service for a client with global customers. In this case, the team quickly identified two major components that performed important roles in the user experience: One provided user pathways through a complex information space presented via facets; the other displayed and allowed progressive filtering for mixed lists of documents, topics, authors, locations, and industries generated by navigation choices made with the facets.

The team spent many weeks designing and documenting minutely different variations of facet structure and display, list ordering, and component interaction, in an attempt to define all the possible states of both elements (even giving them people's names as shorthand). From the outside, it was clear that the individual components were overly complex and poorly resolved, and in combination they were overwhelmingly confusing. Yet during this time, the designers paid only cursory attention to the overall user experience.

Unfortunately, the team spent so much time exploring the intricacies of business rules and variations that they had to skip testing on paper prototypes, and move directly to formalized usability testing on a high fidelity, fully clickable prototype. Scheduled far in advance, this round of testing was a three-week tour in which the team's clients presented the prototype to their customers in several cities around the world, recording sessions and sharing progress toward the planned release.

It was supposed to be a happy trip. Not surprisingly, customer feedback on this "immature" user experience was—to say the least—consistently negative. The clients were embarrassed, the team lead was replaced, and eventually the client put the entire project on hold. In a word, "Ouch!" The team's quest to exhaustively derive and document the many possible variations of individual components obscured the much more important questions of whether these elements were inherently valuable, and whether they worked together coherently and harmoniously within the larger user experience context. In combination with other factors, this mild case of design myopia led to unfortunate consequences.

When using a component-based approach, always remember to balance apparent progress with thinking holistically and systemically about the complete experience, especially during conceptual stages of a design effort.

Notes

Scott, Bill. Interaction Matrix, November 2005, http://looksgoodworkswell.blogspot.com/2005/11/interaction-matrix.html.

Tufte, Edward. *Visual Display of Quantitative Information*. Cheshire: Graphics Press, 2001.

4

C O M B I N E

Up to now, there's been much talk of breaking pages apart, chunking them into component pieces. In the early phases of a design process, initial page designs suggest an array of components.

But once we've identified many chunks, it's time to use those components to construct pages. This chapter will address how to do the following:

- ▶ Assemble components into page layouts.
- ▶ Appreciate how components fit into variations of a single page as well as across the context of many different pages.
- ▶ Take advantage of component relationships, including duplicates, bundles, and page shells.
- ▶ Formulate page regions so that components can be more simply explained and consistently applied.
- ▶ Appreciate the relationship between components in layout and code.

Assembling Pages

No matter the value of components, it is the page that is rendered in a browser. Each time the browser loads a page (or even a portion of a page), a user experiences the content and interactivity of a complete, aggregated view. Sure, the user's glance may home in on and bounce between chunks of interest. But that bounce is around a layout of all the pieces arranged together.

As components evolve, vary, and mature, they must be combined and arranged into the pages serving as the cohesive whole. With components in hand, a designer is better equipped to communicate design through a wider array of page variations. Now it is time to see and confirm what works and what doesn't. Combine components in meaningful layouts, relate chunks together, relate pages together in a flow, and get a feel for what's too complex, what's too simple, and what needs to be rethought from the ground up.

Once pages are divided into sets of independent components, they are generally reassembled with one of two goals: assemble a page based on a collection of components, or convey how a component appears and varies across pages.

A Page of Components

As one communicates a design, participants in design reviews often ask the question "OK, but how would an article appear under these other circumstances?" Even if a designer has created variations that address the display state of every component in question, it's too much to expect others to be able to see the page in their mind's eye. Instead, the designer must be prepared to render additional examples to reinforce the modular nature of the design and answer that question.

For example, an article page could use many different components depending on available content (**Figure 4.1**). Sure, every article includes body content and framing chunks not really related to the article itself (header, footer, sidebar). But many chunks can be optionally included: different types of article titles (in the upper left); inline media, such as photos and videos (in the upper right); and related articles and tasks.

But outside the context of page layouts, so many questions go unanswered. Every article can be printed, shared, and emailed, but where does that widget go? Can the article be mapped to other related articles? If so, where would that list be placed? Can we position an inline video within the article? Where would a photo carousel go? Is that in the same place as the inline photo gallery? How would the article appear if it's part of a special event or ongoing series, like a blog?

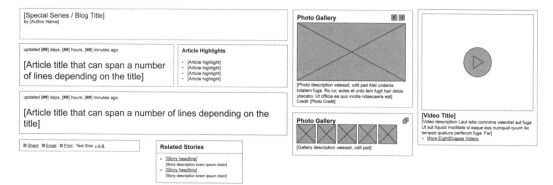

Figure 4.1 Numerous vital components that can be used modularly on an article page, but lack the context of use when they stand alone.

To answer those questions, it's not enough to just design the components individually. We also need to recombine them in viable page layouts to depict applicable scenarios.

Figure 4.2 displays an article page in different circumstances and reinforces the use of all the components in concert. Notice how each article has a title, author, and key tasks, such as print and email. But the vertical location and relationship of those components varies relative to the inclusion or omission of other optional components.

Also implicit in the page layouts is the relative use of components. For example, you can establish the context of the article within a series by placing an additional component above the article title (see variation D, which includes a box above the page title). Additionally, you can clarify that an inline video, photo carousel, and photo gallery should not be used together; instead, you can choose one and only one to include in the upper right of the article body. Keep in mind that you cannot just rely on different pictures to convey these points; also include annotation to reinforce the distinctions.

A Component Across Pages

Additionally, a designer can communicate the range of component use through page variations that demonstrate a single component used in pages with different layout, purpose, or context. These displays reinforce what the designer may have already assumed, but stakeholders may not have realized: Components are indeed reusable!

A **Basic Article**

B **With Inline Video**

C **With Gallery Launch**

D **With Inline Photo Carousel**

Figure 4.2 Article pages of varying depth and component quantity.

Take the video player from the article page, with a few important states as shown in **Figure 4.3.** Sure, inline videos may be associated with an article as helpful, supplemental content. However, videos can be surfaced, played, and related to other content across many different page types.

Therefore, reinforce the video player's flexibility by including it in page layouts across the site. Pages highlighting products, telling a story, or supporting a how-to demonstration can have very distinct layouts (**Figure 4.4**). But the inline video player can easily be reused in each instance.

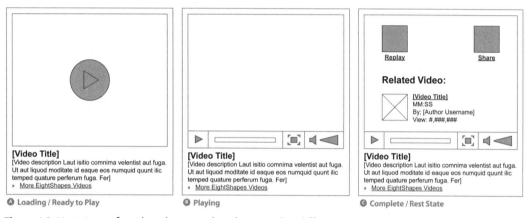

Figure 4.3 Variations of a video player, ready to be reused in different contexts.

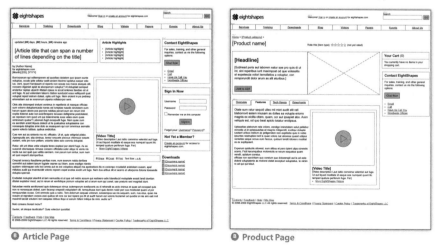

Figure 4.4 A mini video player reused in different page types: article page (on the left) and product features (on the right).

Such scenarios help designers show reuse and negotiate tradeoffs. At times, stakeholders push and push to embed features and displays that limit the component reuse in other contexts. Their goals are clear and justified, but such design decisions can cost an organization more in the long run. Which makes more sense: a team building distinct video players for each scenario, or reusing one common player that ends up meeting 90 percent of everyone's needs?

Additionally, page variations establish how flexibly a component can be repurposed to fit different user needs and page types. Pagination is a common component that displays what page you're on and how many pages there are, and enables navigation across each "page" of results (**Figure 4.5**). Here, a page may not be a browser page, but more a set of any object type, such as search results, photographs, blog entries, users, email, or events. Pagination requires many variations, including first page, last page, and pages in the middle when there are more or fewer page links than can be displayed at one time.

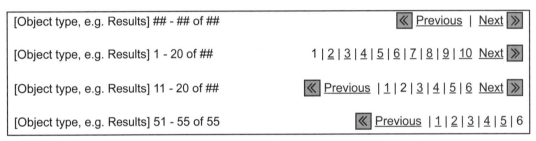

Figure 4.5 Standard variations of a typical pagination component that reveals current page, clarifies overall set quantity, and enables navigation across pages.

Ideally, pagination is consistent across an entire site design. The use of pagination may apply to an entire page's context or to a narrower and tighter single component (such as photographs).

This flexibility is evident in the range of pages where pagination can be used (**Figure 4.6**). Notice how the component is displayed both above and below search results on one page, but only at the base of a sortable table on another page. Each uses the same component, omitting a few elements here and there, and juxtaposing the summary of the page ("Results 11–20 of 55") on the left against the navigation across pages on the right. Showing pagination in each context is helpful in understanding its flexibility: Overall width depends on the container it sits within, and pieces can be included or omitted based on the designer's judgment.

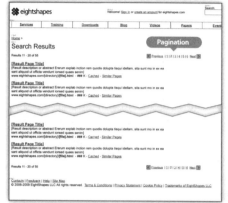

(A) **Search Results**

(B) **User Profiles**

Figure 4.6 A pagination component used in two contexts: search results and data tables.

Rock'em Sock'em Components

AUTHOR: **Keith DuFresne**

ROLE: **Art Director, LivingSocial**

Once your components are created, the fun can really begin. Or can it? As the components are assembled into page views within wireframes or low-fi prototypes, it's hard not to notice a similarity across them. Black text. Larger black text. Some small black text. Maybe a color thrown in for the interactive elements. Not to fret—that's what a visual designer's here for, right?

Yes and no. Component positioning dictates a content hierarchy that is great for getting your ideas across but may confuse the user if visual harmony is absent. Sure, you are mindful of reuse when using components, but a visual designer must also consider position, balance, weight, size, and visual feasibility. Designing a small part of the big picture can quickly lead to disaster if components don't work together.

A couple of years ago, I worked with a talented information architect on an advanced search application. I joined the project after the interface had gone through several iterations and was already signed off. The product had deep business requirements and required a fairly sophisticated solution. The "final" design solution contained many inline interactions and modules, both new and existing. The design was brilliant. Unfortunately, it also broke many aspects of our visual system. The solution completely failed to take into account how it would live within the existing Web site design.

As I translated wireframes into visual comps, the sortable A-Z list and filters running above the content would just not fit in the template. No matter how hard I tried, it was impossible. Flustered, I looked more closely at the wireframes and realized that the wireframes deviated from the standard template to fit the new sort functionality. Sure, the search experience could be a one-off, and I could rationalize that this template infraction did not matter. I could have gotten over it.

However, a larger issue emerged: This template change meant that the sidebar could no longer fit standard components. Plus, two new sidebar components were introduced and they were to be partnered with existing components. In black and white, these components were able to coexist peacefully. Once they donned the site's style and typography, however, they were visually at odds with one another, creating a ping-pong match as eyes bounce back and forth between them. The new pairing didn't work, and we scrambled to adjust in the project's waning moments.

In the end, it is the visual designer who establishes visual hierarchy, and creating balance isn't easy (or even possible) if the component does not follow established guidelines or fit with those around it. A bucketful of components does not give you license to place them willy-nilly. Instead, components must flow together and relate to one another to guide and help the user interact with content and functionality.

Common Combos

While pages are chunked into independent components, you may find that two (or more) adjacent components find themselves used together often. While each component may need to be divided, varied, and documented separately, it may often be positioned with others. That there is a perceived relationship isn't necessarily a bad thing. Even more, you'll want to arrange your design artifacts and reusable items to enable you to add common combinations quickly.

Duplicates

The most common case of combinations is duplicate component use. Here, a component is repeated numerous times vertically, horizontally, or even as a grid across a page.

Figure 4.7 displays a stack of frequently asked questions (FAQs), grouped into categories on a page dedicated to FAQs.

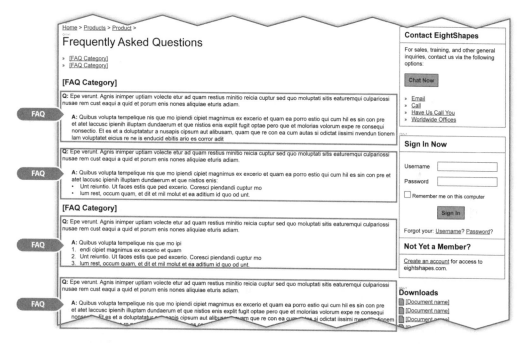

Figure 4.7 A frequently asked question and answer component, repeated once for every question.

Here, the FAQ component consists of two elements: question and answer. Each instance of the component is stacked down the page and includes some variations to communicate the use of bulleted and numbered lists. Communicating the structure of an FAQ is important, answering many questions: What can I include in an FAQ? How do I structure the content? How long can one be? But seeing the FAQs in layout depicts how they fit in the context of categories, anchor links, and other pieces of a page.

> ▶▶ **TIP** Don't take this example as an endorsement of FAQs; in fact, I'm one who rails against the use of FAQs as a crutch for otherwise ineffective content organization. But FAQs happen, and representing common and acceptable FAQ structures ends up being important.

Similarly, suppose you were creating a high-level page that linked to a number of different product types, each featured in a separate but duplicate component (**Figure 4.8**). In this case, you'd repeat the component three times in the page layout. However, each instance adheres to the same guidelines: a general header, thumbnails and links for each item, exactly three features per component, etc. In this case, it may even help to include actual content in place of labels, such as [Product Types] and [Destination], if the rendered page needs to be more specific.

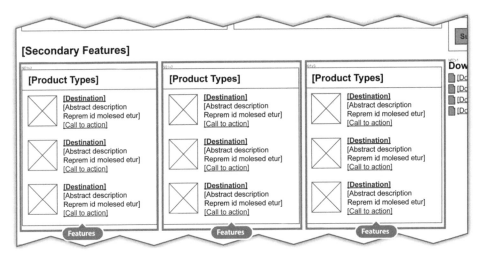

Figure 4.8 A string of feature collections across the body of the page.

Duplicates enable you to define the necessary states, behaviors, and editorial guidelines of a single instance without worrying about or trying to define exactly how many can go on a page. Avoid creating distinct variations for sets of three, four, five, and six instances of an entirely duplicated component. Instead, define it once and establish guidelines on quantity and layout arrangements.

Bundles

In other cases, instead of duplicating the same component, you may want to frequently use a component with one or more other components. A component bundle includes multiple, distinct components, such as a local navigation bar combined with promotions underneath, or a stack of components in a right rail. Such bundled use is often correlated with frequent creation of an individual page or suite of pages.

In the previous examples depicting variations of an article page, did you notice that the components in the right sidebar did not change? The display of those components—Contact Us, Sign In, and Downloads (**Figure 4.9**)—could be highly correlated and repeated across many pages, beyond just articles.

Designers, stakeholders, and engineers will begin to notice such patterns, as will users who start to expect that they are always displayed together. However, clearly all three components have different purposes, different independent states (such as signed in versus not signed in), and may be reused elsewhere alone. So resist the urge to document the entire stack as a single component. Instead, note the correlation and describe when and why they should be used together.

Figure 4.9 A component bundle reused frequently in a sidebar: Contact Us, Sign In, and Downloads.

 TIP Consider including component bundles (such as a library panel or a separate, linkable file) in your library of reusable assets. (See Chapter 5, "Reuse.") Just be mindful that this added efficiency must be balanced with the maintenance cost that arises by including reusable pieces in more than one place.

Shells

Getting started on a new page design should be easy. Open a template, drop in the oft-reused header and footer, and then fill in the details of what makes a page unique.

Given that some of the first components you'll codify and prepare for reuse are the header, footer, and possibly local navigation, it may be worthwhile to create a composite "page shell" out of these items (**Figure 4.10**). That way, starting a new page doesn't require adding seven individual items, but instead dragging and dropping an entire frame.

Once you've added components to your page design, it makes sense to store them on a separate layer and lock the layer. This prohibits you from selecting the components as you work on the remainder of the page. With the layer locked, you won't mistakenly select a fixed portion of the design, whether by clicking on it with your mouse pointer or using Select All.

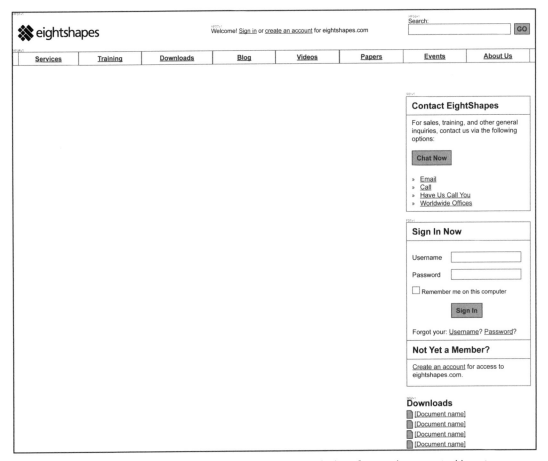

Figure 4.10 A page shell that includes a header and sidebar but lacks a footer whose vertical location depends on body content.

Page shells always contain a page header (such as site logo, utility navigation, site search, and primary navigation) and may contain a left or right sidebar that contains local navigation, contact options, or other common components.

Why not the footer? Well, the footer's location is indeterminate. Page height can vary substantially, moving the footer higher or lower on the page. That said, you could still include a footer in a page shell without locking it with the shell items above it. Footers should definitely be included in a page shell where the user interface has a fixed height.

Some designers suggest that this page shell should be integrated *into* the page design template. That way, you can open a file and the shell will already be placed and locked. This offers significant efficiency in page start-up time, but comes with a few drawbacks, too. What if your site design has more than one type of page shell, such as separate shells for marketing copy, ecommerce, and a member portal? Then you start embedding a lot of unnecessary artwork and the template file—which should be a lightweight starting point—starts to get bogged down.

Additionally, now you are in the business of embedding components into templates, which can become a maintenance nightmare. When components change (even a slight labeling change in a header navigation bar), you now must remember to update not just the reusable component, but every instance where it's been embedded as a starting point for a page design. Plus, other designers may assume that since they have the new header component, their template may not need updating. They may continue to use the template starting point with the now-incorrect header.

Regions

The shell concept hinges on a higher-level breakdown of pages into different, identifiable areas. Most all pages include regions for the header, footer, and body content. That said, many design systems take a regional perspective further, establishing left and/or right rails and even well-defined regions within the body of the layout.

Regions afford a well-defined and understandable way to think of a page as a bento box (**Figure 4.11**). The bento box is a Japanese serving tray partitioned into different areas, each intended to contain a different portion of the meal. To designers using components, the page layout serves as a bento box, with each partitioned area a destination to drop components.

Figure 4.11 A bento box, partitioned into areas in which different portions of a meal are contained. *(Source: http://www.flickr.com/photos/t_trace/2323732013/)*

For many reasons, it is helpful to identify regions, such as the following:

▶ Containers for engineers that transform page layout into high-level markup (commonly, hierarchies of <div>s into which component code is authored)

▶ Identified page areas for documenting where a component can—and cannot—be used

▶ Visual blocks into which a designer can insert components within a layout

▶ Potential component categories when organizing items into a library (refer to Chapter 9, "Organize")

From Projects to Systems

Combining components into pages drifts toward an increasingly formal enterprise. Sure, defining a page as a collection of components is meaningful in its own right. But as more and more components emerge, and more and more pages are constructed, the many-to-many relationships between the two become quite extensive. Component and page design relationships begin to map to HTML/CSS reuse patterns and strategies as well.

Moving Towards Code

A page can be considered as fully composed from components, even to the extent that a page could be considered just one long component sequence. This is much like a Web page's source code. While a layout is apparent in a viewer, in the source code it is just one continuous stream of markup in between two <body> tags. From a design perspective, one could think of pages in the same way.

For example, the article page (**Figure 4.12**) is composed of 14 components. From the header's components at the top to the footer on the bottom, the page can be described as 14 distinct chunks. The HTML behind the scenes may not yet be formed. However, from top to bottom, and left to right, the components could be ordered as displayed in the composition, likely mirroring their order within the page's markup.

That source code, displayed on the right, is how engineers may see a page in their mind's eye: a series of <div> tags containing each bit of content. Pages can be rendered as a series of components that fit into one container (the <body> tag) or a series of subcon-tainers (likely, <div>s corresponding to regions of the overall layout). Suddenly, the bridge from design to development seems a little shorter.

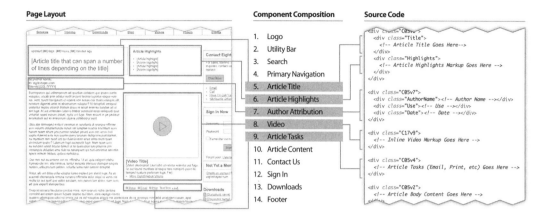

Figure 4.12 A page inventory of components mapped to a layout and to example page markup.

A Worthy Investment

The more you create and share page variations under different conditions or show how many pages use the same component, the more literate your audience will become. You—and your audience—will be able to see the pages in your mind's eye without having to render it as an actual visualization. You'll imagine components within pages without *seeing* the pages, discuss them more efficiently with each other, and save time by reducing the need to create full page designs over and over again. That modular literacy is key for you and your audiences to use components effectively in the long run.

That said, creating mockups of screen designs—whether wireframes or comps—is central to a designer's ability to communicate design. You must be able to do it faster. And better. And consistently. Even in the throes of hectic projects and ridiculous deadlines. That's where increasing your competency to use and build reusable design assets becomes critical.

5

R E U S E

To be modular means you've constructed your components so they are flexible and can be reused. In application development, reuse is a deep, well-researched topic that has occupied the minds of many a software engineer. Designers appreciate reuse, too. However, if designers want to tackle the opportunities of component-based design, they must have a thorough knowledge of software features at their disposal. Armed with sophisticated capabilities, they can then employ more reuse techniques, and even evaluate whether a different tool may be more appropriate for their needs.

This chapter covers core concepts in reusing design within common design software tools, with a focus on the following:

- ▶ Embedding artwork in screen designs via symbol panels and placed files
- ▶ Linking artwork to panels and files to create more extensive reuse
- ▶ Comparing embedded and linked features across common software tools
- ▶ Using linked artwork to relate components and pages
- ▶ Adopting a culture of linked artwork, with its benefits and challenges
- ▶ Unifying design, copy, and deliverables via advanced techniques for linking files

The Curse of Embedded Artwork

Using content in one location and then reusing it somewhere else can be extremely easy and fast. Copy and paste it, right? The copy and paste operation is simple, direct, and available in every design software tool.

Once you've prepared your first page design, just start another by selecting what you created in the first, copy it, and paste in the second. How about the third page? Just copy what you need from pages one and two, and you've got yourself the starting point for page three. But as you design more and more pages and components, you'll start to copy the same elements over and over again. Most commonly, a header and footer seem to find their way into every design. Page titles, breadcrumbs, and other common treatments, too.

The big drawback of embedded artwork is that there is no connection to its source, preventing you from keeping numerous instances of the same thing in sync if it changes over time. Sure, many items won't change on your project. On nearly every project I've worked on, the footer doesn't change. Therefore, embedding a footer in each page layout represents little to no risk.

However, many components do change, even frequently, during a project as requirements shift and your design evolves. That's what this whole book is about: flexible and dynamic reuse. And yet, the files of so many designers don't reflect the same modularity and helpful reuse that their design solution suggests or software tool enables.

Therefore, take advantage of your software tool's techniques for reusing objects. Embedded, manual copies of a design may be quick and easy at first, but using them takes its toll on your productivity, degrades consistency, creates a maintenance morass, and limits collaboration as your design—and design system—matures over time.

A More Dynamic Design

To mitigate the drawbacks of embedded artwork, use features provided by your design software to link and reuse components dynamically to a master version.

Reusing Components Inside a File

Linked reuse can start inside a document, where you can often link multiple component instances to a master symbol. Whenever the master symbol is modified, all linked instances are automatically updated to reflect the change.

Using master symbols can save you significant time and also reduce file size. Suppose your solution includes 32 wireframes that each use the same header. If you add a new button to your primary navigation bar managed as a master symbol, then you only need to update the master to change all 32 wireframes simultaneously. That certainly beats going page to page to make the same change 32 separate times.

Depending on your tool, this feature is called a symbol (Adobe Fireworks and Adobe Illustrator, as shown in **Figure 5.1**), smart object (Adobe Photoshop), or master (Axure and items dragged from a Document Stencil in Microsoft Visio).

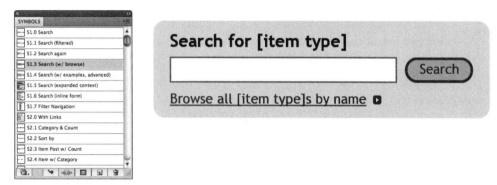

Figure 5.1 The Adobe Illustrator symbol panel, from which a designer can drag and place a symbol instance in artwork but retain the link to the master symbol managed in the panel.

In cases where an instance must be different than the master, you can break the relationship between instance and master to customize the instance's appearance to fit its context. This break might be necessary to extend a generic component to include specific copy, imagery, and other characteristics. For example, you may change header copy from the component's default "[Header]" to "Key Benefits" specific to your page design. However, once you break the link, the instance may no longer reflect any changes to the master.

Reusing Components Across Files

Master/instance object relationships are powerful for establishing and maintaining reusable artwork within a file. But just like all the other art in the document, the masters themselves are embedded within that one file. That makes it harder if not impossible to effectively reuse artwork in other documents you prepare.

Recall those 32 wireframes you've annotated in a document prepared for stakeholder review? If you want to create a clickable prototype using those same visualizations, then you copy and paste those pages—one by one—from your wireframe review document into a new prototype document (or even HTML prototype). Sure, perhaps the new document inherits the master and linked relationships. But wireframes in the prototype document are separate from and not linked to those in the wireframe draft document you started from. You've now got a complete second copy of your artwork.

Creating a prototype that way takes time. Even worse, it's painful when the design changes before you run the test, and you've got more copying and pasting to update the prototype. The problems intensify as someone else prepares a test script before or a testing report after the test: As design changes, artwork copied into those plans gets out of date, too.

Many software tools—notably Adobe Illustrator and Adobe InDesign—allow you to place a linked instance of one file in another document's layout. Linked files remain connected to, but independent of, the file in which they are placed. When you publish a document with linked files, the tool retrieves each linked instance and outputs linked artwork at full resolution.

Using linked files can dramatically widen reuse opportunities and ease maintenance. Using linked files, you can store your components in separate files, and each of your page designs can be in distinct files, too. As you begin to combine components into different page designs, you now have a rich collection of distinct assets that you can combine to create more variations, interesting displays and flows, and use across many deliverables.

Within the document containing linked artwork, you see the artwork but cannot directly select or edit elements. Instead, you use a command like "Edit Original" to open the linked artwork, make and save updates, and return to the document to see the changes. The process of editing linked originals becomes familiar, such that drilling into and out of linked instances feels fluid and natural after a few tries. This operation results in a "hub and spoke" model for maintaining design documents (**Figure 5.2**).

 TIP Set up a keyboard shortcut for editing a linked file (such as for the Object > Edit Original command) so that you can quickly edit the original linked file via a simple keystroke.

Customizing Each Linked Instance

When component artwork is linked to a page design, you can customize component appearance within the page via operations that don't alter the underlying component file, such as the following:

> **Crop:** When rendering variations of the same component, you can arrange them in the same file side by side or in a matrix, and then crop that matrix when you place it in a page design so that you show only the variation of interest. That way, you can maintain variations in one place, quickly make changes that impact all variations at once, and easily place them together into a deliverable to annotate and compare them together.

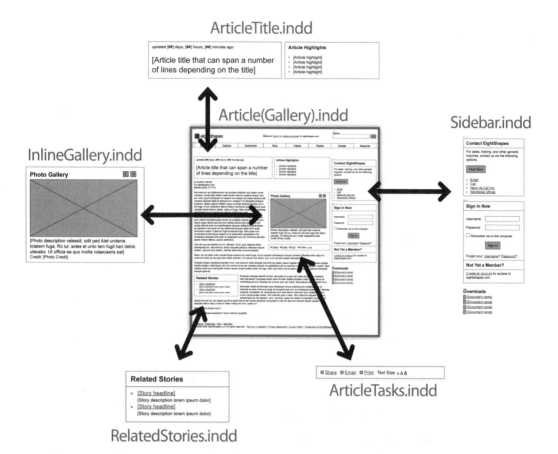

Figure 5.2 Editing files (the "spokes") from a document that aggregates the linked instances (the "hub").

Resize: While a component may be created in a document at actual screen size, resizing lets you increase its size when annotating details or reduce it when including it in a gallery with many other components.

Move: You can position the linked component in whatever location of the document you want. For a component placed in a page design, move and snap it into a region like a page's sidebar. For component variations placed in a deliverable for annotation, position the artwork on the left so that you leave room to annotate the details on the right.

These operations enable you to creatively reuse linked artwork without altering the artwork itself in any way.

TIP   When linking artwork, control display performance of each bit based on your needs. To see a linked instance at its full resolution, display it at "high quality" to view how the final output will appear. However, rendering at a high quality slows the software down. To work faster, render linked assets as "typical" (where a proxy but lower-quality image is shown) or "fast" (where a gray X box is shown in place of the image).

Benefits of Linking Design Assets

Linked symbols and files give rise to many benefits. You can create an environment where your design assets mirror and influence how you—and others, including engineers—break down the design itself. These benefits include the following:

Intelligent Chunking: Linking symbols and files forces you to make good decisions about how to chunk a design for reuse. Those lessons learned—while in the context of reusing design assets—transmit directly to collaborative discussions with engineers and others and can strongly influence how code is partitioned.

Easy Maintenance: You can reduce the time it takes to update designs. With one change, your edit propagates everywhere.

Smaller File Size: As each piece is modularized, symbols and files become pointers to master versions instead of copied pieces replicated everywhere. Therefore, each piece is much smaller—and more reusable.

Independent Annotation: Since each piece of artwork is reusable in different contexts, you can apply annotations relevant to the context where it's presented. In a wireframe review, you can call out how the chunk fits in a design solution, whereas in an editorial document, you can add numerous markers to identify each element in detail. Both documents link to the same underlying artwork.

Broader Reuse: With modular design bits spread across files, you can be increasingly creative with how you reuse each part. For example, a header is linked to numerous page files, but also reused when annotating the header independently as well as communicating related interactions and storyboards that start from a header.

You can reuse component and page designs across projects, and even source artwork for a layout from a standard, shared library. A designer need not even own and manage a file to include it in his design, but can instead just link to it.

Specific Sharing: Does a teammate need to use your header in his file? Now you don't have to send a massive, all-inclusive deliverable document. Instead, just wrap up a simple symbol or send a single file that contains only the header. Whether he is creating page designs, a storyboard, or even authoring cross-project standards, that header is easily shared and reused.

Targeted Deliverables: The rigor in authoring—and maintaining—multiple documents is significantly reduced. Multiple documents can link to the same source artwork, leading to the production of targeted deliverables for different purposes, audiences, and depth of detail. For example, the same page design can be linked to a lightweight design review, a prototype suitable for testing, technical specs for an engineer, and editorial guidelines used by publishers post-launch.

Reuse in Design Software

Most design software tools provide built-in features that let you reuse common, reoccurring items. Often these features are symbol panels and files that can be placed in a layout.

Reuse Through Symbol Panels

Panels are popular for organizing reusable components. Panels let you easily find an item and drag and drop it into the page. Adding an object from a panel is more efficient than jumping between documents to copy and paste pieces over and over again.

Table 5.1 illustrates that different software tools support panels for reusable objects, albeit with different names for the feature.

Table 5.1 Software Tools and Panel Names for Reusable Objects

Software Tool	Name of Panel Feature
Adobe Fireworks CS4	Document and common library
Adobe Illustrator CS4	Symbol library
Adobe InDesign CS4	Object library
Adobe Photoshop CS4	Feature not available
Axure 5.5	Widgets
Microsoft Visio	Stencil
Omnigraffle 5	Stencil

Panels exist as separate files on the disk, and each file contains a set of reusable objects. When you open a panel, it appears in your workspace as a collection of object thumbnails, names, or both (**Figure 5.3**). Closing the panel removes it from the workspace, but the panel's file remains on the disk so you can open it in the workspace again later. This allows you to open and close panels relevant for your particular design work at a given time. Panels are portable, too, in that one designer can send panel files to another designer so both can work off of the same source of reusable objects.

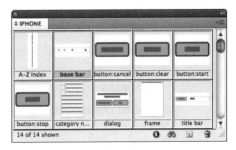

Figure 5.3 Adobe InDesign object library panel for reusing objects across multiple documents.

Panels are used to get the basic elements right every time. This includes page titles, lists, and many form controls such as checkboxes, radio buttons, textboxes, sliders, and buttons. Panels can be helpful for organizing more sophisticated components, too, particularly those that are reused often: the header, footer, navigation, and sidebar components.

Refer to your software tool's help materials to learn more about how to create, use, and manage reusable symbol panels.

Reuse Through Linked Files

Another technique for reusing components is to create a separate file in the tool's native document format.

Design software in the Adobe Creative Suite (including Fireworks, Illustrator, InDesign, and Photoshop) supports placing one file in another via the File > Place operation. For example, you can import a PNG component file created in Adobe Fireworks into a separate Fireworks PNG containing one or more page layouts. Similarly, you can place an InDesign component INDD file into a page INDD document, and place a Photoshop PSD component file as a smart object into a separate Photoshop PSD document used for a page layout. Note that some place operations (such as placing one Fireworks PNG in another) results in embedded artwork instead of linked files.

File placement is performed via the Place dialog or by dragging and dropping a file from Adobe Bridge, Windows Explorer (on Windows), or Finder (on Mac OSX), as displayed in **Figure 5.4**. Adobe Bridge is provided with the Creative Suite and enables you to browse files visually. Bridge offers richer opportunities for organizing, retrieving, and using files via associated metadata, like tagged keywords. In addition, you can position Bridge as if it's a separate panel within a tool's workspace, from which you can directly drag and drop files into a layout.

You can reuse files in Microsoft Visio by inserting each file as an object, but this approach doesn't scale well for numerous inserted objects. Axure and OmniGraffle do not currently support placing files, although OmniGraffle does enable you to place and link PDF and other artwork (just not place one OmniGraffle file into another).

Adobe Bridge   Wireframe Page Design File   File > Place Dialog

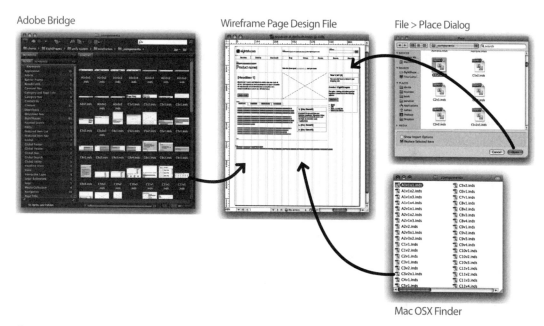

Mac OSX Finder

Figure 5.4 Reusing components within page layouts as files placed via a tool's dialog or directly via drag and drop.

Comparing Software Features

Not every software tool provides the same features for embedding and linking assets. In fact, tools generally refer to the same features by different names.

The table in **Figure 5.5** breaks down software features (as columns) available across many software tools (as rows). No tool is perfect, but each tool has at least one or two effective features to reuse components and pages in design and documentation.

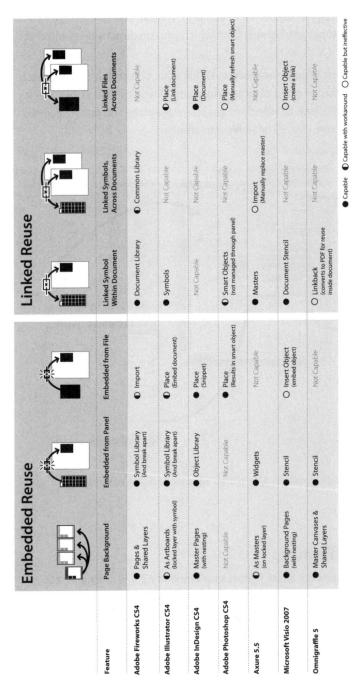

Figure 5.5 A table that compares software features for reuse (as columns) available in different, popular design tools for creating wireframes and comps (as rows).

The various features include the following:

Page Background: Most design tools employ page backgrounds that can be applied to one or more pages and serve as a locked backdrop for the page's content. Axure and Adobe Illustrator enable you to create paginated displays, but lack a direct feature for you to apply a page background to multiple pages at once. For these products, create a reusable master symbol for your background and place it on a bottommost, locked layer across pages it applies to.

Embedded from Panel: Every software tool (except Adobe Photoshop) lets you drag and drop an object from a panel onto a document canvas.

Embedded from File: Adobe products (InDesign, Illustrator, Fireworks, and Photoshop) all support the placement and embedding of native content into another document. The snippet feature in Adobe InDesign is the most direct: When you place a snippet, it directly embeds the artwork and remembers many properties, including styles, layers, and even position. Adobe Fireworks supports the embedding of one PNG in another and remembers layers and styles, too. Finally, Photoshop's placement results in an embedded smart object, which truly feels and behaves like a document inside another document.

Linked Symbol Within Document: Fewer tools support linked objects sourced from a panel in the workspace. However, the behaviors are generally the same across those tools: Place an object, don't break the link, and update the master to propagate the change to every linked instance. The user can break any links to edit a specific instance. The edited instance is treated as an embedded file. Adobe Photoshop offers linked smart objects within a document, although they are managed using the Layers panel instead of a dedicated symbol panel.

Linked Symbols Across Documents: Adobe Fireworks is the only tool that offers a common library panel that enables you to manage linked objects across multiple files.

Linked Files Across Documents: The most flexible option, where each distinct file can be linked into other documents of the same type, is supported by Adobe InDesign and Adobe Illustrator. Adobe InDesign can link to files of any type within the Creative Suite (including INDD, PSD, AI, PDF, and PNG), and supports options for defining the page, layer(s), and layer comps (Photoshop only) of various types. Adobe Illustrator can link to nearly any file type, but cannot customize the linked file's pages and layers, and cropping the placed object is not as direct as just grabbing and resizing by adjusting the object's handles.

Microsoft Visio does support object linking and embedding (OLE), but the feature does not scale well for modular design with many links or a hierarchy of linked files (file A links to file B links to file C). Additionally, performance degrades quickly when one file includes more than just a couple of links. Therefore, Visio's OLE features are generally not recommended for techniques described in this book.

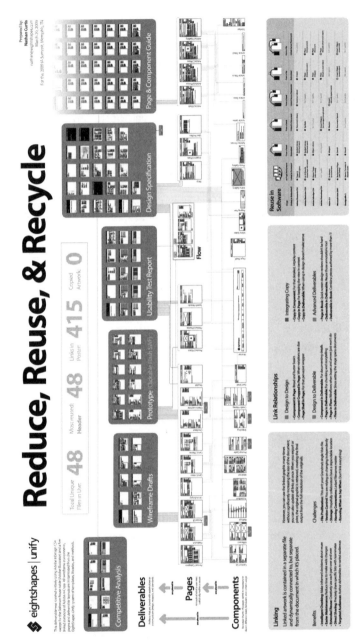

Figure 5.6 "Reduce, Reuse, & Recycle" poster illustrating the many file relationships and opportunities for reuse that result from linking files. The middle portion illustrates linked relationships between pages and component files, both of which are reused extensively for numerous deliverables like a wireframe review, prototype, usability test report, and design specification.

The Essential Links

You can create an array of relationships between components, pages, and deliverables using linked symbols or files. The poster "Reduce, Reuse, & Recycle" (presented at the 2009 IA Summit) illustrated rich and complex relationships across many different linked files (**Figure 5.6**).

While reuse opportunities and relationships are vast and diverse, the most common reuse—and the best place to start—is to link components and pages together.

Component into a Page

Placing a linked component instance in a page layout is the bread and butter of creating modular Web page designs.

A page layout (such as the article page in **Figure 5.7**) can include many different linked components, each linked to a distinct master symbol or file. In fact, the figure doesn't communicate all the linked possibilities, for the header (at the top of the page) and the Related Stories (near the bottom left) could also be linked to a separate file.

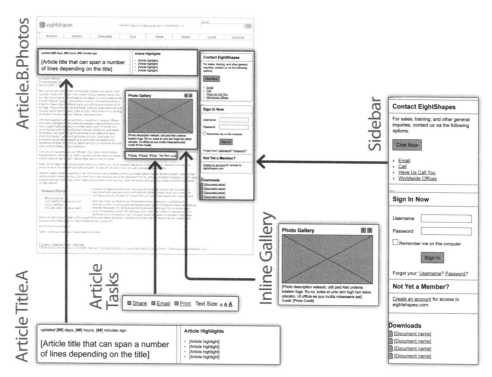

Figure 5.7 A set of components placed and linked into a page layout.

Conversely, article body copy is a poor candidate for a link. The generic content isn't reusable, and the page layout requires the copy to wrap around other component objects inline, such as the article tasks and inline gallery.

Also notice the sidebar as a linked file that contains three components stacked together: Contact EightShapes, Sign In Now, and Downloads. Since each is a separate component, why link the combination together as a single file? Maybe the stack is included on many page variations, and no components are being changed in the project. In fact, since there are no changes or variations of each component, the designer could even simply embed each instance in every page and not even worry about linking files.

Cropped Component into a Page

As we've seen in earlier chapters, varying a component is critical for demonstrating its display under different conditions. One strategy for rendering variations and storing them in linked files is to lay out variations adjacent to one another in one or more rows. That way, you can place the component file in a page layout and crop the artwork to show only one variation, but also place the component file on a separate page to document the variations together.

For example, a sidebar's mini-cart may have a range of variations depending on properties such as quantity of items. **Figure 5.8** shows how you can arrange the variations in a single file, place that file in different page designs, and crop the file to show different variations depending on the story you are trying to tell about the design.

Cropping a linked file can be risky. If you revise the variation layout in the component file, components cropped elsewhere may shift undesirably when documents update to use the component's most recent version. However, you can avoid this by thinking ahead and arranging variations from left to right and top to bottom.

Depending on your software's capabilities, layers provide an alternative to cropping. For example, when placing a component file in Photoshop, Illustrator, or InDesign format into an InDesign document, you can control the layers shown in each linked instance via the Object Layer Options dialog.

When using layers to store variations, size the linked file to the expected component width, ensure enough vertical space to accommodate any variation, and include each variation on a separate layer that can be shown or hidden. **Figure 5.9** illustrates the inline video variations as the three top-most layers of the file.

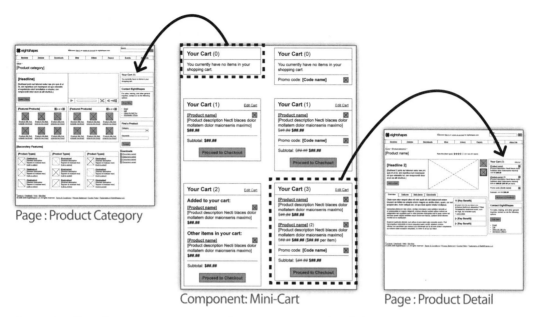

Page : Product Category

Component: Mini-Cart

Page : Product Detail

Figure 5.8 A file with component variations of a mini-cart, cropped and placed into two separate page layouts to demonstrate different mini-art states.

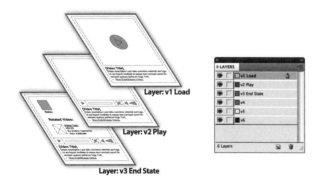

Layer: v1 Load

Layer: v2 Play

Layer: v3 End State

Figure 5.9 Inline video component variations, stored as layers instead of across a single layout.

However, layers are not foolproof. Available variations are obscured since layer names of a placed file are not easily accessed but are buried within the Object Layer Options dialog. Additionally, a placed file's appearance may revert from the customized layer appearance you'd defined for this context to the file's saved layer settings if layers in the linked file change. Therefore, additional layers (v4, v5, and v6) have been included in the file in **Figure 5.9** just in case you must add variations to the file later.

Page Shell into a Page

Chapter 4, "Combine," described different types of component combinations like duplicates, combos, and page shells. A page shell can include a page header and either left navigation or right navigation or both, mirroring the large number of components duplicated in concert across designs that vary within the body of the page. However, omit the footer in a page shell if the footer's vertical location varies significantly based on page content.

The page shell combines all of these components in a single linked file. To use a page shell, place it on its own layer and lock the layer so you don't mistakenly select it while working on other parts of the page.

Figure 5.10 illustrates the use of a page shell for the shopping cart page. The shell includes the header, breadcrumbs, page title, and two sidebar components. This shell is reused across many shopping cart page variations.

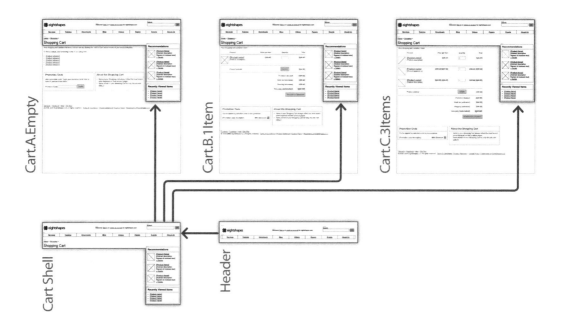

Figure 5.10 A page shell of many components combined, placed, and linked to three variations of a shopping cart page.

Also notice how the header component file is placed in the page shell file. Thus the designer can reuse the header on other pages (or even other shells) independent of the cart shell seen here.

A Culture of Linked Files

There's tremendous power and efficiencies gained by linking files. However, using linked files is usually a shift for designers, so be mindful of challenges that are surmountable with a bit of planning and good communication.

Each Tool Is Different

Most software tools offer incomplete features for linking files, and even tools within the same family (such as the Adobe Creative Suite) don't work exactly the same way or provide the same levels of features that you'd expect. For example, you can choose what layer comp of a PSD you'd like to show when placing it in an Adobe InDesign document. However, when you link an Adobe InDesign document to designs saved as Adobe Fireworks PNG files, you are limited to seeing only the first page within the PNG file instead of choosing what Fireworks page design you'd like to show.

File Proliferation

It's a transition for a designer to move from a single, all-inclusive file containing all artwork to quite the opposite. What began as a separation of a single component (such as a header) from a single page can balloon into scores of interlinked files.

File proliferation requires a designer to organize, label, and store many files. **Figure 5.11** shows two separate folder structures: on the left, a single Microsoft Visio file that includes all wireframes and annotations, and on the right, many different Adobe InDesign files of components, pages, and deliverables.

Collaboration

Collaborative opportunities emerge when a team begins to use linked strategies for its design and deliverable files. Authoring can be shared by federating out different bits to different authors, and teammates can recombine assets in interesting and strategic ways.

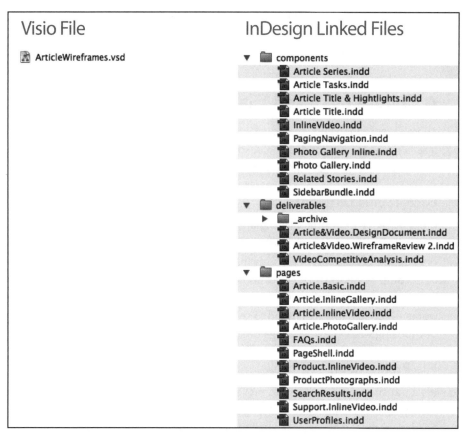

Figure 5.11 Two different folder structures, reflecting a single file in which all design assets are embedded (left) and numerous files and folders across which design and deliverable assets are linked (right).

If two (or more) designers plan to collaborate on a deliverable, they've got to decide three things: who's producing what, how will they link together, and how will they share and maintain files. The answers to the first two questions can come after a brief discussion. The third question—how to jointly share and maintain the files—can be more challenging. Possible solutions depend on the team's IT infrastructure and could include the following:

▶ A version control system, such as Subversion, that enables multiple participants to maintain current and historical document versions with check-in and check-out access. While an available (and sanctioned) server and some setup are required, this is by far the best way to share files across a team over time. Without a server, a team could also use a hosted solution.

▶ Folder(s) on a shared drive from which files can be opened, edited, and closed. Be careful, though: Shared drives typically enable anyone and everyone to delete files, an entire folder, or—even worse—an entire hierarchy of folders. If the team does not have access to a version control system, research other safeguards that prevent consequences like deleted files. For example, determine if you can apply read-only access rights to everyone but the design team working on the project.

▶ An owner identified to organize files and publish the deliverable.

Related to how the numerous files would be shared, a designer must also consider how files would be transported if one works remotely and must transfer files between systems frequently. Sure, this challenge exists with a single file, but it is amplified since a designer needs to think about which files need to be brought home.

Naming Conventions

When sharing files, teammates must discuss file-naming conventions. Designers must name files with labels that precisely reflect the content. Linked file reuse only works when another person can find, distinguish, and use the right artwork. Additionally, many files will be variations of the same item, such as variations A through E of a shopping cart page. When dealing with many files and variations, designers benefit from establishing a consistent yet simple convention like "ShoppingCart.A.Empty.indd" for a shopping cart with no items.

A designer should be mindful of how to archive file instances that are older yet still important enough to be distinguished and retrievable. Since files are linked together, absolutely avoid including the "version number" in the most recent, current version. If you were to change the filename of the current version, then every document that links to that file would need to be updated to link to a new file version. What a pain! Avoid that costly process of updating all your links to point to some new version, and instead leave the current version's name as is, and change the name of versions you archive instead.

For example, suppose you just completed a design review and you need to update your second version of an empty shopping cart. Copy the old version to a subfolder, append a .v2 to the old file's name, and continue using the version in the parent folder as the current version (as shown in **Figure 5.12**). Since the file name of the current version did not change, links to it are not broken.

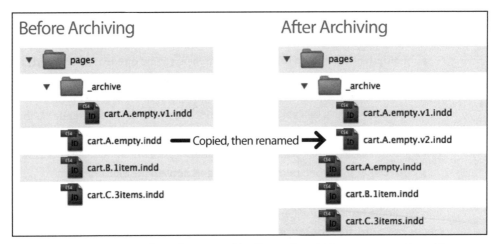

Figure 5.12 An easy process for archiving an older file version yields a current version with an unchanging name. That way, links to the most recent version will not be broken.

To Link or Not to Link, What Is the Question?

Linking files results in all sorts of wonderful reuse opportunities. But be smart about it: Over-linking can cause a system to crash. By *system,* I don't refer to the design software such as Adobe InDesign or Adobe Illustrator. Instead, it's the crash of a designer's brain capacity and patience when he links every single bit of design, from pages to components to elements everywhere. There's rarely a reason to link everything.

A plethora of unnecessary links can litter directories full of little bits with no reuse payoff, cost the designer significant time in creating each one, and create a burden of maintaining many links over time. You'll rue the day too much artwork was linked when you change a directory name or receive a collection of linked artwork from someone else. Imagine the annoyance when you have to re-link an endless array of unnecessarily linked files. No, thanks.

So, be smart when linking artwork. When deciding if you need to link, ask yourself:

Is this artwork going to **change, vary,** or be **independently documented** during the period of its reuse?

Change refers to an update to the artwork, such as adding a link to a global header, adding fields to a form, or editing the interaction design of a video player. If the header, form, or video player is being reused in more than one place—even across variations of the *same* page—then link each instance to a master symbol or file.

On the other hand, if a component will not change during a project, then leave it in each page you design, move on, and don't worry about making a component out of it.

Vary refers to a chunk that has distinct, variable presentations as described in detail in Chapter 3, "Vary." Variations warrant linked reuse so that a designer can do the following:

- ▶ Show the component in different page scenarios
- ▶ Evolve and change component design as a solution matures
- ▶ Document component variations together

Whenever a component has variations, collect the variations in a reusable master symbol or file. If the component is on separate layers, pages, or across a layout, you can crop it when placed.

For example, suppose your design system includes a component that displays a collection of featured items. The feature list has been used across numerous projects over the past year, and its elements have stabilized. Sure, the component is reused three times—in this single page design! But the component is stable, and if you are neither changing it for this project nor annotating this piece elsewhere, then there's no reason to link it. That'd be a waste of time, both now and later as you manage linked files over time. Just embed the feature list three times and move on.

If the reuse candidate does not meet either criterion, then don't bother creating a linked relationship (either intra-document master symbol or inter-document linked file).

Unifying Design and Documentation

Reuse opportunities don't end with the myriad of linked relationships between your page and component designs. Once the door is opened to linking multiple files together, you can present content in a more customized, targeted way for both design and documentation.

Threading Design into Deliverables

Just as your screen designs are threaded together as component and page files, both those files can be repurposed within deliverables to document a design solution.

Components as distinct files provide a great opportunity for you to position each one (or an array of variations) within a page of a deliverable document. **Figure 5.13** shows a set of three billboard variations placed into a design document. Once placed, an author can add annotations, markers, callouts—whatever is necessary to communicate the design. That said, the annotation remains independent of the screen design, so design variations can be reused in other contexts like page designs, too.

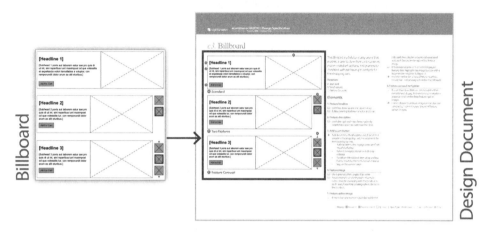

Figure 5.13 A file of billboard component variations placed into a deliverable.

Page designs can be reused in a similar way, added to and annotated in one or more documents. In fact, a single page design can be reused across a range of different documents: an early wireframe review, a test script, a report of testing results, and a detailed design specification.

Pages can also be reused to create interactive prototypes. Most of the time, numerous page designs are linked to a separate, paginated prototype document. The prototype file can then be extended to include hyperlinked and even hovered hotspots that navigate the user from page to page. Ultimately, the prototype is published in a browser-ready format like SWF or HTML for use in dynamic designs or usability tests.

Pages (and even components) can be reused to illustrate the experience design from a higher-level in diagrams like a site map or flow. **Figure 5.14** shows four separate pages, each placed on a deliverable page, connected via arrows, and surrounded by additional annotations to tell the big picture of the design solution.

Wireflow in a Deliverable

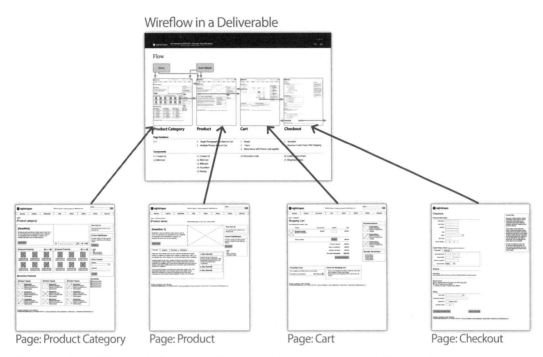

Page: Product Category   Page: Product   Page: Cart   Page: Checkout

Figure 5.14 Four different wireframe page files, placed into a wireflow in a deliverable document.

Prototyping with Components

AUTHOR: **Todd Warfel**

ROLE: **Principal, Messagefirst**

One of the strengths of prototyping is its ability to help you work through your designs, test-driving different solutions. If we look at the example of a shopping cart component, there are a number of different states (for example, before something is added to cart or after something is added to cart). Prototypes help you show those states and explore a number of possible solutions to see how they perform.

A shared strength of prototyping and component-based design is the ability to rapidly design and iterate. By taking a modular approach, you create an assembly framework. That framework is what enables rapid iteration—instead of updating the entire prototype, you only update the component(s) you need and republish. When you have a 60-screen prototype and fix something global like a navigation label, the cost savings of a component-based design is a given. But there is another advantage: the ability to instantly swap out entirely different solutions.

A few years ago, my company, Messagefirst, worked on an ecommerce site that offered discounted pricing for members. There were a number of unknowns—like the best point during the shopping process to display discounts and the how and when to handle discount codes, to show cost savings, or to sell memberships so nonmembers could receive member discounts in the future. As you can imagine, we came up with a number of different design solutions.

How did components fit in? Funny you should ask. Components played a huge role during the initial development, as you might expect. Since there were two of us working on the prototype, it made sense from the beginning to create a set of common components, divide up the work, and incorporate the components. This had all the traditional advantages of components, including increased efficiency and ensured consistency in the design.

The biggest benefit, however, came during testing.

Toward the end of one of our first test sessions, the participant came up with an alternative solution to the two we were testing. I sketched the concept out on paper with the participant to make sure we were on the same page. During the break between test sessions, I made a copy of the existing prototype, opened the shopping cart component, and modified it to reflect the new design, then published the updated prototype to the test machine—all in around 15 minutes.

Since the shopping cart was a component, I was able to open just that file and focus on it without the distractions of the rest of the screen. That also meant I didn't have to open all 60 screens, figure out which ones had the shopping cart, close the rest, then copy and paste the code in manually. Instead, only the pages that had the shopping cart were affected, and they were updated instantly once I saved the shopping cart component file.

Another positive side effect was a reduction in risk. By taking a modular component-based approach, I dealt with fewer lines of code—and fewer lines of code means there's less to go wrong.

Threading Copy into Design

Interaction designers, information architects, and visual designers must work closely in evolving page layout, structures, and behaviors from the ground up. However, content strategists, publishers, and others who write copy for screen designs are often left out of design collaborations.

Most design software tools lack an integrated workflow for designers and copywriters to work together. Some teams have given copywriters access—or even co-ownership—of design files like Microsoft Visio–based wireframes or Photoshop comps in PSD files. Such efforts are generally doomed by a lack of tool proficiency (copywriters find design software too complex), software availability, shared and controlled document access, and—more than anything—trust. What writers and designers need is software in which designers create layout, structure, and behaviors while editors compose copy and flow it into layouts that designers prepare.

Today, the only way to combine wireframing and copywriting is to use Adobe InDesign with copy authored and imported from Adobe InCopy (**Figure 5.15**). Teams that have adopted InDesign as a wireframing tool have piloted the use of InCopy to incorporate copy. Writers contribute linked copy instances to components, page layouts, and design documents that can include tables of messaging and errors for cases beyond those visualized in screen designs. It's no surprise that this workflow fits well in many ways, given the similarities between creating an online experience relative to print material production from which InDesign arose.

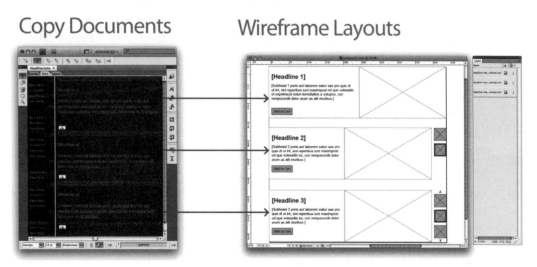

Figure 5.15 Copy documents containing billboard headlines, threaded as linked content into billboard component variations.

Threading Deliverables Together

Adobe InDesign goes the extra mile in providing numerous opportunities to reuse documentation. You can connect different document pieces together to combine contributions or reuse specs, standards, and supplemental information from one document to another.

For example, Adobe InDesign provides a feature where you can arrange multiple documents in a sequence, synchronize properties like page numbers and styles, and then publish the entire collection as one "book." With books, multiple authors contribute portions of content that is aggregated and published as a cohesive, unified PDF document. In effect, the book is a collection of linked pointers to each individual document.

InDesign also enables you to place one InDesign document into another, and identify what page is displayed within the placed artwork. For example, suppose you authored a competitive analysis during a project's discovery phase. The document has lots of detailed examples, but also summarizes findings and sets the tone for design objectives and decision-making.

How can you prevent your stakeholders and engineers from forgetting those key points? Reuse a summary page in other documents, such as a wireframe review or design specification, later on. To reuse a page of a document in InDesign, check the Show Import Options option in the Place dialog. You'll be prompted to define what page of your competitive analysis document to include (and better yet, even what layers of that page to display!). With that simple step, you've now persisted useful content further into the project's life cycle.

Some teams create Web-based documentation for their team's standards and libraries (whether homegrown, through a wiki, or other implementation). However, teams can also leverage reusable documentation chunks to supplement a project-specific design deliverable. One solution is to publish library documentation in PDF form with each item on a separate page.

With that document on hand, a designer can reuse specific pages of component documentation when questions arise. For example, basic standards for the header, tabs, and contact us components may apply across the board and be available from the standards document. For your project, just add pages of that standards document to an appendix.

All of these examples point to advanced techniques for reusing design and documentation within your projects and standards work. With these techniques in mind, the next step is to document your component-based designs. How to tell the story of your design solution depends entirely on your organization's process and preferences. Targeted documentation practices—discerning stakeholder needs, upfront planning, and annotating techniques—is the subject of the next chapter.

6

DOCUMENT

Designs of pages, components, and other aspects of your solution are nothing if they're not properly communicated to those who need to hear your story and understand the details. Often this is achieved through verbal discussion, collaborative brainstorming, and a close relationship throughout a design project. In other situations, such collaboration must be communicated and recorded more formally.

Enter documentation. This chapter will investigate how

- ▶ Documentation can be a key asset or a hindrance in communicating and building a design solution.
- ▶ Recipes enable designers to plan and share expectations for creating documents large and small.
- ▶ Design hierarchies can be a backbone for organizing documentation and drilling into page and component details.
- ▶ Basic tips for rendering documentation can go a long way toward making your communication more effective.

Why Document?

There are common misconceptions in the industry today that software development processes should just flat-out dismiss documentation. Get rid of it. Completely remove documentation from the process altogether. Teams are looking to be leaner and more efficient when producing the best experience for their customers. In that quest, it's important to remove unnecessary steps and focus on artifacts that generate value to a customer (such as software code). That doesn't necessarily mean that documentation lacks value. Instead, we must be smart about why, when, where, and how to produce the right documentation.

Documentation is valuable for communicating a design to people in adjacent cubes, on other teams, or across the world. Why would we document a design? There's a myriad of reasons, including the following:

- ▶ Clarify scope.
- ▶ Tell a story of the overall solution.
- ▶ Close gaps in design knowledge and ambiguous requirements.
- ▶ Communicate and justify decisions.
- ▶ Record progress.
- ▶ Reduce misinterpretation that triggers someone to build something wrong.
- ▶ Avoid heartbreak of a developer who becomes too attached to the wrong code.
- ▶ Accurately plan, prioritize, and schedule subsequent efforts.
- ▶ Ratify decisions.

Summed up, documentation helps us record and reuse knowledge later in the process when we are otherwise not set up for or capable of accurately recalling design communication.

Why Not Document?

On the flip side, why don't we document our designs? In fact, there are numerous barriers to creating effective documentation. First and foremost, some designers are excellent visual communicators but don't like to write, or aren't good at it. Project constraints may limit time available to annotate, and we may be unwilling to rock the boat and change a process to accommodate new types of documentation.

Just as important, stakeholders and engineers who consume the documentation may not be literate enough to utilize it (that's up to the designer to correct). Certainly you don't want your deliverables to be hieroglyphics to someone else. Instead, they must be readable and usable by the variety of audiences that consume them.

Documentation created by a designer may conflict with artifacts that other teammates create, either due to timing (one deliverable precedes another), lack of communication, or outright disagreement between two decision makers. Isn't design about making decisions anyway?

And, although it may be less obvious, documentation may not mature well. What seemed like a lightweight collection of chunked wireframes early in a project may transform over time into an unorganized morass of wireframes, comps, specs, and details. Each piece is progressively added to a document over time in the mantra of "Just put it in the spec." That approach makes it much harder to understand a document later in its life.

The Deliverable Life Cycle

As a deliverable evolves, it typically moves through a series of stages. Ideally, artifacts start from a template with some sense of its purpose and direction. Over time, the deliverable (**Figure 6.1**), along with the design itself, matures from conceptual presentations and strategies to additional variations to increasingly detailed annotations. Design ideas transform into concrete direction. As a document converges on a final version, its strategy, structure, and voice mature. But the document also becomes much less flexible. It's less likely to serve different audiences and project needs.

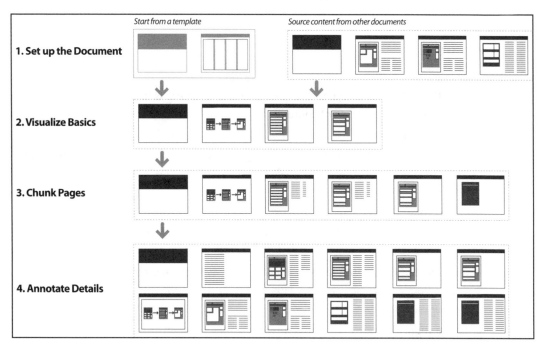

Figure 6.1 A deliverable's evolution as it matures during a project. Documents usually start from a template and/or source content from other documents. Content then gradually evolves as the core experience is chunked out and details are annotated.

Through this life cycle, many factors can disrupt or shift the direction of the artifact's growth. Design iteration can cause large chunks of the design to change—along with any documentation of those chunks. Reducing scope can result in the removal of entire areas of a design from a project. Should this documentation be thrown away and removed from this deliverable or retained but marked as out of scope? Executive input can shift design in completely new directions. Should the documentation have been exposed to such an audience, and what do we do with it now?

Also, the artifact's possible audience grows over time from a few individuals in a narrow team to across an organization. Is your document maturing to address those audiences, speaking to each one in a voice that they understand and find useful? Depending on your workflow and team structure, does your artifact clarify the design enough so that those audience members you communicate with directly can represent the work to the individuals you never meet or talk to?

Understanding a deliverable's audience and lifecycle is critical for the composition and maintenance of a successful design artifact. What can we do to address some of these challenges? Planning and standardizing can go a long way. The remainder of this chapter describes techniques you can use to plan your deliverables at a macro level, as well as to communicate flows, pages, and components in a more organized, efficient way.

Recipes

In every survey we've conducted over the past three years, the most popular response to the question "How do you get started on a new deliverable?" is invariably "I open a previous deliverable, erase irrelevant content, and jump right in."

As designers, our instinct is to solve a design problem, not think about how we're going to document the solution. We start by throwing visuals and annotations into a document without considering the long-range goals or document's life cycle over days, weeks, or even months.

Enter document recipes, which afford us an opportunity to discuss, plan, and assess the relevance of a deliverable before we get started. Through the concept of a recipe, you can discuss all the important aspects of your deliverable:

Ingredients: What visualizations, annotations, research, and other supporting content are included? How many flows, maps, pages, and components do we need? How many variations of each one?

Preparation: How are ingredients mixed and related (such as through modular reuse of design assets), and when is each part added?

Duration: How long does the document take to prepare?

Course: Where does the document fit in our process?

Rationale: Why is the document valuable?

Result: What does the document look like when it's done?

You can concoct a recipe with a quick sketch on the back of a napkin, a casual five-minute conversation between designers, or a formal planning session that includes many participants. Recipe planning often starts by identifying and chunking out a document's parts, organizing each part hierarchically, and graphically depicting their relationships. This is a lot like outlining, but recipes mix in more: preparation, duration, course, rationale, and expected results, too.

All you may need to plan a recipe of an upcoming deliverable could be a quick conversation around a whiteboard, resulting in a sketched plan like that shown in **Figure 6.2**. The whiteboard reveals pages of a document across four sections: front matter (table of contents, change history, etc.); design strategy and research; a flow; and wireframe pages across an ecommerce flow. The team planned to share the workload, in that the design lead (Chris) would author strategy and research content, and two other designers (Nathan and DM) would produce the flow and wireframes.

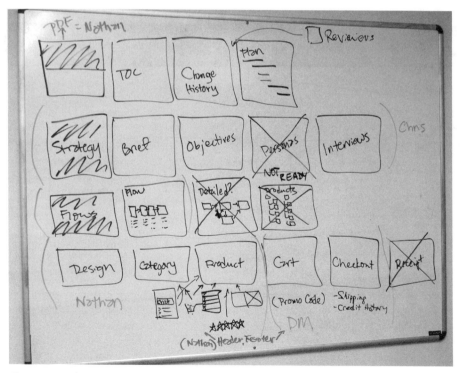

Figure 6.2 A document recipe visualized on a whiteboard during a five-minute discussion among three designers.

The discussion considered but ultimately decided against including personas, a detailed flow, and a receipt page (as indicated by the Xs). Those items were important, but not ready to publish to stakeholders. However, the group remained mindful of the content they'd author in the future so that the document could predictably grow.

The two designers (Nathan and DM) acknowledged shared components (header and footer at the bottom of the whiteboard), so Nathan was assigned to create and share those assets. Finally, the group decided that Nathan would aggregate all the content into a published PDF deliverable (revealed as a note in the upper left).

During the conversation, the group reached agreement on how many screens would be visualized, when they'd be done, and who was creating what—all within the context of delivering to their "user": the stakeholders consuming this particular document.

Recipes are also used to communicate standard deliverables. For example, suppose a design manager anticipates the production of many competitive analyses. A recipe can help formalize the deliverable, communicating standard ingredients, preparation, and purpose (**Figure 6.3**). With recipe in hand, the design manager can communicate the value to stakeholders and set clear expectations for the author responsible for a report.

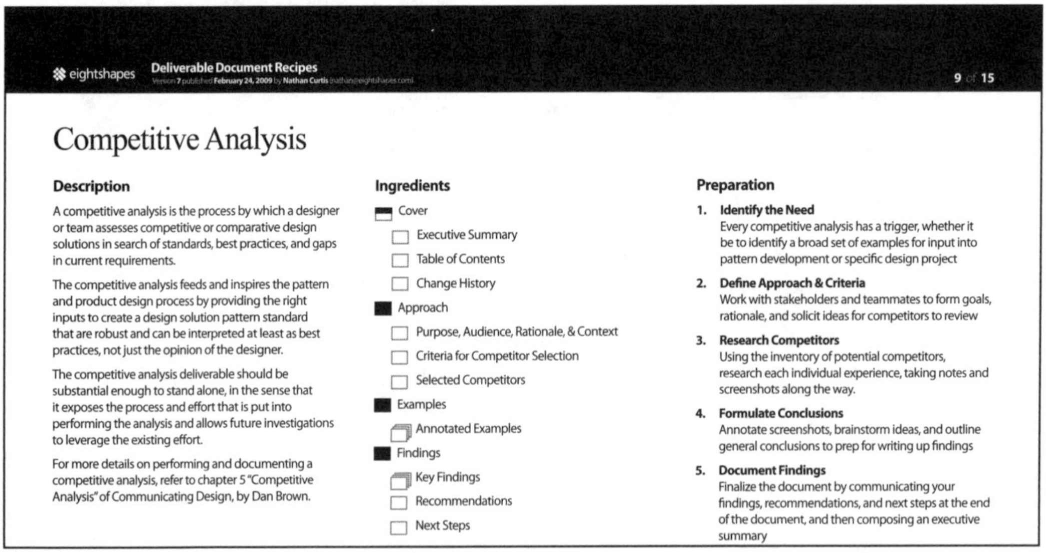

eightshapes **Deliverable Document Recipes**
Version 7 published **February 24, 2009** by **Nathan Curtis** (nathan@eightshapes.com)
9 of 15

Competitive Analysis

Description

A competitive analysis is the process by which a designer or team assesses competitive or comparative design solutions in search of standards, best practices, and gaps in current requirements.

The competitive analysis feeds and inspires the pattern and product design process by providing the right inputs to create a design solution pattern standard that are robust and can be interpreted at least as best practices, not just the opinion of the designer.

The competitive analysis deliverable should be substantial enough to stand alone, in the sense that it exposes the process and effort that is put into performing the analysis and allows future investigations to leverage the existing effort.

For more details on performing and documenting a competitive analysis, refer to chapter 5 "Competitive Analysis" of Communicating Design, by Dan Brown.

Ingredients

- Cover
  - Executive Summary
  - Table of Contents
  - Change History
- Approach
  - Purpose, Audience, Rationale, & Context
  - Criteria for Competitor Selection
  - Selected Competitors
- Examples
  - Annotated Examples
- Findings
  - Key Findings
  - Recommendations
  - Next Steps

Preparation

1. **Identify the Need**
   Every competitive analysis has a trigger, whether it be to identify a broad set of examples for input into pattern development or specific design project
2. **Define Approach & Criteria**
   Work with stakeholders and teammates to form goals, rationale, and solicit ideas for competitors to review
3. **Research Competitors**
   Using the inventory of potential competitors, research each individual experience, taking notes and screenshots along the way.
4. **Formulate Conclusions**
   Annotate screenshots, brainstorm ideas, and outline general conclusions to prep for writing up findings
5. **Document Findings**
   Finalize the document by communicating your findings, recommendations, and next steps at the end of the document, and then composing an executive summary

Figure 6.3 A formal document recipe for producing a competitive analysis, used to establish expectations of authors as well as stakeholders consuming a report.

Fear Not the List

AUTHOR: **Dan Brown**

ROLE: **Principal, EightShapes LLC**

Like an artist facing a blank canvas, you might be a bit anxious about starting a new document. Or, you might be the opposite, diving right into new design problems with unmitigated passion. Those in the latter category may find themselves deep in the weeds before they realize they need to pull back and get the lay of the land.

Even if you follow all the advice in this book to the letter, you may find yourself in this situation. Why? Because all the templates and components in the world can't help you if you don't have a story to tell. (And for those in the latter category, a beautiful wireframe or site map with no context is meaningless to your project team.)

So, before you open your favorite document creation application, do yourself a favor and make two lists. (Lists will be handy throughout the process of modularizing your web design techniques, so best get used to the idea now.) In this case, your first list is everything you want to say in your document, answering the question, "When someone reads this document, what do I want him to take away?"

Good take-away: Readers should understand the pros and cons for each of the three options for the checkout process.

Bad take-away: Readers should appreciate how hard I worked on this design.

What makes a key message good is that it provides measurable direction for you in composing your document. It will help you make tough decisions about what to leave in and what to cut out. And it will help you see when the original purpose of the document is not enough—when you need to expand its scope or create a new document to move the project along.

Two or three key messages is about right. Any more, and your document will be trying to do too much.

The next list you should make is the list of content sections in your document. I say "content sections" because you might decide to do this at different levels—you might decide to think in terms of chapters or in terms of pages. If this is the first time you're thinking about the document, you should put that distinction aside, though, and just ask yourself: What does the structure of this document look like?

Your initial structure for a design specification might look like this:

- ▶ Overview of concept
- ▶ Experience blueprint
- ▶ Product catalog
- ▶ Checkout process

You might make like a screenwriter or novelist and think in terms of beginning-middle-end. You might take a more plot-driven approach and, considering where you want to end up, think about the steps you need to take to get there. As much as we can make our design documents narrative, we should do so because it's a format that resonates with everyone—every client, every team member.

That said, we're dealing with templates, components, site maps, and other things that don't perfectly lend themselves to plotting like a murder, a butler, and a dysfunctional private eye would. If you're stuck and don't know where to begin, start with what you know you have. Arrange that stuff into a list and brainstorm how you might expand each item to explain, in a sense, the story within a story. Here's that first list fleshed out a bit:

- ▶ Reminder of basic requirements
- ▶ Overview of concept
- ▶ Lessons from usability study
- ▶ Experience blueprint
- ▶ Product catalog
- ▶ Close-up of catalog structure
- ▶ Storefront page
- ▶ Category page
- ▶ Product page
- ▶ Checkout process
- ▶ Cart page
- ▶ Forms best practices

As you think through the document further, you'll consider the appropriate order for each of these elements, and how you might need to expand or consolidate any of them. As you massage this list, always be mindful of the first one you made—the key messages—and ask yourself: How does this content or this structure support those messages?

This chapter describes recipes, a concept we use at EightShapes to help us plan and collaborate on documents. Recipes are, at their heart, lists—lists of ingredients and lists of instructions. This book will help you develop your "cookbook" of documents, but keep in mind that making a list of what you need to accomplish and what you have will always be a useful starting point.

Documenting the Hierarchy

A design document's content and depth can vary based on many impacts: project scope, design activities, audience needs, the design's sophistication, and the author's personal style.

That said, most deliverables that communicate screen designs (like wireframes and comps) include visualizations and variations of flows, maps, pages, components, and elements. Not every document includes all these pieces; in fact, many deliverables are much lighter than this. But suppose you were outlining a deep, detailed deliverable, ordered page by page and section by section, to include items such as the following:

1. Cover page

2. "Front matter," including pages like an executive summary, table of contents, change history (if not too detailed; otherwise put it in the back), reviewers, sign off, project plans and/or status, and glossary

3. Strategy, typically in the form of design and project objectives, conceptual models, and research summaries recalling key outcomes from a competitive analysis, interviews, or usability tests

4. Diagrams that depict the experience across many pages, such as maps and navigation flows

5. Pages, and component and element descriptions limited to those pages

6. General components used across an entire design solution

7. Appendices, including standards drawn from a library to make decisions for this project

Notice how the ordering of documents' top-down organization goes from high-level concepts and strategy to low-level details. This allows you to consistently organize your documents and lay out visualizations and annotations in a progressively more detailed way.

A document prepared early in a project to review wireframes (**Figure 6.4**) may be produced more hastily, serving as simply an aggregation of page designs. Producing the document is important, for it provides an artifact that you can distribute, review, and iterate from. The structure here is less formal, and pages are scarcely even related together or chunked out. However, there is still an implicit order (based on when a user would encounter each page in the experience sequentially), and page variations and chunked pages hint at the emerging hierarchy of information.

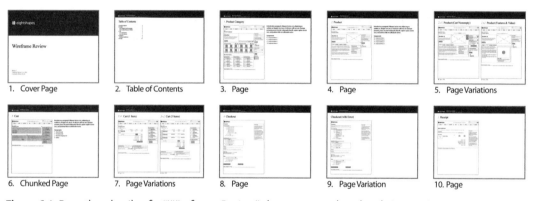

1. Cover Page   2. Table of Contents   3. Page   4. Page   5. Page Variations

6. Chunked Page   7. Page Variations   8. Page   9. Page Variation   10. Page

Figure 6.4 Page thumbnails of a "Wireframe Review" document produced early in a project.

On the other hand, a design specification (such as that shown in **Figure 6.5**) can grow to include a much wider range of content, variations, and annotated details. In this example, strategic project information is summarized near the beginning via a creative brief and design objectives, and a micro project plan is included to reaffirm progress and activities yet to come. A wireflow sets the stage for detailed annotations across the numerous pages and components in the project. At this point, deep annotations are hopefully sufficient for engineers and testers to formulate their approach and accurately develop the solution.

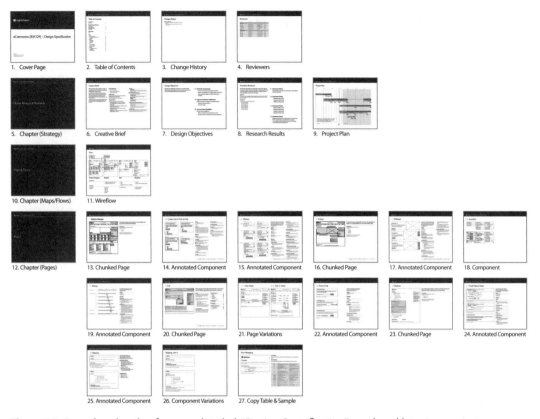

Figure 6.5 Page thumbnails of a more detailed "Design Specification" produced later in a project.

Strategy and Research

Design strategy and research are commonly positioned at the front of a document. Such information is considered applicable across an entire design—the experience itself—and sets the tone, context, and purpose of the design artifacts found later on. Design documents can summarize artifacts like the following:

▶ Creative brief (**Figure 6.6**), design objectives, constraints, and mappings to other requirements

▶ Research results, such as highlights of a competitive analysis, interviews, and other research activities

▶ Conceptual diagrams and summaries of early design brainstorming (such as sketches) to set the context of where the project is now

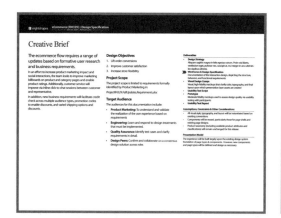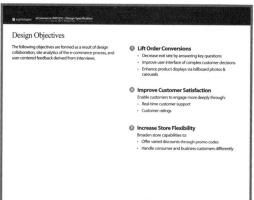

Figure 6.6 Document pages that include a creative brief and design objectives.

The purpose of including strategy and research in design documents of screen designs is simple: Reset context and understanding (if briefly) during design reviews and remind the audience about objectives that influenced the design.

The Big Picture: Maps and Flows

If a design solution spans more than a single page, designers can quickly communicate the "big picture" of a solution via diagrams like site maps and navigation flows of boxes, arrows, and decision points. They can also create "wireflows" and "compflows" that embed screen designs directly in a flow.

Using effective diagrams (as opposed to dense prose few read), readers can quickly grasp the scale and scope of a design solution, and even extract a roadmap for their own work.

Teams can (and often do) linger on diagrams until everyone has a shared understanding. Design reviews often spend a disproportionate amount of time looking at the big picture, and it's important for such diagrams to be powerful, meaningful, and engaging.

A wireflow is an effective tool that blends two techniques—flows and wireframe screen designs—together to visualize a solution at a high level. A wireflow embeds actual page designs into the flow, and connects each one using arrows aligned precisely to interactions within the page layout.

For example, a wireflow of an ecommerce experience (**Figure 6.7**) illustrates four key pages: Product Category, Product, Cart, and Checkout.

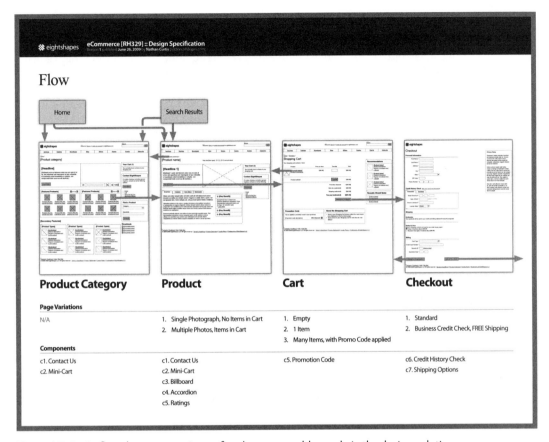

Figure 6.7 A wireflow that communicates four key pages addressed via the design solution.

The page designs are immediately more engaging than four connected boxes with basic page labels. But also notice how the wireflow communicates the lower levels of the design solution, too: different pages that include different components of interest. In addition, the visualization enriches the discussion in other ways:

Scope: The four pages dominate the scene, and should dominate the discussion, too, since they represent the overall project scope. Boxes for Home and Search communicate that those pages are different and less important. In this case, the pages are not in scope, but are the key entry points into impacted pages. Therefore, the visualization shows what *isn't* in scope, too.

Navigation paths: The flow is bi-directional (moving both forward *and* back) with precise connectors that originate at a button or link and end at the resulting page.

Impacts: Via supplemental annotation, a designer can announce impacted components on each page. Implicit here is that the pages themselves are not being wholly redesigned, but instead evolved to meet new requirements. To a product manager, this communicates the specificity of the exercise and limits distraction into other features. For an engineer, this quickly answers the question, "OK, what's the big picture of changes for this project?"

Expectations: The designer can use this page to set up the remaining discussion. If this is the first time the solution is being reviewed, this page is where the designer sets the tone and pacing to cover the rest of the details. If the meeting is a follow-up review, the designer can use the collection to quickly ground the discussion, and then quickly drill into what's changed since the last review.

Maps, flows, and even blander page and component inventories can serve as a project roadmap. In surveys and interviews we've conducted over the last X years with Y organizations, stakeholders, engineers, testers, and even design peers express a strong desire to understand a solution's overall structure. Many admit to looking to the information architect, interaction designer, or design lead to set this framework, but any member of the design team can create such a roadmap.

With a little extra effort, a designer can organize a design solution using flows, maps, and inventories. Teammates can utilize common names (such as the "Product" page and "Accordion" component) and reference numbers (such as "c2" and "1.3.1") throughout a project, resulting in a shared vocabulary that reduces confusion.

Page-level Documentation

While site maps and flows show a range of pages, page-level documentation highlights specific chunks you'll detail at a deeper level. Perhaps you describe all the components that make up a page, only what components are changing, or just a few elements of actual interest.

Some pages may only warrant visualization while others transition to very deep detail. Many end up somewhere in between with vital but spotty annotations. This can result in obvious gaps, but designers do what matters most: convey important aspects of the design within constraints of available time and space.

Documentation of page designs most often takes one of four forms: visualization only, chunked, variations, and detailed annotations.

Page Visualization Only

Early on in a design process—or any time you want an initial reaction to a new page design—position the design within a document even without annotation. This way, you can solicit high-level feedback, discuss basic strategies, and potentially prepare for more detailed notes (**Figure 6.8**).

By including only the page design, you don't invest any further time in annotation when the concept may not be mature or worth the investment. At this stage, you may even avoid creating a formal document at all if all you've created are a few draft wireframes. Instead, you could print out the wireframes one by one or use a different, throwaway document with a setup that maximizes wireframe size in the printout (such as portrait legal size).

Chunked Page

As discussed extensively in previous chapters, page-level annotations chunk a page into components that are marked and named. When choosing which page to chunk, select a page that is either the representative archetype version of that page, or one that includes the most interesting and detailed parts.

For example, when annotating an article page, it's useful to chunk out a page design that includes numerous optional bits like an inline video, related articles, and other pieces (**Figure 6.9**). Those extra parts provide you with the opportunity to chunk more, instead of relying on chunking a basic, vanilla article page with only a few interesting pieces.

The same thing goes for a shopping cart page. Does it make sense to introduce the page to readers as a chunked out version of an empty cart? No way, that is far less interesting and identifies fewer important chunks. Instead, chunk out a version that includes many different items: promotions, different product types, items with different quantities, a cost summary, and more (**Figure 6.10**). That way, you can signal the many distinct parts from the outset.

Page Variations

Good design documentation will at times facilitate comparison and design decisions by positioning different options or examples next to one another.

If you include every design on a separate page of your document, readers have to flip pages back and forth and back and forth through your document to understand differences. Instead, position different page variations side by side so that readers can directly compare the differences. For example, **Figure 6.11** explicitly compares two versions of a shopping cart, calling out that the version on the left is empty while the version on the right includes two or more items. Upon closer inspection, the designer could also use this comparison to call out how the page appears before (on the left) and after (on the right) a promotion code is applied.

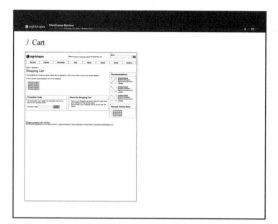

Figure 6.8 A page design positioned within a deliverable document, lacking any annotation beyond a title.

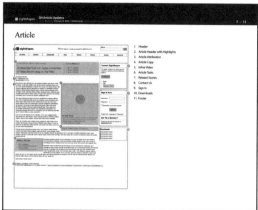

Figure 6.9 A chunked article page revealing many component parts.

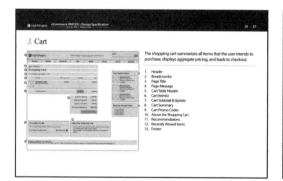

Figure 6.10 A chunked shopping cart page revealing numerous items.

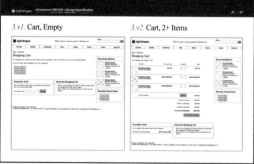

Figure 6.11 Page variations positioned side by side to facilitate comparison.

Detailed Page Annotations

An annotated page can include content like purpose, related pages (such as entry points and exit points), visual style (layout, typography, color), display conditions (such as what components are displayed when), and editorial and behavior guidelines at a page level.

When creating and documenting designs using components, it's important to document each bit at the appropriate level. Therefore, not all the details should be presented at the page level when components could be better annotated independently. As a design solution reuses a component across many pages, documents can also reflect this modularity by documenting component details separate from any particular page.

In the context of component-based design, improve page-level annotations working to do the following:

▶ Connect emerging page designs to items standardized in a component library. A page's component inventory helps readers quickly evaluate the page. Commonly rendered as a list (**Figure 6.12**), an inventory is particularly useful for engineers and librarians who must assemble and integrate the components, respectively.

▶ Distinguish between existing components that aren't changing and those new and updated components that require attention.

▶ Keep it simple when necessary. If your design doesn't need to be broken into components but you need to highlight a few elements instead, then only document the elements. Don't feel that you have to be "true to the hierarchy" if breaking down a page into components doesn't add value.

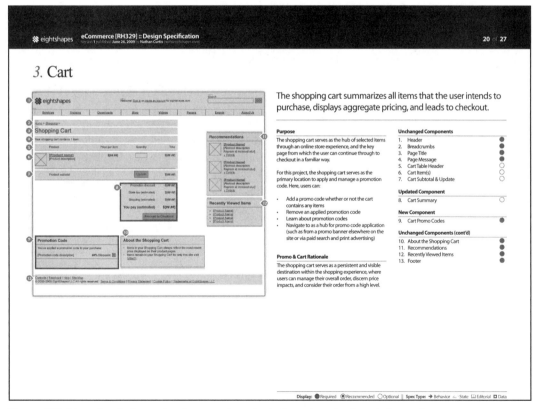

Figure 6.12 More detailed page-level annotations, including a lengthy description and a component inventory indicating new and updated variations and what's required versus optional.

TIP Automate reference tables in your deliverable documents. Engineers, testers, and librarians appreciate lists and tables to reference new and updated components and other inventories. All of your document's readers appreciate a table of contents. Many tools have built-in capabilities to produce reference lists derived from paragraph styles or feature a scripting language that could produce helpful, repeatable lists.

Component Markers

Components can be marked in screen designs with a specific code that enables you—and your document's consumers—to map components back to the formal library and across to other documents. A component marker usually is a simple, small piece of text adjacent to the component that reveals its component code (for more information on organizing a component library using reference codes, refer to Chapter 9, "Organize").

Components that are already in the library and codified in the catalog can be represented visually via unobtrusive text markers (**Figure 6.13**), usually a lighter color (such as orange) consistent with annotation throughout your deliverables. Most often, this text is displayed adjacent to and directly above the component's upper-left corner.

However, circumstances sometimes require a different position. For example, if the component exists within a vertical stack and the interceding marker would create a distracting gap between chunks, then overlay the marker on top of the component (**Figure 6.14**). Ensure that the marker can be read easily and doesn't disrupt or get confused with the component itself.

A design project may lead to new components and variations that are not already in the library.

Figure 6.13 Component markers in the upper left of each component: logo (HF01v1), primary navigation (HF04v1), breadcrumbs (C02v1), and page title (C01v1). Marker codes serve as a visual cue of the component's formality and a unique identifier to map it back to library documentation.

Figure 6.14 A marker displayed on top of a secondary navigation component, since it's stacked directly beneath the primary navigation bar above. This overlaid marker enables the designer to avoid an awkward appearance that positioning the marker between the two bars would cause.

In that case, distinguish them with markers distinct from those embedded with established components. A unique annotation enables quick identification so that others can quickly evaluate the proportion of new versus reused items. When marking new candidates for a library, consider using a solid block with bold text, such as solid block with white type (**Figure 6.15**).

Component markers are distinct from more general annotations, such as the enumerated circles (1, 2, 3 ...) used to chunk out a page or component in documentation. Enumerated circles are specific to that page of a document, outlining elements and connecting them to annotation. By contrast, component markers stick with the screen design wherever it goes. No matter where it gets placed or copied, the component can be connected to its place and role within a library.

That said, if you are chunking a page where each and every component is already identifiable via an embedded marker, then enumerated markers are unnecessary.

> **TIP** Include component markers on a layer separate from the content of your screen design. That way, you can show markers for documents published for engineers and testers, but hide markers for audiences that don't care or would be confused by such formality.

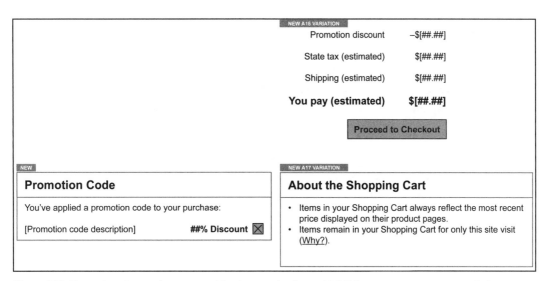

Figure 6.15 Reversing the marker type and background color to highlight a new component, variation, or example to be added to the library.

Components

Similar to how page annotations evolve over a project, traditional layouts for documenting a component include: visualization only, marked visualizations, detailed annotations, and alternative summaries to help set the stage for comparison. Many component layouts are a result of the comparative principles discussed in Chapter 3, "Vary," such as arranging and annotating components.

Component Visualization(s) Only

As with pages, if designs have not yet matured but you need some pointed feedback on component ideas, present the component(s) without annotation.

In this way, you can quickly solicit feedback on a design with a minimum investment in annotation (**Figure 6.16**). Be sure to label different component variations, ideally with labels describing what distinguishes each one, but at least with markers A, B, C, and D so you can refer to each one.

Marking Elements and Annotating Components

Additional component content can include purpose, design considerations, related components, applicable pages, visual style (layout, typography, color), and guidelines of display conditions (how and when elements are shown), editorial, and behaviors at a component level.

Documenting components can feel very similar to documenting pages: Both are supported by the activity of chunking an item into its constituent parts. For components, outlining can identify elements, drill into details, and expose the need for further variation. Outlining components by elements enables a designer to do the following:

- ▶ Establish a consistent pattern of readable and scannable annotation.
- ▶ Guide conversation with stakeholders during design reviews.
- ▶ Identify gaps where adding more detail will improve understanding. For example, you can have questions in mind about states and behaviors, and quiz your audience to see if they "get it" already without explanation or if you need to work harder to fill in more detail.
- ▶ Remember where work left off, so one can return to annotations later and fill in remaining details.

Once the visualization is oriented on the left side of the page, begin outlining layers in more and more detail via three simple steps (**Figures 6.17, 6.18, and 6.19**):

1. Identify each unique element, marking it with a numbered symbol overlaid on the visualization, as well as a numbered list of labeled headers on the right side of the

page (**Figure 6.17**). As opposed to figure labels (such as A, B, and C) that distinguish each variation, use a different system to distinguish each element (such as ascending numbers like 1, 2, and 3).

2. List each relevant property of each element, including states (conditions when it's shown or hidden), events (click, change, load, keypress, hover, etc.), content rules (length, feed, etc.), and editorial guidelines (for publishers that will author copy). Refer to **Figure 6.18** for sample properties of each element.

3. Fill in the details of each property as time and demand warrant (**Figure 6.19**).

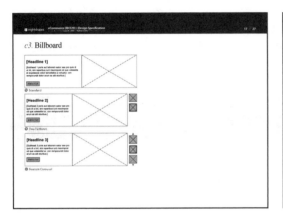

Figure 6.16 Component variations positioned within a document, but lacking any annotation.

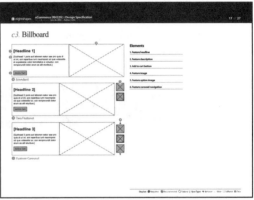

Figure 6.17 Outlining, Step 1: Identify each element using a numbered marker and associated name.

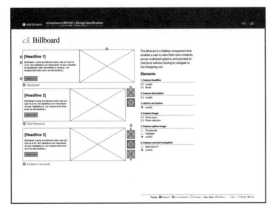

Figure 6.18 Outlining, Step 2: List each relevant property of each element, including states, behaviors, content rules, and editorial guidance.

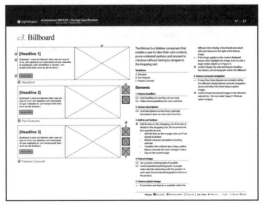

Figure 6.19 Outlining, Step 3: Fill in the details of each property as time permits.

> **TIP**   Long bulleted lists of guidelines stink. Distinguish annotation types (such as states, behaviors, content/data, and editorial guidelines) using different bullet characters. To make this easy, you can create a separate paragraph style for each one. That way, your lists are more scannable, less wordy, and indicative of the similarities—and differences—of guidelines between elements.

Choosing from Alternatives

If you want to work with your stakeholders to select one design alternative from among many, consider creating an alternative summary page. The summary shown in **Figure 6.20** illustrates alternatives by showing and labeling each one, and subsequent pages would drill into variations, sample content, and design considerations (such as pros and cons) of each one, one at a time.

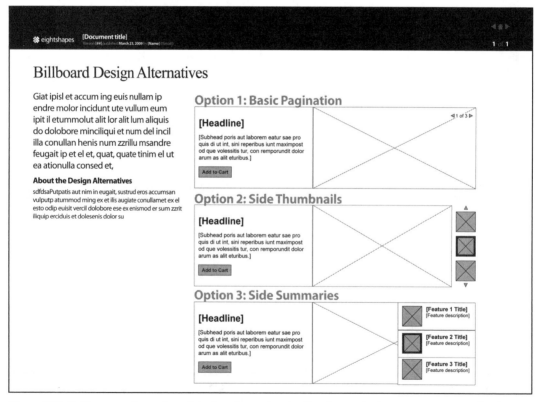

Figure 6.20 Setting up a discussion of design alternatives by showing each alternative next to each other, and leaving details (such as pros and cons) to subsequent pages.

The summary enables a designer to distinctively brand each alternative, establishing its tone and a label everyone uses as a handle for the discussion. While you can use alternative summary for component options, you can use this technique to position design alternatives for flows, pages, or even basic elements, too.

Documentation Tips

When documenting an experience of flows and maps, pages and components, it's easy to get lost in a sea of your own details. Bad habits form early on, and you end up being paralyzed by bad "design decisions" in authoring documents. With that in mind, here are a few tips to keep you focused and effective in communicating both the "big picture" as well as detailed nuances of your design.

#1 One Story Per Page

Try to get a key point across with each page of your document. Don't overload a page with a colossal amount of detail if it obscures or distracts from your main point. This is particularly problematic in pages summarizing strategy, concepts, and research highlights, where a designer's impulse is to embed thorough understanding when a simple, concrete point would be best. Less is more. Even though you may be authoring a design document, if your page needs to feel like a presentation slide with a big idea and a few bullet points, then make it look like a presentation slide. Just because you compose deep specs elsewhere, don't think that 8pt text is required everywhere.

And don't muddle pages with conflicting or dense goals. If a page is meant to introduce a set of design alternatives, then show each one with equal weight, give 'em a label, and call it a day. Save the detailed pros and cons of each one for individual pages or a concluding comparative summary.

#2 Balance Pictures and Words

The whole of effectively combined visuals and annotations is always better than the sum of its parts. The relative balance of each is dictated by project conditions.

Pictures almost always dominate early on in a project's design cycle, growing from low- to high-fidelity as the audience considers strategic design implications. Therefore, documentation should provide a foundation to aggregate and share visualizations even without detailed annotation. Later in a project, if time permits or project complexity warrants details, deepen understanding through annotated specifications.

#3 Set the Stage and Drill Deep

Don't dive deep into details without establishing context. Jumping in too deep, too fast leaves readers hazy on why something is relevant or how it fits into their own understanding of an experience.

Create a framework to tell a story from the top down, from experience strategy through maps and flows, from pages to components and elements contained in each page. At each level, or across all levels, set a stage for discussion by illustrating a design divided into modular parts. Then, with that foundation, you can layer in as much detail as necessary to communicate your solution.

#4 Anticipate Growth

Set up documents, page layouts, and annotation structures to anticipate the gradual growth of visualizations and details. Variations happen. Examples are requested. New elements are added to a design and require their own detailed specs.

Without a plan—and allotted real estate within your document's layouts—you can end up spending way too much time re-factoring your deliverables layout. Even worse, you may reach the point where a once-glamorous, shiny new document just doesn't work, and you have to lay it out from scratch again to accommodate the growth.

Why do spare page and component layouts (like those in **Figure 6.21**) leave abundant whitespace on the right side of the page? The space allows for adding annotated detail without re-factoring the existing layout. Not many readers complain about the space. In fact, some even use it to take notes or sketch ideas.

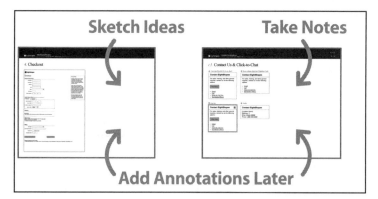

Figure 6.21 Page and component layouts on otherwise spare pages of a design document. Whitespace allows authors and readers to take notes, sketch ideas, and add more detailed annotations later when needed.

#5 Make Documents Usable

There are many ways to improve the usability and effectiveness of design documents, so much so that recommendations could fill a whole book. But they all boil down to one main point: Make your documents useful and usable. Some simple strategies for making your documents usable include the following:

- ▶ Create deliverables that include document title, author name and contact information, published date, and version number—on every page! Repeat that information so that readers can always reorient quickly.

- ▶ Empower readers to easily navigate your document via page numbers, automated table of contents (if supported by your tool), clear page titles and headers, and easy-to-learn reference numbers.

- ▶ Lay out design and annotation consistently using grids and guidelines to control the location and proportional size of pictures and words.

Haphazardly produced documents with inconsistent layouts leave readers unimpressed ("A designer produced this?") if not annoyed and confused as they try to scan and learn about the design. It's sad to see how often deliverables lack any discernible visual structure. A poor document layout can diminish an author's credibility as a designer.

Turning Projects into Standards

Standards documents are different from project-specific documents that include basic collections of screen designs as well as detailed design specification. Projects require that documentation evolve and adapt to changing conditions. On the other hand, standards documentation (whether a document-based style guide or web-based library of components) requires a different approach.

Standards documentation is prepared differently for the following reasons:

- ▶ Audiences are more diverse and less predictable.

- ▶ Guidelines must be flexible and consider wider application.

- ▶ Readers lack context established by participating in a project.

- ▶ Projects succumb to tradeoffs, whereas standards (try to) transcend them.

Projects involve the creation, evolution, and management of a design system that, if worth its weight, needs to be standardized if it's to be persisted. Therefore, design and documentation produced during a project is essential source material for authoring standards.

Near the end of a project, or after it's complete, designers may be tasked with creating design standards. They'll comb through specs and artwork, interview and strategize with designers who worked on the project, and aggregate information to record good design decisions and author tight guidelines.

Therefore, your efforts to divide, vary, combine, and document your design solution will provide a foundation for reusable assets valuable to you, your design team, and your organization at large. With an expansive, mature set of component-based designs, it's time to move on to creating a component library.

II

COMPONENT LIBRARIES

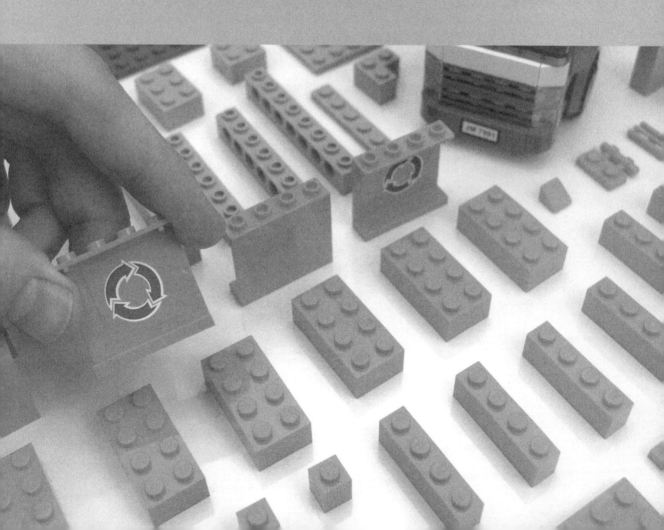

7

A P R A I S E

So, you've started to master designing with components, and you feel like you're ready to build a library of reusable bits to spread far and wide across your organization. A component library—a collection of reusable building blocks for rapidly creating consistent screen designs—can have a great return on investment, but requires assessment and planning.

Before you dive head-first into building out a library, appraise a library's value to you and your organization. This chapter explores key questions to ask before you start, including the following:

- ▶ Why create a library?
- ▶ Are you building the right library?
- ▶ Is your user experience ready for a library?
- ▶ Are you ready for a library?
- ▶ Is your design team ready for a library?
- ▶ Is your organization ready for a library?
- ▶ Is management ready to support a library?

Why Create a Library?

Not everybody wants to build a component library for the same reasons. Interestingly, your motivations can have a significant impact on how you position a library, teach it to others, and use it in your day-to-day processes.

The following motivations are a litmus test for you to understand what drives you and determine how you'll need to position the system to your organization.

Efficiency

Some teams see the main benefit of a component library as speed: Get the design done faster, be more productive, save time, save money! Efficiency is paramount, as managers are constantly pushed to produce more design in less time for less money:

Without a Library	With a Library
You spend considerable time starting a project by creating templates, headers, footers, and other aspects of the design from scratch. Or, you search through old documents looking for artwork to cut and paste (and thus risk repeating the mistakes of the past).	You have a collection of starting points for creative work: Skip the setup, dive into creation, focus on project-specific challenges, and explore alternatives at a greater scale.

Consistency

You want your design efforts to result in a more consistent, predictable experience, from grids, colors, and typographic styles to the common locations, structures, and behaviors of each component you use:

Without a Library	With a Library
You make your best judgment as to where and when to use, locate, vary, and render designs based only on project needs since you lack a broader, more holistic perspective.	You can apply components and leverage past design decisions, resulting in more precise first drafts, faster reviews, and solutions more in line with the holistic site experience.

Efficiency and consistency end up being the top two themes on most motivation lists. However, you may be surprised at how teams actually drift toward one more than the other.

Some teams care more about increasing the scale and volume of design production. Consistency is important, but only so much as starting points that include commonly used design treatments. A governed system of organized components and guidelines may be far less important. Efficiency drives the team's goals.

On the other hand, consistency and governance drive other teams. In their minds, components provide a baseline to maintain a holistic experience. The message still includes how a designer's job is easier and more effective with a system. But, more importantly, the team seeks to converge on a consistent user experience within a formal framework of guidelines, assets, reviews, and cross-disciplinary collaboration.

Both aspects are attractive and can motivate a library. However, the degree to which you are more interested in efficiency than in consistency and governance will dictate how much rigor, formality, and in-depth guidelines you inject into your culture.

Memory

A component library also provides an archive to record and refer to all the design decisions made in creating a large-scale experience:

Without a Library	With a Library
Design decisions (as artwork and annotation) are scattered across documents buried in (and, therefore, almost always irretrievable from) folders on a shared drive, or worse, on the local drives of each person. Therefore, it's very difficult, if not impossible, to recall design decisions and source artwork.	You converge on a central, commonly understood destination where such artwork, decisions, and conventions are recorded, retrieved, and reused.

Portability

Designers come and go. Project priorities change. With many individuals producing designs, your investment in a system should make you more nimble in shifting resourcing and focus:

Without a Library	With a Library
You render designs using a variety of tools, and as resources shift from one priority to another, others recreate artifacts from scratch (and, in the process, perhaps override design decisions long since finalized).	You work within a common framework—and ideally, tool set—to produce artifacts that can be transitioned, reused, and shared more effectively.

Vocabulary

A library affords you an opportunity to establish and promote common understanding that includes terms and reference codes you use for components, page types, codes, and even deliverables:

Without a Library	With a Library
You refer to the Contact Us module in the sidebar that includes a flow in a lightbox. An engineer refers to the same thing as the Let Us Help module from the right rail that triggers a popup form.	You have a shared understanding of terms for components, patterns, page regions, and more. Even better, you establish shorthand for unambiguous references, such as component ID numbers.

Authority

A component library provides a more formal and credible resource on which to make design decisions, prioritize efforts, and refer to conventions in an open, accessible way:

Without a Library	With a Library
You get frustrated when your declaration of "This is just how we do it" doesn't carry much weight with a headstrong stakeholder or new engineer on the team.	You can refer to an established source to educate your teammates, and even be the "good cop" who challenges the system alongside your skeptical stakeholders, recognizing both why standards exist and knowing when to change or diverge from them.

Predictability

A component library provides a framework to plan design projects to cross-experience impacts:

Without a Library	With a Library
A core team kickoff meeting results in divergent understandings of project scale, impacts, and efforts required.	You have a starting point to approximate breadth and impacts, and discuss it with others in a concrete way.

Collaboration

Whether you are looking to amp up collaboration within your design team or across to other groups in your organization, components can be a way to trigger conversations, share knowledge, and learn together:

Without a Library	With a Library
Design is perceived as a black box, where designers make decisions without justification or transparency.	How you expose your evolving system suggests or even requires the participation and contribution of other disciplines.

Ultimately, you shift the conversation from the recurring minutiae of design decisions that have already been made to a more strategic appreciation of a holistic experience. A library provides you with a platform to explore project-specific impacts (such as "How would this component fit elsewhere?") but also broadens awareness of the project-specific impacts to an overall experience.

Are You Building the Right Library?

As described in the first chapter, components are complementary to design patterns, and both can be applied effectively and repeatedly during design projects. Once you start applying patterns and components across many design projects, you may wonder what kind of library is right for you.

Patterns are ideal for teams that design many experiences, such as a team like Yahoo's that designs a plethora of products, each with a unique visual system but needing to adhere to a larger, common brand. Components have proven ideal for other teams, such as Sun Microsystems' Sun.com/webdesign/library that synthesizes a massive collection of pages, sections, teams, and content into a common, single design system and experience.

But, this may not be an either/or question. In fact, one team built libraries for both patterns (for example, Tabs), as well as components (for example, tabbed product details, tabbed content module, tabbed search results, and so on). Other teams have hedged their bets by embedding aspects of one approach into the guidelines and spirit of the other, most commonly via pattern-like guidelines incorporated into the more specific component definitions.

Consider a pattern library especially if your team has the following:

▶ Many visual systems that are intentionally different or will not be reconciled

▶ Capability to document patterns more specific than public libraries already in existence

▶ Known opposition to prescriptive approaches, but a willingness to use common guidelines

Consider a component library especially if your team has the following:

▶ A specific visual design system, including grids, layout, color palettes, and typography

▶ Many reusable components (page "chunks") within that system

▶ Diverse groups (and resources within disciplines) across an organization that must work together to evolve and publish against using that system

▶ Interest in and capability of sustaining that design and code system across groups, projects, and time

▶ Strong, centralized influence to create, deploy, and maintain a library (or plans to centralize influence via a library)

Is Your User Experience Ready for a Library?

OK, so you've got big dreams of incredible efficiencies, consistency, standards, and more. However, just because you've built a big Web site, that doesn't automatically imply that you should build a component library to support it. In fact, there are plenty of Web sites—or at least portions thereof—for which a component library won't net much benefit at all.

Despite your best intentions, you should also take a long, hard look at the scale, maturity, and disparity of your overall user experience to ensure that your experience warrants a component library.

Scale

Component libraries can be invaluable to large, distributed teams evolving an experience over time. On the flip side, the smaller the scale of your site design, the less it makes sense to focus on reuse, consistency, and standards through a component library.

Consider the small startup that focused on building an online music discovery and player experience. Their design included many sophisticated behaviors: Add a song to a playlist, view song details via a hover balloon, mix and share playlists with friends, and so on. There were many interdependent interactions and content displays, like artist, album, playlist, and the player itself. The user interface took months of tinkering, prototyping, and detailed design to get it just right.

Component-based design principles were absolutely essential in design activities. The team focused their attention on important interactions and variations of each page chunk. Wireframes and comp deliverables divided page designs into many, many component designs and annotations. The tight-knit team was definitely thinking and building modularly.

However, once each piece was designed and built, there was no need for reuse. The experience was an integrated collection of transactional pages and centrally managed by a small team working closely together. There were no publishers to publish content. There were no strategists to apply it to other projects. There were no additional engineering teams that needed to grab portions of code and apply them elsewhere. In this setting, a library would have been a self-indulgent, misguided enterprise of creating standards, design assets, and guidelines without an audience to consume them.

This question of scale applies just as much to your organization as it does to the experience. If you are a tight-knit, co-located team in constant, fluid communication across desktops, then there's no need to codify standards. Heck, there's no need to document anything at all—just get real and build stuff collaboratively in real time. Design using component-based principles? Great! Codify components in a library and create reusable design assets and deep guidelines? What a complete waste of time.

Relevance

Even for larger-scale teams and experiences, a comprehensive component library may still not be relevant. One corporation chose to revamp its entire online presence in a massive redesign. The project spanned the entire experience, from marketing products and services to selling products online to managing and supporting those products post-purchase. The redesign touched every page, from product catalogs to registration, from shopping through cart to checkout, and even the account management portal. Some components, notably the header and footer shared across the entire experience, had to be centrally documented and published.

However, many transactional areas of the experience—such as checkout and the account management portal—were unique solutions that didn't reuse many components from other areas of the site. Instead, many of their component designs had no reuse value whatsoever, like checkout's shipping and billing data entry and the portal's dashboard for product usage and service plans. Design activities resulted in complex component displays and variable states. But no other design team or publishing group would ever reuse them in the future. Therefore, the detailed specs and states for checkout and the portal were not relevant to the group's persistent, holistic component library.

Stability

As discussed in more depth in Chapter 8, "Discover," be careful not to componentize your experience too soon. There's a certain stability required to codify a design system. Your page grids (columns, margins, padding, spacing, and so on), typography, and even core components like your header and footer should be stable and mature before you propagate design assets. You can lose much momentum if you work hard to create templates, libraries, and documentation only to throw it away or extensively refactor it just weeks later because things change.

On the other hand, it makes sense in some cases to build a component library progressively during a project. Just temper upfront investment in creating templates, building libraries, and communicating standards relative to its increasing stability over time.

Disparity

Do you actually have more than one experience or design system to build a component library for? Consider a core corporate site that doesn't share grids, typography, and components with additional experiences like your video channel, management portal, or other subsites. Therefore, be open to creating multiple component libraries and blending assets and conventions across experiences only as necessary.

Centrality

Behind the scenes, multiple technical platforms, content management systems, and development teams may support your holistic experience. Multiple environments may each embed their own version of components, grids, style sheets, image libraries, and more. If your design system must be propagated to many systems rather than from a central source, it will be tougher to proliferate standards across teams, projects, and releases.

For example, one massive corporate site was supported by five platforms, each with similar but subtly distinct grids. When a new component was published, it had to be published per platform, one by one, even across design engagements and engineering release cycles. The librarian had to be very conscientious, asking questions like "When can we use this component on platform A?" and "Will that component be personalized or static on platform B?" during design and development reviews.

There was still a viable return on investment, but design projects, cross-functional collaboration, and library management were more complicated. As a result, the team focused on corralling styles into a central style sheet, synced visual style and naming conventions across implementations as best it could, and built practices and procedures that aligned platforms over time.

Are You Ready for a Library?

Building and sustaining a component library takes an evangelizing advocate or two, as described in Chapter 12, "Administer." Since you are reading this book, that person may be you, or at least someone you manage or work with. As you consider and ultimately set out to build a component library, you must be aware of the roles you'll take on, such as the following:

Leader. You'll be a leader of a new way of thinking in your organization, shepherding participants into a common practice and evangelizing the techniques, benefits, and spirit of the library.

Speaker. You'll frequently speak about the library's principles and strategies, as well as demonstrate how to use the library's tools and related techniques. Other "speaking opportunities" will include discussions during reviews, collaborations, and brainstorming sessions where components and standards come into play.

Target. You'll be a lightning rod for the library, and even the cause of controversy in a design organization. Others will point to you as a person who constrains them from being creative. Some may dismiss your ideas even if they have significant merit, or even if they are outside the context of the component library, since they may perceive you as the "standards police" and tune you out if they don't trust you.

Writer. You'll be an author, or at least a contributor and frequent reviewer of others' contributions. Whether you develop component guidelines, library cheat sheets, blog posts, or other pieces, you'll likely be doing quite a bit of writing and editing.

Teacher. You'll be a teacher, espousing principles as well as basic fundamentals about what's where and how to use it. Others will look to you for help and to learn, and those requests can be disruptive since everyone else needs it now, if not hours or days ago. Therefore, you'll have to be patient, determined, and flexible. If you hope to integrate components and a library into their workflow, then note that it'll be mostly on their terms and not yours.

Is Your Design Team Ready for a Library?

A component library can transform how a design team operates. Gone are the days when every project was a blank canvas on which a designer created a beautiful, unique, and exceedingly creative work of art. Instead, designers are equipped with starting points, helpful page chunks, and a framework within which to operate. Those constraints can be simultaneously welcome and controversial.

Above all, you'll have to get your team over the hurdle that a library is about constraining innovation. You want to—you need to—stop reinventing the wheel with each effort. Templates with grids, libraries, styles, and premade page chunks don't turn designers into robotic automatons. But they often react that way. You'll have to work to convince designers that these starting points focus their innovation. Templates and libraries remove the chaff and rigor of getting started, save you time, and get you significantly closer to a consistent, effective design rendering within the context of a holistic experience.

Other factors can help you judge whether your team is ready for a component library:

Size. How big is your design team? The larger the team, the more likely it is that your deliverables, design solutions, and communication styles vary. Component libraries and templates can get your team synced up and communicating more consistently.

Overlap. How much do their design solutions overlap with shared components? If your team is designing toward a common experience, a component library can be a key pillar of a holistic strategy.

Distribution. Is your team spread out geographically? Standard design assets can be one approach to replace the lack of face-to-face conversations and collaboration.

Adaptability. Will your team be able to adapt to design practices that involve a library? Additionally, the bigger the library, the more team members need to learn and the more often it'll change, grow, and contract. It'll be up to designers to recognize—or know when to ask—if a component is emerging, stable, active, or even nearing the end of its life cycle.

Stability. How stable is your team? Do designers come and go often? Learning the ins and outs of a component library is an investment with a return that increases the longer each designer uses it.

Advocacy. Are some members of your team especially jazzed about or knowledgeable of component-based approaches? Without those advocates serving as in-team champions of the effort, you'll be positioned as the "bad cop" more and more often. It's incredibly helpful to have allies who can help you tell the story of components and flavor it with their own unique perspectives and experiences.

Is Your Organization Ready for a Library?

You should be ready to engage and communicate goals to other teams if necessary. Is your library simply meant to be a set of designer starting points and shortcuts to faster, more efficient design? Then cross-disciplinary impacts may be limited, but others may still inquire as to what the "new wireframes" or "new comps" are all about.

Is your library meant to catalog emerging standards, or even transform the way you communicate with other teams? Then you have your work cut out for you. At that point, it becomes less about what software tools you use to draw boxes or paint pixels. Instead, you must think more deeply about how different teams blend their workflows, and how components will change how work gets done.

Every organization is different, and to assert a one-size-fits-all recommendation for cross-disciplinary collaboration would be foolish. However, without a doubt, your library can impact how teams communicate, plan, collaborate, participate, document, and believe in a process that includes components.

Communication

Everyone else will want to know—in simple terms—what this component library is all about, how it works, and what it means to them. Your story must be simple, concrete, direct, and focused on how each group and individual may be affected. Is your organization receptive to changes in approach? Can they adapt to new nomenclature and communication methods, whether verbal or via the artifacts they produce and consume over the course of a project?

One team aimed to start small, using the component library as one of many "pillars" of how a team of information architects was transforming its practice of methods, tools, and standards. The goal wasn't to take over the world with components, but instead to use components as a foundation for communicating design solutions in a more consistent, structured way. Over the course of three to six months, other teams—namely, visual designers, engineering, and product management—were exposed to new deliverables, new annotation styles, and new ways of how the IA team was thinking modularly within each project. Gradually, the new techniques took hold, via an implicit "communications plan" that exposed the practices on a grassroots level.

Workflow

Component libraries impact at least two critical workflows: how you produce a design solution for each project versus how you maintain your library's assets, guidelines, and documentation across projects. Ultimately, managing the library is up to library owners. But changes to a project workflow affect everyone.

Depending on how much your library spreads into the activities of cross-functional teams, you'll need to map out those impacts and come together across teams to decide how milestones, artifacts, expectations, and participation will need to shift. Refer to Chapter 15, "Integrate," for more details about common impacts and changes in a workflow.

Collaboration

Do key team members—such as engineers and designers—have a common vocabulary and structure on which to discuss design and development work? A component library can be one way for teams to improve collaboration. That said, be mindful that different disciplines may see a library in different lights. So don't try to a fit a square peg in a round hole, but seek to maximize collaboration and participation in your effort.

One organization had efforts underway for both the design team and development team to build what turned out to be distinct libraries of reusable assets. Each team had its own goals, perspectives, and conceptual approaches of how a library could best benefit its team. But there seemed to be some kind of opportunity for a consolidated library, and they discussed (and discussed, and discussed, and discussed...) how to map their efforts together.

After much discussion, they recognized that their two libraries served different purposes and couldn't blend together into a single, synthesized set of assets. However, the discussions yielded positive results that strengthened relationships between strategies, collections, and people so that the teams could collaborate more effectively.

Participation

Component libraries can galvanize groups yearning for opportunities to synthesize their efforts and deliverables more tightly with others. Design and engineering teams commonly lead and own library development. But other participants can benefit from, learn from, contribute to, or even immerse their work in the foundation created by the library, too. Product managers start to author Product Requirement Documents or product backlogs that refer to components. QA begins to bind test cases to component codes and variations. Copywriters write copy, variations, and error messages mapped concretely to modular design treatments.

The component library's collaborative nature—not the design assets, but underlying principles of modular thinking and standards—can appeal to many disciplines as a platform into which to inject their influence. For starters, there's a well-defined structure to which you can map your own work. Depending on your software, maybe there's a way for you to fluidly blend copy, images, annotations—whatever your contribution is—into design assets.

Documentation

Clearly, component-based design approaches can impact how you annotate and communicate a design solution to other teams. The more broadly the library spreads to other teams, the more common it becomes to see mentions of specific components—even specific references to component IDs—in their artifacts. As you roll out a library, will deliverables change dramatically, be thrown away, or even be invented from the ground up?

One team of interaction designers and visual designers lived in a world tied very tightly to traditional software development life cycle processes. Their organization depended, quite heavily, on use cases, functional requirements, and other nonvisual artifacts authored in Microsoft Word. The introduction of moderate fidelity wireframes and highly structured comps as key deliverables was quite a shift for others to adapt to. So the design team chose to balance production of new artifacts—wireframes and component-based comps—with traditional deliverables not only to smooth the transition, but also to compare the effectiveness of deliverables old and new.

Another organization was further along. Designers and technologists had incorporated components, a library, and sophisticated nomenclature into their conversations. Deliverables like wireframes and HTML page templates were assembled in large part with components. For that team, the discussion became less what components are called or what items are in the library, but which deliverable documented what and who it was for. Valid questions emerged about what should be maintained once HTML page templates were created. Should wireframe updates be made anymore?

Actually, yes—both artifacts had to be maintained for different reasons. HTML was the essential gold standard for engineers and QA to implement the solution correctly. However, HTML page templates wholly lacked any annotation or explanation of how to put pages together, author targeted content, or adhere to the page and component objectives. Therefore, annotated wireframes were invaluable for publishers, engineers, and even product owners to understand the templates once implemented and perpetuate template use for product launches and other publishing cycles.

Reinvention

A large-scale redesign can be an effective time to introduce a new way of getting work done. The business—or at least its Web-facing identity and support system—is undergoing a facelift, and an organization may be doing just as much soul-searching, process reconsideration, and internal transformation.

One organization built a personalized platform from the ground up in order to publish targeted content to key customer segments. Everything was on the table: a new technical platform, a new way of thinking about content, and a new design system with updated grids, page layouts, subsite architectures, and visual style. Change was in the air, and seemingly every part of the organization was involved.

Insert a component library. Using the redesign project as a backdrop, the director of user experience began to assert the use of components as design and code standards. The selling was soft initially, more so to educate partners in engineering, marketing, and branding. But over time, the message became more and more refined, commonplace, and integrated as a part of the way everyone talked about emerging design solutions.

Is Management Ready to Support a Library?

Creating all but the most trivial of component libraries should not be taken lightly. It requires dedication, focus, and an investment of resources, time, and money to get the library going and support it over time.

Therefore, all the assessment and planning you do—of your rationale, your experience, yourself, your design team, and your organization—doesn't matter if you lack the support of your management. That support must be a vocal, public belief in your effort just as much as a tangible investment of funding and resources.

The preceding sections of this chapter provide you with good fodder to think about impacts of a library, and the remainder of this book will teach you the steps you'll traverse in building, publishing, and maintaining it. You'll need to transform this into a concrete plan of action as to who'll need to be accountable, responsible for, consulted, and informed of your progress. It's up to you to communicate that plan—and the return on that investment—and to sell your management on why components matter.

Upfront and Ongoing Investments

Usually an investment is communicated in two parts: Create and maintain.

Creating a library requires you to discover what's needed, plan the involvement of a range of participants (likely mapped to the kinds of design assets you'll produce), organize the library into a mature collection, build the assets, and ultimately deploy them across your organization. Often lumped into "creation" activities are initial face-to-face training sessions, documentation describing how to get started, and—at a minimum—some initial component guidelines.

To maintain a library requires librarians and additional contributors to curate and grow the collection over time. They'll administer asset distribution, manage activities like writing guidelines and integrating artwork, and dedicate time to teaching, answering questions, and reviewing emerging designs. Administrative costs occur gradually over time to sustain the library. Focused attention will be required to ensure that it remains a vibrant, fresh part of your design process.

Know Your Customers

AUTHOR: **Martin Hardee**

ROLE: **Director Cisco.com User Experience, Cisco Systems, Inc.**

It's hard to overestimate the benefits of components to a Web or software delivery organization. Over the years, I have seen components save many hundreds of design and engineering hours and hundreds of thousands of dollars, as well as improve customer experience and brand identity through consistency.

But let's be honest: Components by themselves are not an exciting sell to most executives. One reason is that there's no sizzle: Components aren't glamorous or sexy. A bigger reason is that some of your biggest stakeholders in a component discussion are highly business-focused and probably don't think first about design or customer experience. And, let's face it, if you're reading this book, you probably come from a design, customer experience, or architectural background so you have a double communications hurdle to overcome.

Executives

So how do you sell components to your execs and get the ball rolling on an effective program?

The answer is that you need to speak their language, and the language each key stakeholder speaks may be slightly different. In general, your VPs probably care most about key performance indicators (KPIs), such as cost, customers acquired, acquiring cost, churn, conversion to sale, size of deal, customer profitability, customer satisfaction, and support costs/case avoidance. To make things more complex, different VPs care about different things, and the pitch that works with your VP of IT is likely to be different from the one that works with your VP of Marketing or Brand.

IT and Engineering

For your IT and engineering executives, emphasize cost savings and flexibility:

▶ Cost savings from reuse

▶ Compatibility with bulletproof open source libraries

▶ Lower training costs of technical staff

▶ Lower quality assurance (QA) costs during release (since components are usually pre-tested)

▶ Lower costs to support the code over time

▶ Ability to scale up quickly to outsource new projects due to better documentation

You can use the following quotes to make your case:

▶ "I know your team must be on top of components since it's such a big trend. We're looking forward to the flexibility, speed, and cost savings they'll provide."

▶ "I can't believe we're going to spend time and money reinventing the code for each project. A solid component system would promote reuse and make us all heroes with the company."

▶ "I don't understand why I can't reuse this accordion from section x of the site in area y. Don't we just drop it in? It worked in Photoshop!" (However, with this last one you will be the secret butt of jokes in IT for a few weeks even though you will have made your point.)

Brand and Marketing

For your brand and marketing executives, emphasize the ability to use kitchen-tested widgets throughout your site:

▶ Improved engagement (time on site, "funnel tractors" such as wizards and video)

▶ Better conversion (by using well-honed, time-tested, proven high-conversion winners)

▶ Consistent visual and interaction identity for the brand, by baking the rules into the components

▶ Huge time-to-market advantages, since the designs and code already exist

▶ Lower costs with vendors, since they won't be charging you to reinvent the wheel with each new project

You can use the following quotes:

- ▶ "We know we're only going to have a couple of weeks to plan the next launch... wouldn't it be nice if our design vendor could speed things along by using ready-to-eat templates and components?"

- ▶ "I'm sick of these expensive design agencies cooking up custom designs every time that are impossible to implement and blow the schedule. We need to give them a kit to speed up the process, ensure a consistent product, and save us money."

- ▶ "Look, we've already A/B tested the last design and we came up with some great conversion winners. Let's bottle that formula in a component set so we can get the same wins every time."

- ▶ "I need my agency spending more time on creative and less time redrawing boxes."

Sales

For sales, emphasize conversion and the ability to move prospects into the buying funnel by using standard, tested capabilities. A quote you can use with sales leads: "We've developed a great bag of tricks for engagement conversion. We need to package it up so we can reuse these things like an online selling kit."

Finance or Operations

For your finance or operations execs, emphasize the cost saving advantages mentioned above, as well as the lead generation possibilities. With operations, you could stress things like "operational excellence," while with finance you could say things like the following:

- ▶ "Our vendors tell us they spend 10 percent of their projects reinventing the wheel, and I'll bet it's really 20 percent. If we made them use standard templates and components, we could negotiate better rates."

- ▶ "There's a lot of rework in our internal processes. If we had components, we could avoid some of that and maybe we wouldn't have to go outside so much."

An interesting twist in all of this is that you will often find your design staff and agencies welcoming components, because the templates and documentation system allow them to do work at a higher level—instead of spending all day redrawing boxes!

Management Pitfalls

It's up to you to plan, execute, and manage activities that create and maintain the library. But over the course of many component library adoptions, I've found that you've got to communicate to and rely on management to effectively support you, too. Management support can break down sometimes, most commonly in the form of the issues that follow.

Insufficient Hardware and Software Support

Most of the time, designers aren't buying their own computers and software applications. Instead, it's up to managers to coordinate and ensure that capable devices have the right software installed in a timely way. No failure is easier to spot than the designer's inability to use a component library due to insufficient hardware and software. You'll have to keep a closer eye on this than you think. My confusion at a designer's poor turnaround time and indifferent attitude was transformed into empathy when I sat in his cube and watched for TEN MINUTES as the software tool launched on his out-of-date laptop. My query of "This is unacceptable. Haven't you asked for an update?" was met with "You can only ask so many times" and a shrug.

Lack of Priority

It can happen to the best of teams. You get your top talent together, you start roughing out a library framework, and then projects hit. You get distracted. And status meetings always end up pushing the component library to the back of the priority queue. It's up to your management to carve out sufficient time for you to support the library, or else it'll become stale and ineffective.

Leadership and Evangelism

It's up to you to be the leading voice of why the component library matters and how different people can benefit in different ways. But it sure helps to have management on message, too. It can be downright destructive if management undermines your efforts by selling the concept too softly. It was like the rug was pulled out from under a library launch when an executive's opening words positioned it as "another good idea that, if it doesn't work for you, shouldn't disrupt your own personal approach if you feel your way is more effective." C'mon, really, that's how you unify your organization?

Background Support

As important as public declarations are, the back-channel efforts they'll make on behalf of the library are even more important. Your managers will need to open doors for you, connect you with key players and partners in other organizations, and create an environment in which you can be successful. That's a two-way street, and management can't support you if they don't know that there are obstacles. So help your managers understand where and why you need the most help.

So, Are You Really Ready to Build a Library?

If you are ready, know your mission, and have a plan of attack, then it's time to get started.

The remainder of Part II of this book describes strategies and techniques involved in creating a component library for your organization. You'll discover what goes into your library and why, as well as how to organize it into a catalog of assets, set up your design (or development) tools to assemble each piece, and build out components one by one.

Once you've packaged and distributed your library, it becomes a living, evolving collection that you'll need to administer over time. Users of your library will need to know how to apply assets you provide, and you'll need to facilitate the authoring and publishing of guidelines for each item of the library and the tools that support it. You'll be front and center in fostering adoption of the system, and—in the end—you may play a key role in how the library integrates into the day-to-day activities of how design and development occurs.

So, get ready to discover your library!

8

DISCOVER

Once you've committed to creating a library, you need to concretely identify each component you'd like to include. During this period, you'll answer key questions such as the following:

- ▶ When is the most appropriate time to discover a library?
- ▶ Which components should we include in the library?
- ▶ What area(s) of our experience will the library apply to?
- ▶ How do we identify each one?

Discovering, identifying, and prioritizing the full collection can be completed via targeted efforts and activities that can focus a library's scope and optimize its value.

Approaches

You can discover a new component library organically as a design system evolves or via independent study and workshop exercises to analyze an existing site design. Often, techniques can be mixed and matched based on the strengths and relationships of individuals in an organization, as well as the design's quality, maturity, and stability.

During Design

You can identify emerging components during any stage of creating a new site or redesigning an existing experience. Whether you just participate in meetings reviewing designs or are creating the design yourself, you can establish and evolve a library in parallel with ongoing design activities.

Key Benefits

Creating a component library during the design process has many benefits, including the following:

Planning: Organizing components in a library can be a foundation for documentation and delivery of the design to developers, quality assurance analysts, copywriters, publishers, and others.

Combined Efforts: Instead of a waterfall process of defining design first and organizing it in a library later, the team can define the library in real time.

Focus: Other stakeholders are focused on design *during* design and may care less about or not have time to help establish component standards after a project is completed.

Challenges

Creating an optimal design solution is difficult enough. Now you are taking on an additional challenge of creating—and maintaining—a library at the same time. This takes extra effort, focus, and dedication. If you and your team are eager to try this approach, be prepared for challenges like the following:

Evolving Components: Components identified early (such as a header navigation bar) tend to be the most reused but also continue to change frequently, making it difficult for a team to stay in sync.

Changing Models: Early organizational models (like categories and variations) may seem straightforward and stable, but then evolve as the design matures and library grows.

Unstable Design System: Components are much more effective when formalized and distributed within established grids and type styles, but formal grids and styles may not stabilize or even be considered until later and/or may shift significantly during a tumultuous design effort.

Loss of Focus: You can be very committed to a library early in a project. But when project deadlines hit, you can get bogged down with finalizing a design solution and not have enough time to maintain the library simultaneously.

This last challenge presents the most risk. As you work to establish the credibility and value of components, stakeholders may lose faith in a formal library if you can't maintain momentum during the project. To you, delivering the project solution was an obvious first priority, but stakeholders could perceive that the library isn't important at all. If you find yourself in that situation during a project, then reset expectations and communicate that the library is still a long-term goal.

Design Analysis

You can also analyze an existing design system to identify components. For such an analysis, you review relevant pages within an existing experience and recommend a library based on your own expertise and understanding. Analysis activities can be fast and focused since the design system already exists, scope is well defined, and constraints and technical tradeoffs are already incorporated into the final solution.

To conduct the analysis, annotate comps, screenshots of existing pages, and other materials (refer to the Scope section later in this chapter) to identify the possible components in each layout, as shown in **Figure 8.1**. Be sure to clearly identify each component so that reviewers can easily discern each chunk. Usually, annotated rectangles, outlines, and callouts are a good place to start. Once each component is visually marked, you can add descriptive information like names, categories, priorities, and other criteria adjacent to each annotated layout.

Figure 8.1 An annotated screenshot that identifies possible components.

Alternatively, screenshots of individual components can be very powerful tools, in that an analyst can name files with relevant names and/or codes, group files into folders, and tag items. In addition, those same screenshots can be reused for creating deliverables to communicate the library and create component assets during the build process later on. **Figure 8.2** shows a collection of screenshots that have been named and tagged with relevant labels and categories, respectively.

Beware of the limited perspective of just one designer. While providing a consistent approach for organizing the library, you may not be familiar with an entire experience and/or may have a distinct perspective relative to other designers and stakeholders. Therefore, it's important for the analysis to include collaboration, reviews, and feedback to ensure a comprehensive and balanced library. That said, deliverables must focus on establishing a library as opposed to delivering project-specific feedback. Sure, recommendations provided during project meetings and comments added to project-specific documents can be very helpful. However, a component analysis must transcend project-specific goals and get everyone in the mindset of an ongoing, holistic library.

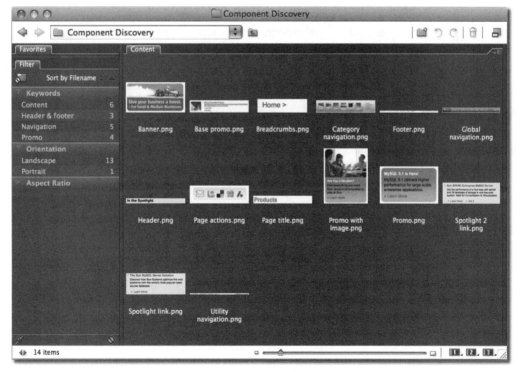

Figure 8.2 Screenshots of potential components from the page design annotated in Figure 8.1, with filenames reflecting suggested component names and keywords (seen in the Filter panel on the left) applied as potential categories.

Additionally, you can augment your analysis with the start of a component catalog that records each item in an inventory. (For more information, see the section entitled "The Component Catalog" in Chapter 9, "Organize.")

Code Analysis

Depending on the quality of a site's code, components can be identified from existing HTML and CSS markup, the framework of a content management system, or other technical architecture. While the preferred modularity of your design may not align perfectly with how technical teams see the system, there are many advantages to adopting or at least learning from a technical baseline to discover reusable components.

Most importantly, HTML and CSS markup is a tangible, established result of the design solution built by the team with whom you want to collaborate the most: the engineers. By deriving a component library from their architecture—and their model of how to modularize the design—you increase the likelihood that both teams can blend an approach partially or completely together. A shared library across both teams is far more powerful than two disparate models that require translation from one to another with each and every project.

Such an effort requires technical expertise. Namely, you must be familiar with the code architecture and know how to decipher HTML markup to identify where a component starts and ends in markup. If HTML is clean and readable, then this task can be straightforward, as with the code shown in **Figure 8.3**. However, if markup is poorly organized or even obfuscated such that it is difficult to interpret, then deriving effective page chunks may be impossible.

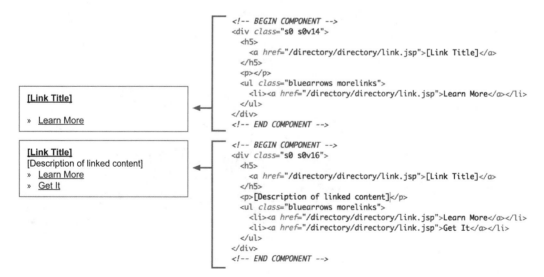

Figure 8.3 HTML markup connoting the code divisions typical to components.

Additionally, you can work directly with developers to organize coded components into a suitable system for your library. Be aware that not all markup is written to be page chunks for easy assembly into an entire page. Instead, developers may have modularized markup based on other objectives, models, and patterns of reuse that may not map cleanly to a component-based approach.

What's the bottom line? If you can establish a shared vision, taxonomy, and foundation of components across design *and* engineering, then your organization can reap the benefits of increased collaboration, productivity, and consistency across the board. Without that shared vision, components are still valuable to a design organization, but will not reach their full potential.

Standard Module Pattern (or The Web Is Rectangles)

AUTHOR: **Nate Koechley**

ROLE: **Senior Frontend Engineer, Yahoo! Inc.**

Web pages are collections of rectangles. Rounded corners and decorative flourishes don't alter the boxy skeleton. Lists of links, tab boxes, login forms, speech balloons, comments— even full articles share the same underlying rectangular structure: They are all modules.

Until earlier this decade, browsers' meager and divergent capabilities required developers to sacrifice lucid code for visual fidelity; maintaining structural modularity was arduous. In contrast, contemporary web development employs HTML correctly. The pages' rectangles—modules—use HTML's <div> element as the mechanism for adding structure to documents (http://www.w3.org/TR/html4/struct/global.html#edef-DIV).

Each module, or chunk of the page, has a consistent structure: Each has a main body area, each usually has a header area, and each sometimes has a footer area. In the case of a Top Stories module, the title "Top Stories" is the header area of the module, the linked headlines to the individual stories are the body area, and the "More stories..." link at the bottom of the module is the footer.

At Yahoo!, we've recognized this common structure with a markup pattern we call Standard Module Format (SMF). The container is given a class indicating that it's a module ("mod"), and classes for the head ("hd"), body ("bd"), and footer ("ft") regions. When a module doesn't have header or footer content, we omit those regions, but the sole remaining region still lives within the "bd" div. It looks like this:

```
<div class="mod">
<div class="hd"></div>
<div class="bd"></div>
<div class="ft"></div>
</div>
```

The outer container's "mod" class comes from Standard Module Format, but because Web Standards allow the class attribute to contain multiple space-separated values, the "mod" value doesn't limit expressiveness:

```
<div class="mod news reuters" id="top-stories">
```

The container's ID is useful when adding Cascading Style Sheets (CSS) and JavaScript throughout the module's life. And because IDs are fragment identifiers, users may jump to or bookmark specific modules (e.g., news.html#top-stories).

Of course, SMF doesn't replace the need for meaningful markup to enrich the content itself. HTML elements have rich semantics that should be fully exploited, including elements like headers (Hn), paragraphs (P), citations (CITE), and list items (LI).

```
<div class="mod">
  <div class="hd">
    <h1>Top Stories</h1>
  </div>
  <div class="bd">
    <ul>
      <li>Story One</li>
      <li>Story Two</li>
      <li>Story Three</li>
    </ul>
  </div>
  <div class="ft">
    <a href="more.html">More stories...</a>
  </div>
</div>
```

Adopting this pattern has several benefits:

1. It neatly encapsulates content within easily identifiable boundaries. We can define the visual presentation and/or modify the interactive behavior of a module without knowing details about its contents. We don't need to know if the content is a first-level (H1) or second-level (H2) header if we already know that it's within the header area (div.hd) of a module. This makes templates more versatile and development more efficient.

2. This encapsulation allows us to manage the powerful—and tricky—cascading nature of CSS while also helping us limit the impact of expensive JavaScript routines. In CSS, we can avoid indiscriminately setting styles for all links on the page by targeting only the links that are within a particular SMF region. In JavaScript, we can limit event listeners and reactions to those associated with regions or modules. Both these techniques recognize the module's general purpose instead of its particular content, increasing leverage and longevity.

   Together, these first benefits promote reuse and portability.

3. (And this one is key!) SMF creates a richer Document Object Model (DOM), or node structure. Instead of just an H2 for the header and a P for the body, I also have the nodes of the SMF itself. Abundant nodes are useful for attaching JavaScript behavior and CSS presentation. Having the .hd wrapping the H2, for example, gives me an extra node to attach CSS declarations. These extra nodes make everything from rounded corners to drop shadows easier and faster.

4. The SMF pattern jump-starts prototyping. For example, several years ago the My Yahoo! site was able to quickly create a drag-and-drop prototype without modifying the existing page. With SMF in place, JavaScript could "find the boundaries of each module (.mod) on the page," then "make the module draggable," then "find the header region of each module (.hd) and make it the drag handle." Done in moments without modifying the underlying page.

All together, our investment in this pattern has paid dividends. By recognizing the broad patterns underlying today's particular pixels—in this case, the rectangular skeleton—we can align our design and technology with the natural modularity of the Web.

Workshops

Nothing beats the energy of getting a team together to mutually deconstruct an existing design system and arrive at a component library together. You can use a two-hour or even a half-day workshop to do the following:

▸ Teach the team about what components are and why they are valuable.

▸ Discuss the opportunities and challenges of using components in your organization.

▸ Conduct exercises that identify concrete component candidates.

Use a workshop to generate momentum internally toward a component-based strategy, establish consensus, brainstorm together, set expectations, and even kick off a project to build a library. In a sense, get project stakeholders around a table to collaborate, as shown in **Figure 8.4**.

Figure 8.4 Workshop participants cut up printed pages to identify, organize, and prioritize component candidates.

The workshop can center around a tangible, real exercise that enables participants to "get their hands dirty" with your design by cutting up page screenshots with scissors and then grouping, labeling, prioritizing, and archiving a collection of candidate components for your library.

Planning

To prepare for the workshop, organize and print out a collection of page comps or screenshots from the live site. From the home page to search results, product pages to checkout, tabular displays to multi-page forms, choose pages that represent the breadth of the experience. Most importantly, select pages that cover the range of potential components you anticipate for your library.

Each page should be printed on a separate sheet of paper—ideally legal size, portrait orientation to accommodate taller pages—and at the same relative resolution. Usually 80 to 120 pages are sufficient to get started for larger sites, but you can get valuable results using as few as 15 to 20 pages.

Once participants cut up pages into components, it's painstaking and impractical to recall where the component came from unless you've got an easy way to trace the cutout back to its source. Therefore, assign each page a unique number and print that number in small type repeatedly across the back of the page printout, as shown in **Figure 8.5**.

Figure 8.5 Pages with a number repeated on the back, so that component cutouts can be mapped back to the page source.

Invite anyone who will influence or benefit from the component library. Participation of the user experience team is critical. However, you'll benefit from inviting other key stakeholders and potential champions, too, for the workshop is a big event and can get many diverse stakeholders energized about the effort. Other important participants can include design technologists (such as HTML/CSS gurus), engineers, site strategists, testers, product managers, copywriters, project management, and even willing executive sponsors.

Assign participants to teams of three to six members each—big enough to have diverse opinions but small enough to make quick progress and not get bogged down. Consider assigning participants to teams before they arrive so you can deliberately mix up roles, personalities, and perspectives on standards and formality. For example, team up an interaction designer, developer, publisher, and product manager together. This way, individuals can be exposed to diverse viewpoints, be sensitive to others' needs, and work on explaining and identifying components from their distinct perspectives. A spreadsheet roster can help you organize participants, manage RSVPs, and assign participants to teams (**Figure 8.6**).

You can even mirror real project teams or relationships. If possible, align subsets of 15- to 25-page printouts with teams knowledgeable of or interested in an area of the experience. For example, if a team focuses on the customer support experience, then allocate screenshots from the support section to that team. Generally, don't distribute printouts in a haphazard way that will confuse participants or raise more questions than answers from participants who are unfamiliar with or don't care about certain pages. If your site doesn't have many unique page and component types, have more than one team cut up the same collection and compare results afterwards.

Name	Role	Email Address	Department/Team	Site Areas of Focus	Experience Level	Workshop Team
	Information Architect Interaction Designer Visual Designer Content Strategist Producer/PM UI Tech (HTML) Developer QA Manager Director VP or above		This connotes the broader organization, such as UXD, Development, and Product Marketing. This is also where you can appropriately identify vendors, along with the name of the vendor (such as "Vendor:EightShapes").	Often, team members may focus on a part of an experience, such as Checkout, My Account, Marketing Site, Product Selection & Cart, Portal, etc. If appropriate, this enables us to define appropriate collections of pages for participants to focus on.	This may be defined by number of years with the team, number of years experience in a career, or more simply with designations such as junior, senior, lead.	
Jane Brown	Interaction Designer	jane.brown@acme.com	User Experience	Support	Senior	A
John Smith	Visual Designer	jsmith@acme.com	User Experience	Support	Junior	B
Janet Chen	Interaction Designer	jchen@acme.com	User Experience	Products	Junior	A
Steve Barker	Visual Designer	steve.barker@acme.com	User Experience	Products	Senior	B
Andy Moore	Interaction Designer	andy@acme.com	User Experience	Training	Junior	A
Jackson Stewart	Visual Designer	jstewart@acme.com	User Experience	Training	Senior	B
Denise Gilbert	Manager, UX	denise@acme.com	User Experience		Manager	A
Kristen Wiley	Content Strategist	kwiley@acme.com	Content Strategy	Products & Solutions	Junior	B
Craig Wolf	Manager, Content	craig@acme.com	Content Strategy		Manager	A
David Lin	Content Strategist	dlin@acme.com	Content Strategy	Training & Support	Senior	B

Figure 8.6 Roster of invited workshop participants that enables a facilitator to plan a workshop and allocate participants to teams during the exercise.

You'll need to stock up for the workshop by purchasing scissors, Post-it® Notes, Post-it® Small Flags, Sharpies large and small, Scotch tape, and blank paper, as shown in **Figure 8.7**. Be sure to buy more than one item per team, so that participants don't sit idly as a single person cuts everything with the only pair of scissors. Usually at least one item for every two participants is sufficient (for example, three pairs of scissors for a team of six).

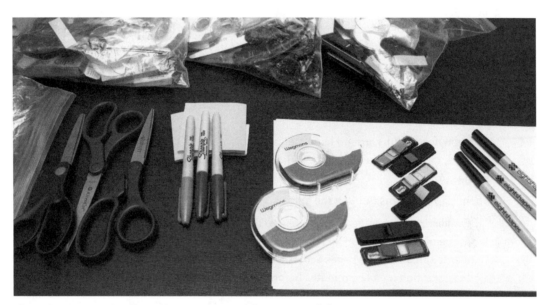

Figure 8.7 Basic materials used in a component discovery workshop.

Facilitation

Workshop leads should drift between teams during exercises, answering questions and listening for common themes and challenges across teams. Watch for participants who struggle or lack confidence in cutting out each component. You can turn those uncertainties—or even components they've cut out already—into mini-lessons on how you may have taken a different approach and whether their decision is OK or incorrect.

If one team is confused by a portion of the exercise or makes a significant discovery, announce solutions and/or findings to the whole group. However, don't disrupt progress across all teams with a constant barrage of distracting comments—save many of them for the discussion afterwards (and even take notes to remind yourself of what topics came up).

The duration of your workshop depends on how much time you can keep the group together and how many screenshots you plan to cut up. Usually, an hour or two of lecture and collaborative discussion precedes the actual exercise. But once you introduce the exercise and split the group into teams, the activity typically lasts between one and two hours. About half of that time should be spent cutting up the printouts and arranging them on tables (steps 2 and 3 in the following section), and the remaining time spent on classifying, archiving, prioritizing, and labeling items. Be sure to leave at least 15 minutes for discussion afterwards.

Finally, it's up to the facilitator to remind groups of how much time remains. In general, you can announce periodic reminders of how much time is left (such as 30, 10, and 5 minutes remaining) to help teams stay on course. If you notice that a team is drastically behind, then encourage them to move on with what they've got so that they can get through each step. If a team is way ahead of schedule, encourage them to dig deeper.

Exercise Steps

To begin, form teams around large tables and distribute sets of page printouts, as well as scissors, tape, pens, Post-it® Notes and Small Flags, and large blank sheets of paper to each team.

Then, lead the teams through the following steps:

1. **Familiarize:** Encourage teams to review the pages to become comfortable with the scope of their collection and identify components that are reused frequently. Some teams spread out the pages across a table (**Figure 8.8**) for a bird's-eye view, pondering the collection for a few minutes before proceeding to the next step.

Figure 8.8 Page screenshots laid out across a table so participants can familiarize themselves with the collection.

2. **Identify:** Participants cut up each and every page into components (**Figure 8.9**), separating each component on the table. During this stage, participants will often ask and need clarity on questions like "How granular should I cut this up? Should it be this bigger section or just these few elements?" Workshop leads can educate participants in real time as to how to cut each component up, as well as relate different variations of the same component based on recommendations gleaned in earlier chapters of this book.

Figure 8.9 Identify components by cutting apart a page screenshot into chunks.

As duplicate components (such as a common header on every page) arise, discard them by throwing each on the floor. Similarly, discard undesirable components that aren't appropriate for the library. Participants enjoy this the most, crumpling up inappropriate components as they throw them to the floor, symbolically disposing of examples of what not to standardize. Just plan to clean up the mess on the floor after the workshop is over.

3. **Group:** As many pages are cut up, teams should begin to group components on the table (**Figure 8.10**). For example, group all the header and footer components in one area, all navigation components in another, and all common sidebar components separately, too. Once all pages are cut out, teams should focus on grouping all components into meaningful categories before proceeding to archive and prioritize items.

Figure 8.10 Organize components by moving cutouts into groups on the table.

4. **Classify:** Use Post-it® Notes with big labels to name each of the groups you've formed (**Figure 8.11**), such as Header and Footer, Content, Navigation, Promos, and Sidebar.

Figure 8.11 Classify components by naming each group.

5. **Archive:** Teams should tape grouped components to plain pieces of white paper (ideally, tabloid size) so that leads can walk out of the workshop with tangible, organized results of the exercise (**Figure 8.12**).

Figure 8.12 Ensure that facilitators can leave the workshop with organized components by taping components to sheets of white paper.

6. **Prioritize:** Using Post-it® Small Flags, prioritize how important each component is to the overall library (**Figure 8.13**). Usually, green is used for "must have" components, yellow is for "nice to have" items, and red is for "less important" candidates. Encourage participants to balance the quantity of each priority. If everything is a green "must have," then the prioritization isn't particularly helpful.

Figure 8.13 Prioritize components by applying a color-coded flag next to each one.

7. **Label:** Teams can use their remaining time to record common names used to refer to each component (**Figure 8.14**), such as "Base of Page" and "Footer Promo." Participants can write labels on the paper adjacent to the taped cutout. This step enables participants to discuss common terms used to refer to each item, informing the nomenclature of the formal catalog.

Figure 8.14 Label individual components to record internal nomenclature.

Wrap Up

After the teams complete the steps, reconvene the entire group to discuss the exercise, compare results, and brainstorm creatively about what lies ahead. If nothing else, you can reaffirm goals and next steps. You can draw out specific challenges to illustrate bigger points, such as how every team tackled the header and footer first, but different teams may have cut it up slightly differently.

But more important, use the discussion as an open forum on the value and direction of using components. Discovering components together in a workshop setting can be an enlightening experience, and participants may have many questions about the opportunities and challenges that await them. Some teams react with lots of enthusiasm, as the workshop demonstrates how they can modularize and reuse aspects of their design system. Others react with restrained optimism, correctly perceiving the constraints that standards and libraries could place on their design freedom.

Most of all, you can use the workshop setting—component cutouts, tactile tools like scissors and Post-it™ Notes, and discarded paper littering the floors—to communicate that what's next will require the group to roll up its sleeves. Investing in a library requires rigor, investment, and determination to stick with such a set of standards, and you'll need to communicate the proper scale and scope of the effort.

Library Scope

The component library scope is the extent to which a library covers a well-defined range of page types, sections, or portions of a site design system.

Most often, a team hopes to cover an entire experience by including any and all possible components used in a design solution. In this case, no page is left untouched, and all possible components are identified, prioritized, and potentially built out. On the other hand, a comprehensive library may be difficult or too ambitious to build in one project if the scale is simply too massive to tackle in one pass. In that case, you can narrow library scope to the following:

- ▶ Section(s) of an experience
- ▶ Depth, such as the first three "levels" of a site hierarchy from home page, section landing pages, and tertiary category pages
- ▶ Critical page(s) (such as section landing pages) or key flow(s) (such as checkout or search)

For example, suppose you were tasked with creating a library for a vast experience of over a million pages that cover products, services, solutions, support, training, entertainment, account management, registration, ecommerce cart and checkout, and corporate information. If the overwhelming share of site traffic, organizational focus, and return on investment is covered by creating a component library for just the product catalog, shopping cart, and checkout experience, then by all means create a library to cover only that area. With a narrower focus, the team can build a library faster and cheaper, and use that experience to more accurately predict the cost of extending the library to other areas later on.

Defining what the library includes—and doesn't include—should be accomplished early. If you don't nail down what you are trying to cover, the library becomes a moving target that requires constant rescaling, is difficult to clearly communicate to stakeholders, and lacks well-defined boundaries that you can drive to complete.

As-Is, As-Intended, or Will-Be?

When creating a library based on an existing site design, teams may not know just what library should be made available. You have the following options:

As-Is: The production site reflects the current state of the experience, including all the tradeoffs made during design and development. As such, the experience may not be optimized and may reflect how pages will be built in the future.

As-Intended: Even though tradeoffs were made during a project, a team may have design artwork and specifications that reflect a preferred, optimal experience.

Will-Be: While a site may already be in production, there are either new designs emerging or there is planning underway to redesign a part of the existing experience.

Deciding on what kind of library you should build can be a tough balancing act, one that may even blend more than one of these alternatives. How do you decide? Generally, think about your library objectives and fully understand what component reuse really means to your team.

Will designers, publishers, and others continue to update existing pages and create new ones that employ as-is components without changing them? Then it makes sense to catalog and publish as-is components.

Will your group be launching updates to the experience to move toward a more optimal design? Then include as-intended components in your library. If not, then avoid as-intended components. Our best intentions and dreams are not useful to those working within the reality—and constraints—of an implemented system.

Will a new site design that includes a range of to-be components be launching soon, but other team members cannot utilize the new components until six months later when the site is live? Then refrain from adding to-be components to your library until others can benefit from them.

Clarifying Scope

A team can clarify library scope using one or more of the following techniques, in descending order of preferred priority:

▶ Create a comprehensive page inventory of all pages, representative page samples, or page types, based on URL or other unique reference code that enables librarians to retrieve, view, and catalog the page.

- Organize polished comp files (JPG, PSD, PNG, etc.) of production-grade visual design, from which components can be derived and built.

- Capture screenshots of applicable page types by browsing relevant sections or pages within the experience and recording the URL and/or page title for each screenshot.

- Identify URL portions based on directories, such as "All pages in [site].com/products/ and [site].com/solutions/".

- Detail expectations via text descriptions (paragraphs, bulleted lists, etc.), providing sufficient and unambiguous information about page types, flows, and navigation structures so that you can successfully discover, catalog, and build components.

- Identify site areas via labels used in navigation structures, for example, referring to a global navigation bar and declaring "Our library will include Products, Support, Shopping Cart, and My Account."

- Refer to existing or burgeoning design documentation by file name, page number, figure labels, and more detailed specifications.

In general, you want to clarify scope—and components—as accurately and unambiguously as you can, and the order of the steps above starts with the most precise and effective techniques.

Wireframes and other artifacts of similar or lower fidelity represent a design solution that is not finished enough to serve as input to a standardized library. Such artwork does not capture refined visual style like typography, width, grids, and other aspects that you should embed in the styles and layout of a formal component-based wireframing system later.

Therefore, avoid using wireframes as source material for a library of templates and components. Instead, source your library's artwork from existing comps or screenshots of actual pages, and establish your library's visual foundation and standards from higher-fidelity artwork.

Value

Many criteria can influence how you can judge a component's value and whether to include it in a library. You can make these value judgments in isolation or via consensus of and collaboration with a broader team during activities like design reviews and component discovery workshops.

Use the criteria shown in **Figure 8.15** to influence your decision-making and employ the common questions to uncover the value of each candidate for your library.

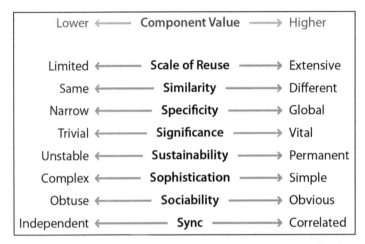

Figure 8.15 Decisive criteria that help judge the relative value of each component and whether it's worth including in a library.

Scale of Reuse

A component's scale of reuse addresses how widely it is used across pages, sections, flows, and throughout an experience. Generally, the more a component is reused, the more beneficial it will be to include it in the library. However, if a component will be built for one page and will *never* be reused again, then omit it from your library.

Common questions you'll need to answer include the following:

▶ How much will the component be reused across experience?

▶ How many different types of page could use this component?

Similarity

Assess the return on investment of adding a new component to a library when an existing component or variation would be sufficient to solve the same design problem. Similarity can also impact how a new component is cataloged, such that what someone may pose as a new component may be instead a needed variation of a component already in the library.

Common questions you'll need to answer include the following:

▶ How similar is this component candidate to existing components?

▶ What makes this component justifiably different than other components?

Specificity

While similar to a component's scale of reuse, specificity addresses the intent to limit a component to a specific site area or context. For example, a site's home page often contains components that may not—under any circumstances—be repurposed for other page types. In another case, a list of training products with unique content and layout may be inappropriate for listing software products.

Common questions you'll need to answer include the following:

▶ Is this component specific to a page, section, content type, or context?

▶ May I use this component in a different context, and if not, why not?

Significance

Different components may be important for different people. Since a team may need to reduce scope or prioritize components built in a project, judging significance plays a key role in conversations and decisions about tradeoffs.

For an information architect, optimizing global navigation is absolutely critical. For a product manager, getting a branded billboard is essential. For an executive, obvious links to corporate governance seem essential even if the content is findable via a less emphasized solution and site visitors express no interest in the content.

Common questions you'll need to answer include the following:

▶ How important is this component relative to our design objectives?

▶ Is this component important to a sponsor or executive?

▶ What are the impacts of making tradeoffs regarding this component?

▶ Can you prioritize these components, from most to least important?

Stability

Building a library is a long-term investment, and adding each component takes effort. Therefore, be mindful of the long-term value of a component. No librarian likes to maintain a large collection of one-offs, and updating unstable components that are always "in play" and change frequently is often not worth the effort.

Common questions you'll need to answer include the following:

▶ How often do you think the component will change?

▶ Are there ongoing or future projects that could impact this component?

Sophistication

The more complex a component is, the higher the cost of building it and incorporating it into the library. And, although not always the case, the more complex a component, the less likely it'll be reused. Don't get caught up adding a fancy widget to the library if it isn't worth the expense or will distract you from adding other items that are more important.

Common questions you'll need to answer include the following:

▶ Do you anticipate reusing existing styles/CSS or creating many new styles?

▶ Are there specific technologies, tools, or frameworks that would need to be utilized (for example, videos or flash) beyond standard CSS and HTML markup?

▶ Are there many behaviors and states that need extensive development and testing, or is implementation straightforward?

Sociability

Components are only as valuable as an organization's ability to meaningfully and appropriately reuse them. If you can't formalize a component's usage, guidelines, and rationale in a way that others can "get it" and use it appropriately, you may want to reconsider adding it to your library.

Common questions you'll need to answer include the following::

▶ How easy is it to explain the component's purpose?

▶ How simple are the structures, behaviors, and content attributes?

▶ Do some stakeholders have difficulty "getting it" immediately?

▶ How strictly would you govern the usage of this component? Would you need extensive editorial or interactive guidelines to ensure that it's used correctly, or simple guidelines that enable flexible use?

Sync

How much a component's use and behaviors are related to other components can have an important impact on how it is categorized, related to other components, or even combined with other items into a larger reusable chunk.

Common questions you'll need to answer include the following:

▶ Is this item a variation of an existing component?

▶ Is this component related to or always used with another component?

▶ Can this component be documented on its own?

▶ Is this component limited to one page type, or can it be used in many places?

9

ORGANIZE

When creating a component library, you must ensure that designers and stakeholders can find and use components during the design process. Just as important, a librarian must be prepared to manage what can become a growing collection. Invariably the conversation turns to how best to organize a library for the long term.

Adopting sound organizational principles enables the team to do the following:

- ▶ Refer to items in a precise and succinct way in discussions, plans, screen designs, tests, assessments, and documentation.

- ▶ Improve findability and retrieval during design so that designers navigate the library to choose components easily.

- ▶ Establish a scalable framework to manage the library over time, extend the system, and store each item.

- ▶ Create ways to connect documents together predictably for projects (such as a design specification) and standards (such as a style guide or Web-based library) using well-defined names and references.

This chapter details ways to organize components in a library that is easy to use and maintain.

The Component Catalog

In order to create and sustain a library of reusable components, you'll need a system to organize, classify, and code each item. Your component catalog serves as the library index and management tool for identifying, arranging, and classifying every component. Sure, you'll want to avoid going overboard and creating a monstrous classification system that's impossible to maintain and impenetrable to new users. But although it's dismissed by some, and contains many details never seen by anyone but the librarian(s), the component catalog is an essential tool for organizing and managing a library.

A component catalog is a compilation of records, with each record describing an item of the collection. From a high level, think of it as a reference table. Rows correspond to each item, and columns correspond to each property used to define and track each item.

An online spreadsheet, structured like the table displayed in **Figure 9.1**, has proven to be an excellent solution, where multiple participants (with varied access permissions and a revision history) can collaborate without worrying about sending a file back and forth.

Some teams have been wary of—or simply prohibited from—using an online spreadsheet outside a corporate firewall, so a spreadsheet file stored on a shared drive has served as a workable alternative. Since it's on a shared drive, all team members could access the file when needed, and they were also able to apply write permissions for the file that limited editing to a few select users. With the team controlling who could see and edit the file, the file was more valuable to a larger group and had a longer, persisted lifespan.

	Discovery		Taxonomy				Build		Management	
	Build ID	Source	Collection	Category	Code	Component Name	Build Status	Build Assigned To	Status	Phase
			Consumer Developers Portal	Header & footer Navigation Content Window Form Tables			Identified Assigned Drafted Reviewed Complete	(name)	Designed Designed (postponed) In Development Pilot Launched Retired	
	32	003_Home	Consumer	Content	TBD	Home billboard	Identified		Designed	2
	56	004_My Account	Consumer	Navigation	TBD	Product list	Identified		Designed	2
	74	004_My Account	Consumer	Content	TBD	Feature list	Assigned	John	Designed	1
	23	004_My Account	Consumer	Content	TBD	Get started	Assigned	John	Designed	1
	49	004_My Account	Consumer	Form	TBD	Log in	Assigned	John	Designed	1
	43	003_Home	Consumer	Header & footer	TBD	Logo	Drafted	Jane	Designed	1
	44	003_Home	Consumer	Header & footer	TBD	Utility navigation	Drafted	Jane	Designed	1
	45	003_Home	Consumer	Header & footer	TBD	Search	Drafted	Jane	Designed	1
	47	003_Home	Consumer	Header & footer	TBD	Primary navigation	Drafted	Jane	Designed	1
	60	007_Contact Us	Consumer	Content	TBD	Contact	Identified		Designed	2
	135	009_Training	Consumer	Content	TBD	Billboard	Assigned	Jane	Designed	1
	138	009_Training	Consumer	Content	TBD	Key Benefits	Assigned	Jane	Designed	1
	128	012_TrainingCatego	Consumer	Navigation	TBD	Product list	Assigned	Jane	Designed	1
	134	009_Training	Consumer	Content	TBD	Billboard	Assigned	Jane	Designed	1
	127	012_TrainingCatego	Consumer	Content	TBD	Secondary Billboard	Assigned	Jane	Designed	1

Figure 9.1 A component catalog managed via a Google Docs spreadsheet.

Depending on the complexity, delegation, and shared management of your library, a more sophisticated solution (such as a database) may be warranted, but it isn't common. Regardless, create an environment where librarian(s) can update and manage the collection while others can access and view the catalog for reviews, comments, prioritization, and other tasks.

A catalog enables you to track many properties of each item throughout a component's life cycle, including the following:

Discovery Properties. Where did an item originate, what do people call it, and can I trace where it came from? You'll want to track where a component came from so you can reference its context of origin. Activities for discovering components are described in Chapter 8, "Discover."

Taxonomy Properties. What is this item called? How is it classified? How is it related to other components? These properties are defined as a component's place in the library is formalized, described later in this chapter.

Build Properties. Who is assembling this item? What progress has been made? The process of building component assets is described in Chapter 11, "Build."

Administration Properties. How important is this item? Who is authoring guidelines about it? Where can this item be used? Is this component active or retired? Over the course of a component's life, the team's value, focus, and activities around the component will vary. Administration of a component library over this life cycle is covered in Chapter 12, "Administer."

Additional Notes. These can include URLs, helpful supplemental information, and other reminders that you need to keep somewhere as you manage the library.

Discovery Properties

Once you consider adding a component to the library, add it to the catalog so you can track it and trace where it came from. In this sense, the catalog is a helpful tool for a "candidate" component, even if it doesn't have a formal code or concrete location in the catalog's hierarchy.

When you discover items for the catalog, assign each one a "Build ID" (as shown in **Figure 9.2**). This ID number serves as a unique reference number until an item is given a more formal component code. Using the Build ID, you can bridge documentation and communication (e.g., email) by referring to the same item with the same number everywhere. That is, component #95 referenced in an email is the same as the component #95 annotated in a screenshot, which is the same as the component #95 in your draft set of component artwork. Everyone knows what component #95 is, and this unambiguous reference is fundamental when you are organizing, prioritizing, and building the library.

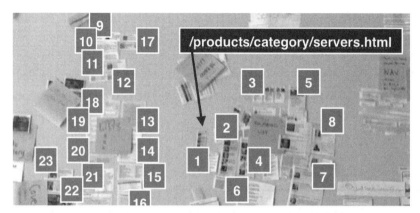

Figure 9.2 Outputs of a component discovery exercise, where items are subsequently encoded with a Build ID (in the orange box) and their source recorded.

Invariably, stakeholders—or even you—will forget where a component came from. To mitigate this risk, track the component's source (be it a URL, page name, or screenshot file name) to trace back to where you found the item. This mapping is vital, since many may ask you later to identify "Where did that component variation come from?" Without recording this mapping, the context may be lost as you cut out and create component artwork without the broader context of a page or experience. Track the source, so you can avoid time-consuming exercises of searching for that component later amid a site design or collection of screenshots.

Taxonomy Properties

The most important role of a catalog is to manage the library's namespace: names, IDs, categories, and other organizing principles embraced by your team. The catalog serves as *the* authoritative source for establishing a hierarchical taxonomy and maintaining it over time. It's up to the librarian to ensure each item has a unique, unambiguous, and single place in that hierarchy, and a meaningful taxonomy goes a long way.

As detailed in subsequent sections of this chapter, **Figure 9.3** illustrates the levels that have proven effective for classifying components into a concrete, cohesive taxonomy with properties that include the following:

- ▶ Category (such as header and footer)
- ▶ Component name (such as utility bar)
- ▶ Variation name (such as logged in)

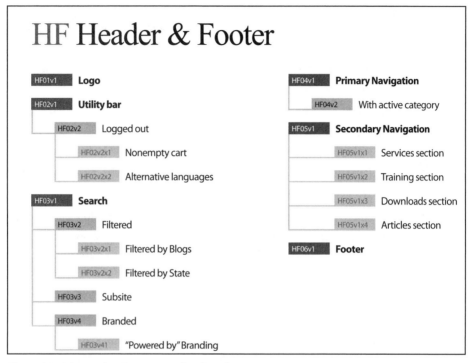

Figure 9.3 A hierarchical taxonomy for classifying components.

▶ Example name (such as logged in with alternative languages)

▶ Code (such as HF02v2x2)

Build Properties

As artwork and/or markup for a component library is assembled, you can use the catalog to assign an item to a contributing designer, and track completeness via a sequence of steps: identified, assigned, drafted, reviewed, and complete.

Within the catalog, a librarian could use one cell to denote the current step, or separate contiguous columns for each step, each marked with "Done" and/or color as the step is completed.

Administration Properties

Designers and stakeholders typically don't need to know the gory details of library management. However, a catalog is a great place for librarians to manage component activities like authoring guidelines, producing artwork, and managing releases. The catalog can also be used to track progress, priority, and other properties including the following:

Status, such as In Development (not yet released), Pilot (limited release), Active (available for open use), or Retired (no longer in use)

Phase, such as 1, 2, and 3 in cases when working across multiple build cycles

Priority, such as high, medium, or low, so that stakeholders can assess and influence what's most important to be added

Platform(s) used to classify items if they are only usable with a specific content management system, application platform, or style sheet

Well-defined management properties enable a librarian to sort, filter, and report on the library's status and growth. Leave at least one column for general notes, and add temporary columns for stakeholder feedback. Once the library incorporates that feedback, the temporary column can be removed.

Retiring Components

Not every candidate component will make it into a formal, published library. In fact, often 50 percent or more of the candidate components are discarded before the library's launch. Even if an item is assigned a formal component code and gets published, it may fall out of favor and eventually be retired. Even if it remains in use on existing pages, the item's retirement communicates to designers and stakeholders that an item should no longer be applied to future design solutions (**Figure 9.4**).

	D	E	F	G	H	I	J	K L
1	**Taxonomy**						**Build**	**Management**
2	**Collection**	**Category**	**Code**	**Component Name**	**Variation Name**	**Example Name**	**Build Status**	**Status**
3	Consumer Developers Portal	Header & footer Navigation Content Window Form Tables					Identified Assigned Drafted Reviewed Complete	Designed Designed (postponed) In Development Pilot Launched Retired
19	Consumer	Header & footer	HF01v1	Search bar	General		Complete	Launched
20	Consumer	Header & footer	HF01v2	Search bar	Section-specific		Complete	Launched
21	Consumer	Header & footer	HF02v1	Logo	Standard		Complete	Launched
22	Consumer	Header & footer	HF03v1	Account bar	Non-personalized		Complete	Retired
23	Consumer	Header & footer	HF03v2	Account bar	Personalized	Not logged in	Complete	Launched
24	Consumer	Header & footer	HF03v2x1	Account bar	Personalized	Logged in	Complete	Launched
25	Consumer	Header & footer	HF04v1	Primary navigation	No section active		Complete	Launched
26	Consumer	Header & footer	HF04v2	Primary navigation	No section active		Complete	Launched
27	Consumer	Header & footer	HF04v3	Primary navigation	Active section		Complete	Launched
28	Consumer	Header & footer	HF04v3	Primary navigation	Active section	Products section	Complete	Launched
29	Consumer	Header & footer	HF05v1	Footer	Standard footer		Complete	Launched
30	Consumer	Header & footer	HF05v2	Footer	Thin footer		Complete	Launched

Figure 9.4 Lines for retired components are changed to gray to reduce emphasis yet keep the records in the catalog.

No matter what, be sure to *retain those records* in your catalog. Do not remove any lines from your spreadsheet (even if you need to change their appearance via color or other formatting). Keep each record in the catalog because discarded items may be added back later, and retired component codes are permanently reserved and should not be mistakenly applied to future items. For both discarded and retired items, you may later want to refer to where they came from or even use them as examples of what not to do.

Categories

The first step in organizing components is to group all items into meaningful categories. You can begin a discussion of categorization with whether page regions would make a good organizing principle. **Figure 9.5** illustrates high-level areas like header and footer, body content, navigation (such as left or local), billboard (at the top of the content space), and a sidebar that provide a good baseline from which to consider component categories.

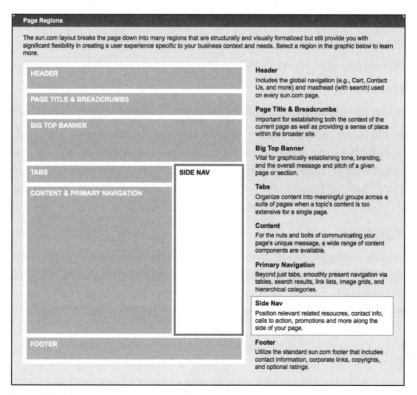

Figure 9.5 The Sun.com page layout broken down into regions that suggest component categories. (*Courtesy Sun.com/webdesign*)

In fact, many browser-based site designs have all five of these key page regions, even if teams refer to these areas with distinct, organization-specific names. Other user interface contexts (such as desktop software or a mobile device) also have layout regions that are useful for grouping components, such as navigation/menus and body content.

And while regions provide a good basis for categorization, other categories can be valuable for grouping components, such as a search category for an ecommerce site with many displays for search submission and results. The following sections describe categories used most frequently and components that are traditionally classified into each one.

Header and Footer

Within most Web sites, the page header and footer include the site's primary branding, structure, and navigation options. A header and footer category often contains the following:

▶ Site logo/title (which often doubles as a link to the homepage)

▶ Utility navigation (such as About Us, Contact Us, and/or links to Worldwide Sites and translations)

▶ Primary navigation (such as links to the site's main sections)

▶ Site search

▶ Footer navigation bar(s), including additional links and legal information

A header and footer category usually contains the fewest distinct components of any category, but is the most important to create first as a foundation for any subsequent page design. With a header and footer, designers can start a new page design within a consistently rendered framework.

Body Content

Almost always the category with the most components, the body content category begins with simple items like page titles, paragraphs, section headers, bulleted lists, and numeric lists. Once the fundamentals are covered, this category grows rapidly to include a wide range of diverse components depending on your site design.

Navigation

Navigation components commonly include links and other basic controls (e.g., drop-down menus) that take a user from the current page to a distinct, separate place. Most often, this category is used for link collections (such as the article links in **Figure 9.6**), breadcrumbs, and more.

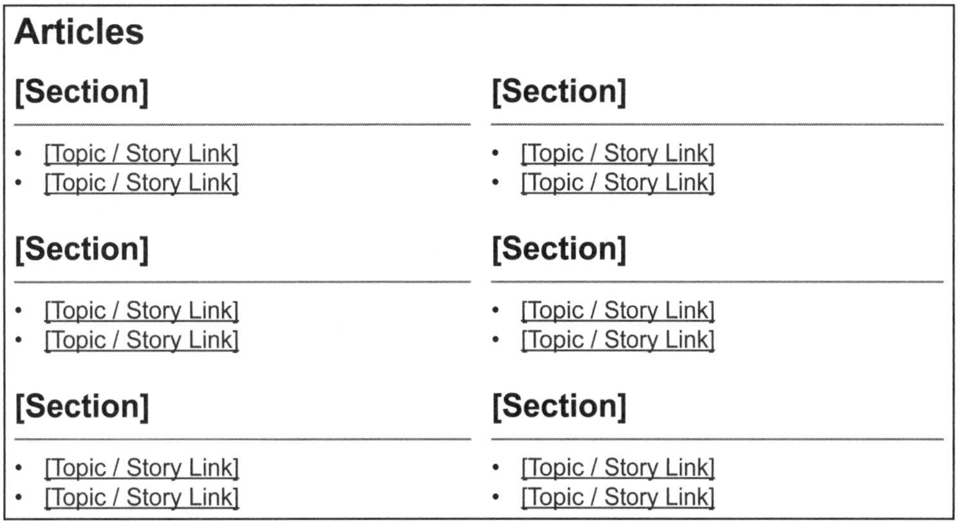

Articles	
[Section]	**[Section]**
• [Topic / Story Link] • [Topic / Story Link]	• [Topic / Story Link] • [Topic / Story Link]
[Section]	**[Section]**
• [Topic / Story Link] • [Topic / Story Link]	• [Topic / Story Link] • [Topic / Story Link]
[Section]	**[Section]**
• [Topic / Story Link] • [Topic / Story Link]	• [Topic / Story Link] • [Topic / Story Link]

Figure 9.6 A navigation component for categorized article links, suitable for a higher-level page that links to articles across six different sections.

Sidebar

Also referred to as right rail, right navigation, or related navigation, the sidebar is frequently included as an area for tertiary navigation, links to related content, calls to action such as Contact Us, and promotional banners and ads. If a site does not have a sidebar region for such components, then this category is unnecessary.

Billboard

Also referred to as dynamic lead, hero, spotlight, or big top banner, this key area of site messaging, branding, and promotion often occupies disproportionate amounts of a team's effort. Generally positioned above the body content, a billboard spotlight warrants a separate category due to its significance, dominant visual position, often sophisticated interactions, and frequency of change.

Other Categories

Depending on the design system, a component library can include other categories specific to your experience. Examples of other categories include the following:

► Windows (pop-ups, hovers, lightboxes, confirmation dialogs, and more)

► Search (for search submission with various sets of fields, as well as search results that can include lists, filtering, sorting, maps, and more)

► Tables (including both common row and column header configurations, as well as related interface components like pagination, sorting, and filtering)

► Portal or Personalization (for components that are limited to and fit into customizable portal pages distinct from other page types)

► Application widgets (for more highly transactional applications, particularly intranet apps)

Overlapping Categories

Invariably, some categories may overlap in definition and purpose. For example, two of the most common categories—navigation and body content—can be the hardest to distinguish if a component is used in the body content region but also provides navigation to other pages within the experience. Why separate them? Otherwise the content category can become ridiculously large relative to the other categories, so create enough categories so that any one category doesn't have far more than all other categories combined.

While organizing, make an effort to classify a component in the category that is most specific to its use while also amending or evolving the definition of each category to be as precise as possible. Instead of navigation acting as a category based only on where a component is located within a page design, perhaps navigation components are those that enable users to "navigate to a different destination beyond the current page," whereas body content components generally keep you within the context of the current page.

Such distinctions may be lost on some library users, but don't be too concerned unless your categorization inhibits findability, causes significant confusion, or leads to inappropriate use.

Variations

With components organized into high-level categories, the next step is to group related components together when they share a common mission or specific purpose. When assessing relationships between components, ask yourself if the two items are really alternatives that meet the same design objective. If two items have the same objective and a very similar appearance, but differ due to wording, subtle visual style, link destinations, supporting markup, or some other criteria, you can classify both as variations of the same component.

Variations can often be fairly easy to recognize. Consider the page title variations shown in **Figure 9.7**: stand-alone, with subtitle, and with quantity of search results or products. These aren't three distinct components. Instead, they represent three variations of the same component: Page Title. A page can include only one page title component, and a designer would want to determine and use the most appropriate variation.

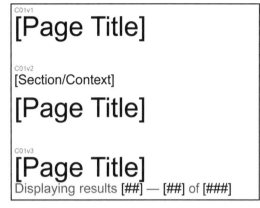

Figure 9.7 Page title variations.

Variations enable designers and other participants to review and choose from alternatives when making design decisions. During the design process, variations enable you to quickly try an alternative in the context of a page. Variations also enable you to communicate how broadly you can change a component to fit different conditions. Finally, variations help to organize similar components as they are added to and retired from a library over time.

Variations can represent a more complex array of alternatives, too. Consider a utility bar at the top of the page. **Figure 9.8** depicts many versions for different country sites (United States versus other worldwide sites), different states (not signed in, signed in as a guest, signed in as a member), different languages, and even different quantities of items in a shopping cart. Even though each instance has a distinct set of content, links, and states, it's sensible to group them together as variations of a single utility bar component.

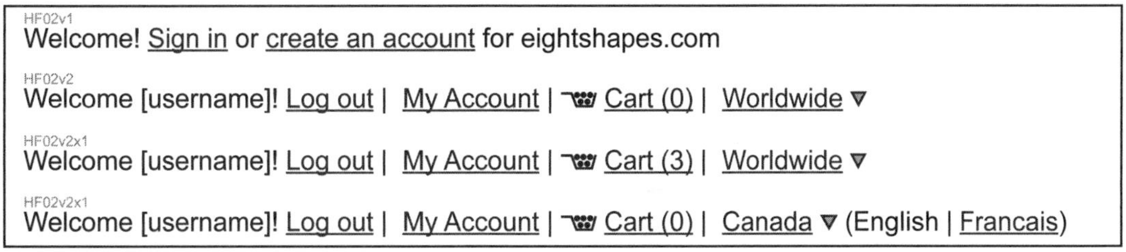

HF02v1
Welcome! Sign in or create an account for eightshapes.com

HF02v2
Welcome [username]! Log out | My Account | 🛒 Cart (0) | Worldwide ▼

HF02v2x1
Welcome [username]! Log out | My Account | 🛒 Cart (3) | Worldwide ▼

HF02v2x1
Welcome [username]! Log out | My Account | 🛒 Cart (0) | Canada ▼ (English | Francais)

Figure 9.8 Utility bar variations.

Keep in mind that you can use the same component variation more than once on a page, or even variations of the same component on the same page, too. A designer could choose to repeat a banner component three times in a vertical sidebar by stacking a banner variation with a graphic two times above a banner variation without the graphic (**Figure 9.9**). Therefore, a page's sidebar could include three banners stacked together, each a variation of the same component.

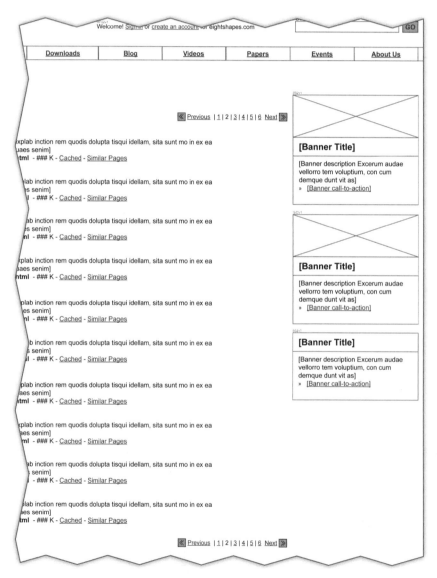

Figure 9.9 A page sidebar that repeats the same banner component three times: two with a graphic, and a third without the graphic.

Avoid creating and classifying every component state as a separate variation. Recall the designer's motivation: Add a component in the screen design and go from there. In that case, often the default or initial state will suffice.

For example, there's no need to include a variation for every star level of the customer rating shown in **Figure 9.10**. Instead, include representative variations (such as unrated and rating applied) and leave the detailed states of each level (such as a stored score of one through five, hover interactions) and supplemental text to the guidelines instead of the reusable wireframe and comp artwork.

Figure 9.10 Customer ratings variations.

Relating Components as Variations

Figure 9.11 displays a navigation bar that—when hovered—displays a menu that presents navigation options. The menu is only used in connection with the navigation bar, and isn't permitted in any other context.

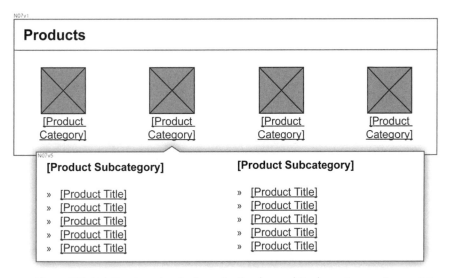

Figure 9.11 Relating two chunks (a navigation bar and its dynamic menu) as variations of the same component.

Therefore, organize the two chunks as variations of the *same* overall component. Sure, a menu panel isn't truly a variation of the navigation bar. However, the benefit of organizing the two items together to powerfully communicate their connection outweighs our need to classify all the components.

Another common opportunity for relating components as variations is when a structure can be divided into smaller reusable chunks that are always used in concert.

Consider tabs. A tabbed component may seem straightforward: just a simple bar of alternative navigation options that group content. However, from a component perspective, tabs can become a more sophisticated array of reusable chunks: primary tabs, optional secondary and tertiary tab navigation, tabbed containers, and other reusable tab chunks, such as menus for filtering and sorting. For engineers creating component markup for tabs, they may even need invisible component chunks to close a container (via closing <div> tags), since from a code perspective, tabs actually contain other content nested within. **Figure 9.12** illustrates the range of visible tab component variations, stacked together.

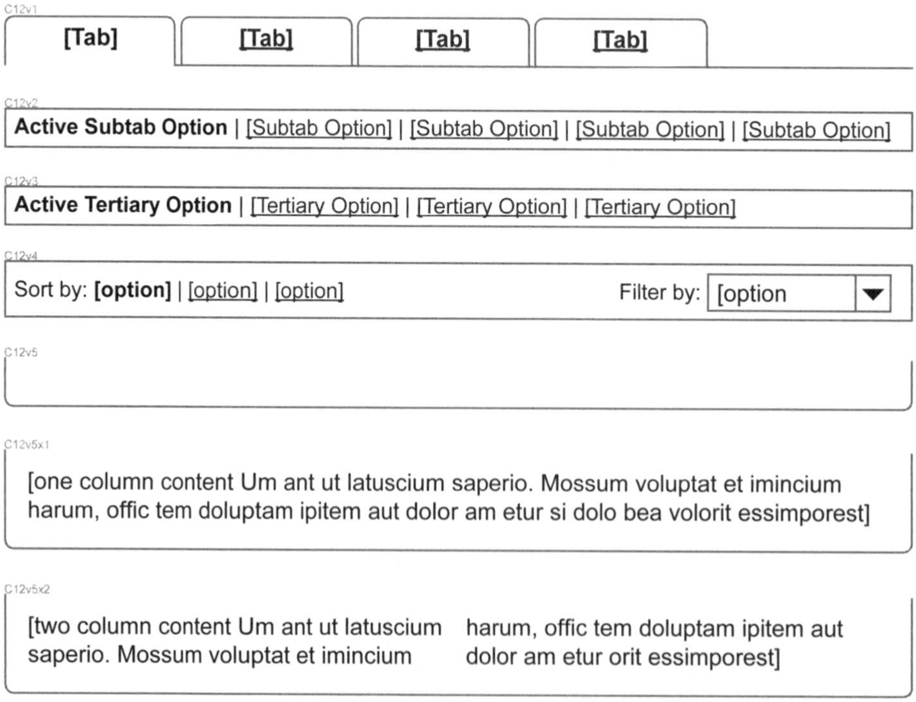

Figure 9.12 A stack of reusable tab chunks, organized as variations within a single tab component.

Although different, all these chunks are relevant to one design goal: assembling a tabbed structure. So group these items as variations of the same component.

Also, avoid grouping components together as variations just because they have a similar structure, interaction, or visual style. If one item has a different or far more specific purpose than another item that is otherwise similar, it may be useful to distinguish the two as separate components.

Figure 9.13 contrasts two different components usable in a page's sidebar: a general, labeled list of related links, as well as a module for downloads where each link is preceded by an icon and followed by file size and type. In this case, the sidebar category should offer a component specifically used for downloads, separate from a more generic component for any set of related links.

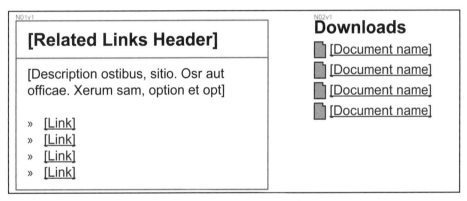

Figure 9.13 Different components for specific downloads versus generic related links.

Examples

At times, it may be necessary to document or create examples of a component variation where you want to include real content or branded imagery. In that case, it makes sense to include this instance as an example of the variation.

For example, consider common tab sets found in a site design like the primary tabs shown in **Figure 9.14**. For designers creating products and solutions pages often using the component system, it's valuable to also catalog two examples of primary tabs to illustrate examples of typical quantity, labels, and order of primary tabs for those page types.

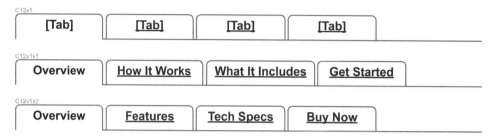

Figure 9.14 Tab examples.

Similarly, a Contact Us component could be customized depending on the available contact mechanisms employed for different types of customers or product lines. The component itself doesn't change, but depending on circumstances, some links may not be included. **Figure 9.15** shows how examples can differ.

Examples are powerful tools for reinforcing context and appropriate component use. While components—and even variations—may be rendered with generic copy, an example is real. Examples also enable quicker application of an oft-utilized component, such as the active category of a navigation bar or a standard tab set for product pages.

The structural, behavioral, and general appearance of a component or variation is the same across every example. However, examples are different because they do the following:

▶ Add content (such as more links in a list)

▶ Remove content (such as omitting a checkbox or help link)

▶ Include sample images (such as a custom background of a navigation bar)

▶ Include sample copy (such as well-written headlines)

Figure 9.15 Contact Us examples.

Every example in your catalog should be based on an existing component or variation. Therefore, if you find yourself adding an example that has no corresponding, more generic item, then add the generic version, too.

Taking the Engineer's Perspective

Examples also enable a designer and librarian to communicate the range of variability to an engineer building HTML and CSS markup. Each example should *not* require engineers to build more stuff, but instead enable them to assess the flexibility of the code they already have.

A great way to understand examples is from a code perspective. For each example, HTML tags (like <div>) and CSS classes and IDs would not change. However, the content *inside* that markup would be different, such as the words within a paragraph (<p> tag) or list item (<li> tag) or image within a reference (such as the src attribute of an <img> tag or <div> background).

Conversely, if a component sample requires other distinct HTML tags or CSS coding, then it's probably not an example, but truly a different component or variation.

Codes

Once your library grows beyond the simplest of collections (such as 20 or 30 items), consider assigning a reference code to each component, variation, and example. Each reference code, such as S03v1x1, enables you to refer to an item more succinctly and precisely. The reference code is used not only as a marker on visualized screen designs and within annotated documentation, but also for verbal communication between team members.

As components are increasingly embedded in a team's communications, rapid reference to individual items becomes commonplace, if not essential for success. In my first meeting with one new client, the team drilled into project details quickly and within five minutes was talking in a foreign language of codes and references. "Excuse me," I interrupted. "What is the S03v1?"

The team paused, and then the publisher explained, "That's our Contact Us component for the sidebar—S refers to the sidebar category, and the rest of the numbers refer to the code we all use to refer to it." She gave me the URL where I could find a component index (and lots of documentation). From then on, I knew exactly what they were talking about, and if I didn't, the answer was one quick lookup away. What's more precise and efficient— explaining that you are referring to "The first example of the first default variation of the Contact Us in the sidebar" or succinctly saying "S03v1x1"?

The shorthand code can be derived directly from the taxonomy of categories, components, variations, and examples. Consider a "search bar" component of the "header and footer" category, which has four variations for default, filtered, subsite, and branded. Then a variation of that component could be codified in the library as HF04v2x1 based on the following:

- ▶ HF: header and footer category
- ▶ 04: 4th component within that category (search bar)
- ▶ v2: 2nd variation (filtered)
- ▶ x1: 1st example (by blogs)

Such a component could be amid a wider range of variations and examples as illustrated in **Figure 9.16**:

- ▶ HF04v1.SearchBar.Default
- ▶ HF04v2.SearchBar.Filtered
- ▶ HF04v2x1.SearchBar.FilteredByBlogs
- ▶ HF04v2x2.SearchBar.FilteredByState
- ▶ HF04v3.SearchBar.Subsite
- ▶ HF04v4.SearchBar.Branded
- ▶ HF04v4x1.SearchBar.BrandedPartner

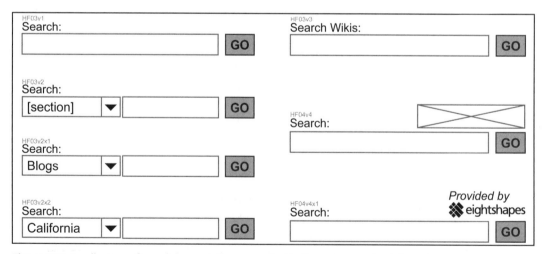

Figure 9.16 A collection of search bar variations recorded in the component catalog.

But Aren't Codes Cryptic?

Yes, codes can seem cryptic when first encountered. Stakeholders new to component codes must be taught the basic structure. Even many designers initially respond that codes are overly vague, unnecessarily dogmatic, and indicative of the threat to their "freedom to design" an experience.

However, this teachable moment takes less than a minute to explain what each part of the code represents. Those same stakeholders and designers can be quick to value codes when scanning for components reused in artwork and annotations across many pages or engaging in conversation in a fluent, efficient way.

Despite the initial learning curve, component codes can be used to do the following:

▶ Serve as written and verbal shorthand for fast and precise identification.

▶ Enable faster lookup within reference materials and asset libraries.

▶ Mark components within screen designs in a minimally obtrusive way.

▶ Map screen designs to adjacent annotations.

▶ Provide structure for easier-to-use specifications.

▶ Establish predictable names for pages, chapters, and files.

▶ Filter, sort, and retrieve artifacts within a library setting.

▶ Connect artifacts together via shared references, such as wireframes, comps, markup, technical analysis, and QA test plans being created in parallel by different people.

Creating Component Codes

Creating codes for components in your library is a quick, self-contained exercise, and will serve as a foundation for scaling and managing the library over time in a predictable, organized way.

However, don't start assigning codes too early. You could waste time if you start applying formal codes during a project while component designs are unstable, nomenclature is evolving, and new requirements and variations are emerging. The early stages of a project's design cycle can be a tumultuous time, at least for a librarian trying to manage a coded naming architecture.

Instead, pause before establishing formal codes. Apply codes only when the library has stabilized or just before you are to publish the library for the first time.

Once you are ready to create the coded taxonomy, follow these steps:

1. Validate that your catalog contains a record for each item needing a code.

2. Move items (records) into a meaningful order based on your taxonomy, such as by category, then by component within category, then by variation within component, then by example within variation. Why care so much about ordering the components so hierarchically? Because typing in the codes next, line by line, becomes a simple process of enter code, press return, enter code, press return in a similarly hierarchical order.

3. Starting at the top, assign a code to each item row by row, as illustrated in **Figure 9.17**.

	Collection	Category	Code	Component Name	Variation Name	Example Name
1	**Taxonomy**					
2	**Collection**	**Category**	**Code**	**Component Name**	**Variation Name**	**Example Name**
3	Consumer Developers Portal	Header & footer Navigation Content Window Form Tables				
20	Consumer	Header & footer	HF01v1	Logo		
21	Consumer	Header & footer	HF02v1	Utility bar	Logged out	
22	Consumer	Header & footer	HF02v2	Utility bar	Logged in	
23	Consumer	Header & footer	HF02v2x1	Utility bar	Logged in	Nonempty cart
24	Consumer	Header & footer	HF02v2x2	Utility bar	Logged in	Alternative languages
25	Consumer	Header & footer	HF03v1	Search	Standard	
26	Consumer	Header & footer	HF03v2	Search	Filtered	
27	Consumer	Header & footer	HF03v2x1	Search	Filtered	Filtered by blogs
28	Consumer	Header & footer	HF03v2x2	Search	Filtered	Filtered by state
29	Consumer	Header & footer	HF03v3	Search	Subsite	
30	Consumer	Header & footer	HF03v4	Search	Branded	
31	Consumer	Header & footer	HF03v4x1	Search	Branded	Powered by
32	Consumer	Header & footer		Primary navigation	Standard	
33	Consumer	Header & footer		Primary navigation	With active category	
34	Consumer	Header & footer		Secondary navigation	Standard	
35	Consumer	Header & footer		Secondary navigation	Standard	Services
36	Consumer	Header & footer		Secondary navigation	Standard	Training
37	Consumer	Header & footer		Secondary navigation	Standard	Downloads
38	Consumer	Header & footer		Secondary navigation	Standard	Articles
39	Consumer	Header & footer		Footer		

Figure 9.17 When you're ready, use the catalog to finalize the library's organization and then apply component codes in one pass.

If multiple individuals will manage the library, consider creating component codes together as a team. During such an exercise, the team can not only discuss the best way to organize the library, but also brainstorm on nomenclature, additional component candidates to consider, and more.

Code Guidelines

The following guidelines will help you maintain a healthy, coded taxonomy:

Category Codes

▶ Represent a category with one or two letters, usually the first letter of the category name (such as "C" for Content).

- ▶ When multiple categories start with the same letter, use a single letter to refer to the most important category (such as "S" for Sidebar) and utilize two or more letters for other, less important categories (such as "SE" for Search).

Component Codes

- ▶ Use a unique number for each component.
- ▶ Start component numbering in each category with 1 and ascend.
- ▶ Assign the lowest numbers to components likely to be extensively reused.
- ▶ For example, common content components , such as generic elements, page title, and breadcrumbs, should be assigned low numbers such as C01, C02, and C03. When adding new components to an already established base of codes, don't worry about low numbers. Instead, just assign the next available number to the next component.
- ▶ Avoid changing or reusing a number once it has been assigned.
- ▶ For example, if you have components C01 through C04 and C03 is retired, then C03 is permanently unavailable. Imagine the confusion if C03 once referred to a video player that was retired, and then a photograph component was added to the library as C03 two months later. If an older wireframe was opened that included the retired video player marked as C03, some might get confused.
- ▶ Append a leading 0 (zero) to the first nine component numbers.
- ▶ By including a leading zero, you can improve scanning and sorting components in a sequence like C08, C09, C10, and C11.

Variation Codes

- ▶ Use a unique number for each variation of a component.
- ▶ Start variation numbering for each component with 1 and ascend.
- ▶ Avoid changing or reusing a variation number once it has been assigned.
- ▶ Append a leading 0 (zero) to the first nine variation numbers.

▶▶ **TIP** In your screen design, include component code markers on a separate layer that you can manage and hide if necessary. Separating codes from designs allows designers to hide markers when using the artwork for executive reviews, prototypes in usability tests, or final image slicing. However, for the rest of the design process, keep codes visible to precisely identify items.

The Power of Mumbo Jumbo

AUTHOR: **Andrew Payne**

ROLE: **Design Technologist, Sun.com**

Component codes are the key to making a component system work. They are not fancy or exciting, but they are the thread that ties everything together. From wireframes, HTML, and CSS class names to image file names, the common language of component codes enables you to easily identify and communicate the components you're using.

Managing Images

Aside from using component codes in wireframes, using them in places such as image file names offers many benefits. Not only does it help with image file management, but it also sends a clear message to publishers that a given image is specific for that component and should not be used in any other context.

To embed a namespace into images, prepend a component code to the image (such as go4_myimage.jpg or go4v1_myVariationImage.jpg) and use directories based on component codes to organize a central repository of component-related images (such as /images/go4/go4_myimage.jpg).

The Secret Is in the Sauce

The real value of component codes comes in the CSS and HTML. As you build and evolve a component system, you will face the reality that the descriptive component names change. As you add variations and update components to meet new needs, descriptive names can become dated and confusing.

This may seem counterintuitive to those who follow the school of semantic class naming, which prefers class names such as *header, footer, globalnav,* or *promo.* However, there is no difference. Component codes only add a layer of abstraction to the semantics, so Ao1 can be a header and Ao2 can be the global navigation. Literal class names don't have to be abandoned. Instead, use component codes to define component containers and use literal class names in comments and inside containers to make things more readable.

For example, you can create a main container class in the HTML:

```
<div class="g04"> ...foo... </div>
```

And then a variation of that class:

```
<div class="g04 g04v1"> ...foo... </div>
```

And even use the variation as a container ID as well:

```
<div id="g04v1"> ...foo... </div>
```

When you use DIVs for styling, don't get hung up on style-related class names like *leftcorner*. Use the component code instead, with a label like *"w#"* to identify wrapper elements that exist only for styling:

```
<div class="g04 g04v1">
<div class="g04w1"> <div class="g04w2">
...foo...
</div> </div>
</div>
```

Components change over time, and sometimes you cannot make a new component and also end the support for an existing component at the same time. When the CSS must support both new and old versions, you can use a class name to indicate the component revision number:

```
<div id="g04v1 g04v1r1"> ...foo... </div>
```

If You Build It, They Will Follow

It takes a leap of faith to take on a component system and introduce a somewhat cryptic naming convention. From my own experience, I can tell you there is nothing to fear. If people resist at first, they will soon forget all of that when you create a cool component that everyone wants to use. Then they will all be begging for the G04, asking for it by name, and wondering when you'll make the shiny new G05.

Names

Names are critical in establishing a common, plain language, and function as unambiguous labels to communicate what components are and how they're used. A component's name is vital to define an item and to relate it to other components, grids and locations, best practices, and visual and editorial standards.

However, despite the value of names at each catalog level (category, component, variation, and example), my experience with many large UX teams suggests that as designers acclimate to a library over time, they rely less on names and more on coded references and visual techniques like scanning a collection of thumbnails.

Browsing a view of component thumbnails often enables a designer to more rapidly find and use a variation. The "Aha" moment of finding a component visually or exclaiming "I want *that* one!" by pointing at a printed contact sheet can be a more powerful and gratifying experience relative to trying to discern and remember what "Secondary Navigation" means and where exactly it's supposed to fit in a page design. Sorting files or symbol libraries based on codes can enable a designer to pick the needle out of the haystack.

And other stakeholders, such as developers, may be less efficient in repeatedly typing out long names in communications, documentation, and code. Instead, component codes offer a shorter—and more precise—reference than the long labels of component names. The codes also result in far fewer reference errors, since natural language labels can shift as they are being retyped or remembered, but codes don't afford such language shifts.

That said, consider ways of combining component names and codes. If components are retrieved as individual files, concatenate the component code and name together in a filename like G04v2x1.SearchBar.FilteredByBlogs.inds (in this case, an InDesign snippet). Similarly, label the component symbol as G04v2x1.SearchBar.FilteredByBlogs in a stencil or symbol panel. Finally, use names for any features that your software tool supports for searching and filtering. This is especially helpful if your tool supports tagging an item with keywords.

Keywords

Depending on your software tool(s) of choice, you may be able to apply keywords to components (files or symbols) that make it easier to learn, retrieve, and use components.

If your software or Web-based documentation enables you to apply and retrieve components based on keywords, then go for it. For example, Adobe Bridge enables you to apply keywords to a range of files within the Adobe Creative Suite, and its Filter panel enables you to see one or more directories of assets simultaneously and filter files based on keywords (**Figure 9.18**).

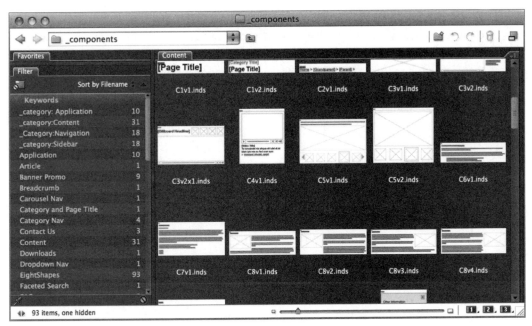

Figure 9.18 An Adobe Bridge view of a component library, with keywords applied to each file and used to filter components via the Filter panel.

At a minimum, apply individual keywords for the category, component name, and variation name of each item. This way, a designer can filter the library at any level, for example, "Show me all components in the Sidebar category" or "Show me only the Contact Us components."

When keyword quantity increases, it becomes difficult to identify higher-level keywords, such as for a category. In that case, consider preceding keywords with a prefix like "_category:" so those keywords are distinguished and display first in lists. Additionally, reinforce other aspects of the taxonomy, such as the shorthand code for each category, by including those in keywords, too. For example, you could apply "_category:Sidebar (S)" to every component in the sidebar category to reinforce that S stands for Sidebar.

Keywords are very powerful for revealing other important properties that distinguish when a component can or can't be used, such as by the following:

Publishing platform (such as "_platform:Portal" and "_platform:CMS")

Grid (such as "_grid:full width," "_grid:two column," and "_grid:two column with sidebar")

Page region (such as "_region:billboard" or "_region:sidebar")

Page type (such as "_pagetype:navigationClass" or "_pagetype:article")

Additionally, apply keywords that serve as synonyms within your team's vocabulary, especially since synonyms don't appear in a component's formal name. For example, consider a component used for showing time-sensitive messages at the top of a page that is referred to formally as the "Messaging" component. Depending on how your team refers to the component, you could also apply keywords such as "Notifications" and "Time-Sensitive Messaging."

10

SETUP

Make sure you're prepared with a solid foundation to build on before indiscriminately starting to build a component library. That foundation is laid with informed decisions and team consensus, and this chapter will discuss key preparations for building a library, including:

- ▶ Choosing software tool(s)
- ▶ Creating page templates with predefined grids, backgrounds, and layers
- ▶ Discerning which—and how many—styles to embed
- ▶ Establishing design conventions

Tools

As teams prepare to produce components, be ready for an important and perhaps emotional discussion about selecting a software tool. Creating a component library requires an entire team to standardize on one or a few software applications. Your strategy must consider organizational culture, individual capabilities, willingness to collaborate, available hardware, and ultimately your team's ability to adapt and embrace a new tool for getting the work done.

Culture and Capabilities

As you plan for your library, get a feel for the culture via team surveys, brainstorming, and personal conversations that answer questions like the following:

- ▶ What tools are already installed and in use? If we chose new tools, how much would they cost and how long would they take to procure?

- ▶ What operating system(s) are used: Windows XP, Windows Vista, Mac OS X, others? Will vendors use the system as much as internal resources? Does that change what operating systems we must support?

- ▶ Who will need to create or update designs based on the component library? Are there people outside our own team who will also need to install and learn a new software tool?

- ▶ What artifacts will be produced using the system, beyond wireframes, comps, or HTML/CSS? Will the tool need to produce specifications or design strategy documents? How about diagrams, such as flows, site maps, and concept models? Standards documents, such as a style guide? Reports, such as a competitive analysis or usability readout?

- ▶ What artifacts should not be produced using the system? For example, should we still continue to produce use cases in Microsoft Word even if screen designs are produced using the tool that includes the component library?

- ▶ Are there internal resources that can serve as experts and/or support?

Different people use their software in different ways. It's important to understand the range of skill levels among everyone who will use the library, as well as the differences in how they work. Some things to look for include

- ▶ Workspace and environment setup, including menus, panels, and windows

- Document setup, including page setup/canvas size, units of measurement, layers, grids, guidelines, pages, frames, and states
- Drawing using shapes, vectors, anchors, direct selection, pen, and line tools
- Operations including grouping, locking, alignment, pathfinder, snap and glue, and arranging items above and below other items
- Typography, including character, paragraph, and table formatting and styles
- Color, including swatches, gradients, and color spaces
- Use of symbols, stencils, snippets, and linked files

Platforms and Products

When selecting a software tool, sometimes you'll find that a single tool won't provide all the features you need. In other cases, a software tool may be sufficient but not particularly modular or integrated with other tools that would round out your set. In either case, consider opportunities to blend tools together to optimally address the needs of your library.

- For example, Microsoft Visio is an optimal diagramming tool, familiar to those already using Microsoft Office, and a very popular tool for creating annotated wireframes. However, Microsoft Visio is Windows-only, wireframes are embedded in documents and cannot be easily reused, and content generally cannot be integrated with other design tools.
- Another very popular tool, Adobe Photoshop, is a powerful design tool, has great features for layers and artwork organization, and enables you to reuse artwork across other Adobe Creative Suite applications. However, Adobe Photoshop is not made for wireframing and is incapable of easily producing an elegant, paginated deliverable without blending with another tool like Adobe InDesign.

To address this challenge, consider blending multiple products together to meet the needs of multiple roles (for example, information architect and visual designer) as shown in **Figure 10.1**.

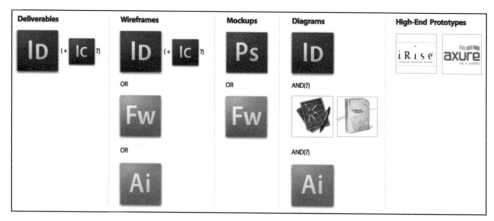

Figure 10.1 Diagram software icons for considering different tool roles for producing design and documentation.

Every type of artifact has unique properties and needs, so choose software tools that work best together to create artifacts such as those described here:

Deliverables: Paginated documents that include all types of artwork and diagrams, delivered as versioned PDFs. Examples include: annotated wireframes, design specification, style guide, usability report, and competitive analysis.

Wireframes: Low-fidelity designs rendered as boxes, symbols, and type hierarchy to communicate screen layout, structure, and behaviors, but without annotation and content describing the design.

Comps: High-fidelity screen designs with precise layout, color, typography, and style, but without annotation and content describing the design.

HTML/CSS: The source code for the presentation layer.

Diagrams: Any conceptual illustration, including site maps, concept models, navigation flows, mental models, and more. Diagramming tools are likely to be left to a designer's preference (such as preparing a concept model in OmniGraffle for PDF and placement within a separate InDesign deliverable).

Prototypes: Any interactive document that links screen designs together, such as an interactive HTML, Flash, or PDF export from a design tool.

Markup and Other Assets: Documents that contain HTML, style sheets, scripting, compiled interactive experiences (for example, SWF), and production images (for example, JPGs and GIFs).

Component libraries are often built in the context of large design organizations looking to promote consistency across many people. The larger the team, the more likely multiple operating systems (both Microsoft Windows and Mac OS X) are in play, particularly if both internal staff and vendors use the system.

However, many tools are platform-specific. For wireframes, Microsoft Visio and Axure RP work only on Microsoft Windows, whereas OmniGraffle works only on Mac OS X. For some teams, that's just fine since all resources are constrained to a single platform and already used to a single tool. In other instances, platform-specific products are quickly dismissed in favor of applications within the Adobe Creative Suite.

Using more than one Adobe Creative Suite product is often associated with a desire for wider adoption across larger organizations and participating vendors. One large team had standardized on Microsoft Windows XP internally, but all of their vendors used Apple OS X. That team decided to use Adobe CS because it works on both platforms, enabling the team to build out one library as well as share files between internal and external team members.

The Adobe Creative Suite provides a range of powerful and cross-platform design applications (for example, Photoshop, InDesign, Illustrator, Fireworks) that work well together with helpful support tools (for example, Bridge). The choice of tools in the Adobe Creative Suite comes with a price, however: Adobe CS (particularly if many products are used in combination) may cost more per seat and require more dedicated training and a longer adoption period.

Resistance to Change

Over the past three years, we've facilitated surveys and observed behavior of over 200 designers that reveal some interesting perspectives and behaviors. As an individual cultivates proficiency with software over the course of a career, a strong attachment to one or more tools may develop. Some designers are fearful of management recommending—or mandating—a standard tool and systematic approach for producing designs. Such fear extends beyond being bound by standards that seem to constrain (but are intended to focus) innovation. More simply, individuals feel comfortable and effective using their tool of choice and are resistant to the cost of switching tools. Nobody wants to be perceived as less productive, less efficient, and thus less valuable to an organization.

There is a strong correlation between experience level and resistance to change. Such resistance among senior designers is unfortunate, since they are leaders of design projects, more effective at communicating design, and potential champions of the approach.

By contrast, less experienced team members often exhibit a strong desire to learn more effective techniques and tools to broaden skills, if given sufficient time to learn and adapt.

Assembling a library in multiple tools is one technique to counter resistance and increase adoption. In effect, you replicate an entire library in two or more software applications so that designers can choose a tool to produce screen designs, such as using Microsoft Visio and OmniGraffle to produce wireframes. Be careful with this approach, for assembling in multiple tools exposes a team to the following risks:

▶ Maintaining multiple instances of the same library costs more, and it takes more time to create, package, and distribute each version.

▶ Tools have different capabilities, so consistent production is potentially compromised due to disparate features.

▶ Designers use the existence of different tools to justify creating and communicating design differently, which runs counter to the goals of unifying a team around a component library.

Another approach to mitigating resistance is to find the tool that represents the best compromise of all teams. This, too, is risky. By compromising everyone's needs and trying to select a one-size-fits-all tool, you may end up diluting the power of any individual discipline (for example, visual design) and/or capability to produce a type of artifact (comps vs. wireframes vs. annotated specification or report).

Selling the system too softly, and the potential cost of switching to a new tool, can undermine your effort. A director of a large UX team was acutely aware of dissident designers groaning about the tool switch. So, on launch day, the director began the training session with something akin to "we're here to learn about a system that, if you like it, can help you design. But we don't want to disrupt your preferred workflow." With that, right out of the gate, the opportunity to transform the team and culture was lost. Contrarian designers tuned out the training, instead working and checking email. The director could have openly recognized challenges, inspired the team with a rousing strategy, and invited the designers to identify gaps that the group could have closed together.

Ultimately, it is open communication that most effectively mitigates resistance to change. Frank discussion must acknowledge the resistance and provide opportunities for contrary voices to be heard. When creating a library, there's ample opportunity during the project: the kickoff meeting, discovery workshops, reviews of survey results, workshop sessions, coaching clinics, and most importantly, private conversations. These events are a platform for cynics to challenge the system, identify its gaps and weaknesses, recognize viable alternatives and solutions, and ultimately trigger teachable moments that help everyone understand the constraints—but more so the opportunities—of a new system.

Templates

Once you've selected a tool, then it's time to starting thinking about templates. For wire-frames and comps, document templates are a standard starting point for screen designs and annotations that include preset page height and width, grids and guidelines, text with styles, standard layers, and other implied conventions.

If you want to create consistent, modular design, solid templates are a must. Templates start the designer with an established foundation to design with components and document their designs.

Separating Design and Deliverables

Remember that age-old tenet of separating content from presentation? Ever been per-plexed by the complexity of blending canvas grid setups between the screen designs you create and the annotations around them? Have you noticed that a style called "header" in a screen design may mean something entirely different from a "header" of a paragraph in your design annotations?

If your design software enables you to dynamically link documents (or you can maintain the separation via more manual operations), consider creating distinct templates and libraries for screen designs versus deliverable documents. With different templates and libraries as illustrated in **Figure 10.2**, you afford yourself the opportunity to use one set of styles, grids, layers, and document sizes for screen designs and another set to annotate those designs.

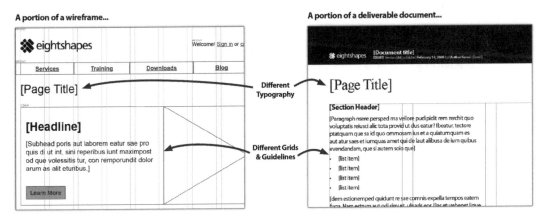

Figure 10.2 Use different templates for screen designs (here, wireframes) and deliverable documents.

For screen designs, you can set up the canvas size to match your design system, such as a page width of 800 or 980 pixels. Guidelines can match one or more standard layouts within your design system. And typography styles can map directly to your experience's style guide.

Conversely, deliverable documents can have a distinct collection of masters or backgrounds, each with relevant guidelines, typographic styles, and layers oriented to how you document your design.

Modular reuse of screen designs by placing them one or more times into a deliverable document enables separation of content (in this case, screen designs) and presentation (in this case, paginated documents). Such separation increases flexibility and collaboration: First, John the design lead could create a wireframe that Paul the researcher and Stacy the production designer could each include in their research report and design specification, respectively. Second, if the wireframe is linked to the deliverable, then any subsequent changes by John would be automatically updated when Paul and Stacy publish a new version of their deliverables.

Document Setup for Design Templates

When setting up a template, mirror the context and constraints of the page layout and grid as closely as possible. Tips for optimal document setup include the following:

Units of Measurement: Set up ruler units of measurements—both horizontal and vertical—as pixels if possible, since ultimately the design is rendered and measured using pixels of a screen. Otherwise, choose points. Avoid inches, unless the design's primary medium is print.

Ratio of Document Size to Actual Screen Size: Create a simple ratio between the canvas size and the actual size of your layout. A 1:1 ratio is preferred. If your design system's grid is 800 pixels wide, then your canvas size should also be. When screen designs are embedded in the same document with annotations (common when using Microsoft Visio) and a 1:1 ratio is not possible, try to create an easy-to-remember ratio, such as 2:1. With that, you do the simple math transformation in your head, such as converting from 800-pixel-wide screen design to a 400-point width within the template.

Without an easy transformation, you will become increasingly frustrated at the non-stop conversions of type size and object size when trying to design within a relative scale that is poorly defined. Imagine if 9.3586pt size in your design file corresponded to 13pt type size within your screen design. Nonsense!

Grids and Guidelines

A template usually has one or more grid columns, commonly established via vertical guidelines. By embedding a grid into your template, you provide a visible framework for designers to organize components on a page and snap components into place. When your design system provides multiple grid options as displayed in **Figure 10.3**, you enable the designer to quickly apply the right grid and start a screen design from an appropriate foundation.

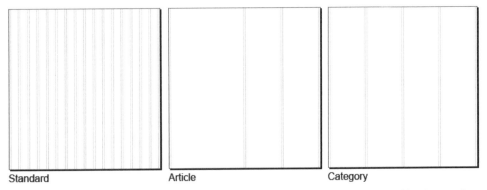

Standard   Article   Category

Figure 10.3 Multiple-page layout grids, each made available as a separate, named background in the software tool.

Tips for setting up grids include the following:

Names: Include descriptive, unambiguous names for each grid alternative, such as "Two Column without Sidebar" versus "Two Column with Sidebar." A designer should be able to open a template, quickly choose a grid, and start design.

Backgrounds: Make each grid available as a separate, frozen background for the page design so that guidelines and other metadata are reused across pages and don't get jumbled page-specific content. This feature has different labels across software tools: background (Visio), canvas (OmniGraffle), master (Adobe Fireworks, Adobe InDesign). If your software tool doesn't support backgrounds, then use one layer (or more) that can be locked and hidden if necessary.

Grid Annotations: Include grid metadata, such as column widths and/or names, on a separate layer, but hide the layer by default.

Setting up grids and guidelines is downright crucial before building your component library. Be wary of unstable grids, since changes to page width, columns, and other aspects of the layout can trigger significant refactoring of both templates and the component library. Unstable grids should not prevent formalizing a template, but should prevent you from creating a template too early.

Layers

Keep layers simple in templates. Designers will organize layers when creating screen designs using their own mental model (if they organize layers at all, which many don't). This will leave many efforts for sophisticated layer standards as exercises in frustration. That said, a few basic layers, such as content, grids, and annotation markers could keep designers aligned, and enable one designer to open another's document and not be completely confused (**Figure 10.4**).

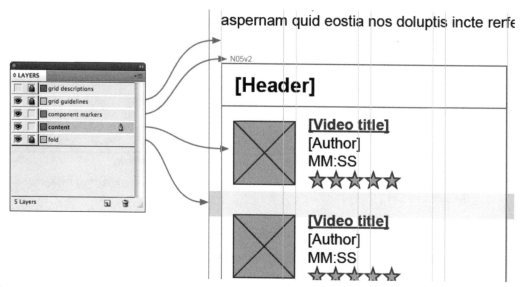

Figure 10.4 InDesign layers panel positioned adjacent to elements on each layer of a wireframe: grid guidelines, component marker (No5v2), content (an image), and the fold band.

In addition, minimize layer quantity in design files. Layers tend to obscure document organization to those who didn't create the layers. Also, some Adobe CS products enable you to control what layers display in one document when it's placed in another document, but the value of such a feature diminishes when designers can't recall or understand the layer structure they themselves created. In my own practice, wireframe content rarely spans more than a single layer, with shapes and text instead arranged forward and backward within that layer.

Tips for setting up layers include the following:

Document Structure: Create separate layers for content (the actual screen design), component markers, grid information, and annotations so that you can show and hide each independently.

Markers: Add component markers to a specific marker layer when a component is placed from a library. That way, if you want to share a design with team members not familiar with a component library, or if you want to hide the markers when designs are used in a prototype, just hide the component marker layer.

Fold: If necessary, add a layer to depict the fold so that designers know the boundary beyond which content will be initially hidden and require scrolling to view. As of this writing, the standard web page fold at a 1024x768 resolution ranges from 590px to 610px from the top of the page, depending on browser and platform combination. This results in a "fold band" rather than a fold line.

Styles

A style is a predefined set of formatting that can be applied to shapes and text in a design, including color, font, alignment, opacity, size, weight, and more. Depending on your software tool, you can create styles for paragraphs, characters, shapes, tables, and cells in a table.

Really? Styles? If we're talking wireframes, then why do styles matter?

Whether you are creating wireframes or comps or HTML/CSS libraries, styles embedded in your templates are crucial for quickly creating designs and easily maintaining the visual system. While wireframes are not meant to be pixel-perfect, a wireframe library should accurately mirror the typography of a design system so that designers can quickly create—and communicate—consistent screen designs. For a library of high-fidelity, pixel-precise comps, the value of styles increases even more. On the code side, one or more cascading style sheets are the bedrock on which a component library rests.

When at the outset of building a component library, after you've resolved that grids are sufficiently stable, the next critical question is: What typographic and layout standards have been defined and documented? By defining a set of template styles based upon conventional names, your templates can bridge to the team's collective understanding of the design system. Don't leave designers guessing at how to appropriately format a basic paragraph, bulleted list, or page title.

To get started, use an existing style guide that includes typography and color palettes. Project documents and specifications contain style details as well. You can also review cascading style sheets of live pages to discern common type treatments. Without that baseline, use your best judgment to establish a reasonable type hierarchy from scratch.

 TIP   Speed up your ability to evaluate styles of live pages by using a bookmarklet, which is a small utility you can embed as a simple bookmark in a web browser. Bookmarklets enable you to quickly identify formats like font family and font style without drilling through complex source code. Using a bookmarklet is simple: Just highlight a portion of a page (such as a piece of text) and select the bookmarklet to reveal details such as font size, weight, color, and more. Useful bookmarklets can be found at Square Free's site at https://www.squarefree.com/bookmarklets/webdevel.html, or via a basic search for terms like bookmarklet, style, and CSS.

Type Styles

Communicating structure in wireframes and comps is essential to good design, and a core yet limited set of standard type styles can help designers be more consistent. With type styles that are easy to distinguish and apply correctly, designers have an accurate starting point and can map templates to standards like those found in a style guide.

Stock your library with organized type styles for the following:

Paragraphs: Usually normal, small, and large paragraphs suffice, but add additional sizes as necessary.

Lists: Include bulleted and numeric lists of various sizes, plus other common lists found within the design system, such as a stacked list of links preceded by "»" as the bullet character.

Titles and Headers: Include one or more section headers, as well as the page and other common titles.

Tables: If table text differs from paragraph styles, then consider a separate set of table text styles.

Forms and Errors: Include form labels, supplemental text, error text (usually the only red text within a wireframe library), and text that appears as a value within a form control like a text box or list box.

Links: Use blue, underlined links for wireframe libraries so that linked interactions stand out. Since links often appear within a paragraph, they are better formatted via a character style applied inline to only a portion of text rather than a paragraph style that applies to an entire paragraph.

Gray: Although type color is not often used to communicate structure in wireframes, 50% gray text (for supplemental text on a form like formats, for example) can also be useful as an inline style.

Applying a text style quickly from a menu or simple command is paramount for designers to be willing to adopt text styles. Most design tools have one or more type style panel(s) (such as those shown in **Figure 10.5** from Adobe InDesign); a designer selects a chunk of text and then applies the style by clicking it in the panel.

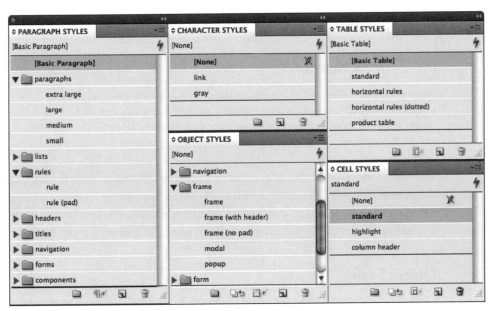

Figure 10.5 InDesign panels of interrelated styles that enable a designer to create wireframes based on existing conventions.

Some tools, such as Adobe InDesign, also enable keyboard shortcuts to "Quick Apply" the style by typing the first few characters of the style name only. Such shortcuts dramatically reduce the time and rigor when applying styles.

Depending on available features of your software tool, you can set up tab stops for form labels and controls in a single text frame (**Figure 10.6**).

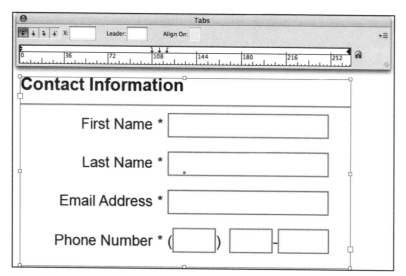

Figure 10.6 InDesign form layout inline inside a single text frame with inline form controls and tab stops to align labels (right-aligned), required fields (center-aligned), and form controls (left-aligned).

Each stop can ensure proper alignment (left or right), control spacing between labels and controls, and enable a designer to shift all elements in a form quickly and consistently by selecting the entire passage and moving tab stops left and right. For longer forms, this can be much more efficient than moving each label and control independently.

Object Styles

Consider object styles to encapsulate common formatting attributes of shapes. Common objects that can use styles include the following:

Frames: Of course, frames! Those white boxes with a gray border to distinguish a particular chunk of a page. Although using at least one frame style is essential, advanced wireframe libraries include a range of frame border styles based on common formats of the design system, varying the box by stroke/line width (from 1px to 5px to 10px), and varying padding, alignment, and style of type within the frame.

Buttons: Usually you'll have standard button styles, including type size and padding. For wireframes, define buttons as blue with lighter text label as well as text inset padding if possible; this way, they'll stand out as interactions just as links do, and be easy to create and resize from scratch. For comps, embed standard colors, corner styles, gradients, and other graphical treatments.

Relating Styles

When setting up type and object styles, consider the relationships you can create across styles to better manage a collection of styles and quickly apply a series of related styles.

Figure 10.7 shows a common wireframe chunk that includes a header, horizontal rule, and then normal paragraph content.

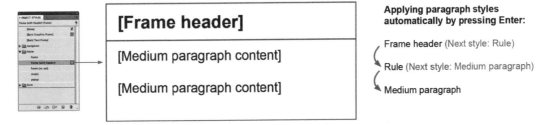

Figure 10.7 A common wireframe chunk—with header, rule, and paragraphs—constructed via a single object style and paragraph styles related via Next style.

Here, an object style formats a first line with a "frame header" paragraph style. The defined next style for "frame header" is "rule" so that when you press return, the next line will be defined as a horizontal rule. Pressing return from a line styled as "rule" will then yield a subsequent line styled as "medium paragraph." That way, you can type in the header of the frame, press the enter key (which creates a subsequent line as a horizontal rule), press enter again, and begin typing the normal content. In just a few keystrokes, you've created a standard wireframe box with content!

Take Control

AUTHOR: **Andrew Payne**

ROLE: **Design Technologist, Sun.com**

A component system is all about taking control of your website. How can you maintain order and control over a component library?

1. Document Everything

Documentation of HTML components is essential for keeping all parties informed of what is available for use and how the components should be used. Forget screenshots and PDFs; use live HTML examples for component documentation and keep a singular "gold" repository—that is, authoritative and finalized code—of all components.

2. Leave the Design to the Designers

Unlike most CSS methodologies, a component-based CSS should confine styles to each component. Avoid making the CSS a grab bag of styles for publishers to use. Letting them concentrate on components allows them to focus on content rather than style.

3. Keep the CSS Under Wraps

When you own CSS styles and consolidate them to one place, you can maintain design system integrity. If your site is distributed across servers or sub sites, consider versioning the CSS and releasing it on a regular basis. New features will keep site owners coming back for more, and thus they'll be motivated to keep their CSS files up-to-date.

4. Respect Component Authority

It can be difficult to let go of a carefree past, but all parties need to agree to live and die by the component library. If something is not in the library, it shouldn't exist. Of course there are exceptions. The key is that each new request should be evaluated first to determine if it is component-worthy. If it is not, a one-off solution may be the right answer. However, most things that start as one-off eventually multiply. That'll change your mind about one-offs.

5. The Style Guide Is Dead. Long Live the Style Guide!

Building out a components system is all about letting go of the status quo. The days of PDFs that define a website's style with font callouts and little red arrows are over. The new style guide is all about components that have the style embedded in the code. The formality and purity of your component library becomes the only "style guide" you'll need.

Conventions

As templates stabilize, discuss design conventions to be adopted by the entire team. Conventions are critical for successfully using a template system for consistently designing screens, and will help stakeholders learn whatever the designs do—or do not—represent.

Wireframe Conventions

For wireframes, conventions have evolved over time and remain distinct across individuals and organizations. A review of my own portfolio reveals a transition from highly styled wireframes to simpler presentations over time to more simply communicate structure and behavior without implying or constraining visual design. **Figure 10.8** reflects this range of wireframe personalities, where earlier wireframes had included numerous colors, many levels of grayscale, and rounded corners. That said, wireframes produced within the context of a well-formed system can include well-defined

Figure 10.8 Diagram of different wireframe conventions, opting for simple frames and white backgrounds relative to grayscale frames, colored frames, and unnecessary rounded corners.

visual standards, such as positioning, typography, and other layout details that remove ambiguity of structure and behavior.

Common wireframe conventions include the following:

Simple gray scale: Wireframes include gray outlines, white backgrounds, and clear, black type hierarchy to reveal structure and behavior of a screen design. Beware of gray backgrounds that can (a) inordinately emphasize page regions (instead, use annotation for that), (b) confuse consumers into believing it's closer to a final color treatment, and (c) simply be difficult to interpret. Minimize backgrounds using different shades of gray to connote hierarchy. Instead, rely on position and type to reveal hierarchy.

Use Arial. Only Arial!: No matter what font family or families you use in your site design or for your deliverables and annotations, limit wireframes to Arial. Many site designs use Arial anyway. Arial is available across both Mac and PC platforms, and Arial provides a strong distinction between normal and bold weight. Resist the temptation to integrate many font families in wireframes; instead, standardize on Arial as a recognized typeface to minimize confusion with more formal typography in your visual system.

Blue for interactivity: With your wireframe consisting of black, white, and level(s) of gray, use blue as an obvious cue for linked text and regions (such as a button). When you do this, you tell a consumer that "everything's black and white, except for things that you can interact with, which are blue."

X marks the image: Use boxes with an X to represent images, such as a collection of three thumbnails in a list of articles, or a big banner image in a page's billboard (**Figure 10.9**).

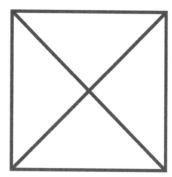

Figure 10.9 Use a standard X box to indicate image placement.

 TIP Minimize unnecessary visual detail: Rounded corners, gradient backgrounds, varying stroke weights, and type variations almost never have anything to do with the core purpose of wireframes, which is to communicate structure and behavior. But such visual cues almost always degrade early, strategic design discussions into annoying conversations of visual style long before they're appropriate. Therefore, avoid embedding unnecessary graphical details.

Comp Conventions

For comps, conventions take on a different tone. The comp library need not standardize on a way to represent an image (with an X) or link (such as a blue underline), since the comp components should depict exactly how the design should appear for a design system. Some standard conventions to be discussed include the following:

- ▶ Screen resolution
- ▶ Use of layers and layer groups
- ▶ System versus rasterized text
- ▶ Effects, layout, and other customization of specific elements such as form controls
- ▶ Typography, including font families, weight, leading, kerning, and more
- ▶ Color palette(s), gradients, interactions of different colors, and color coding (such as hex values)

These and other comp conventions are strongly mapped to the style guide and overall visual system and should be embedded into templates, libraries, and styles as much as possible.

Representing Copy

During the design process, copy is almost certainly not final. However, decisions on interaction design labels, editorial standards, and branded messaging will find their way into a design over time. As designers place components into their screen design, the default representation of each copy element can go a long way toward helping the designer decide whether to change copy, and how to communicate content requirements to others.

As you prepare to build out a library of components, represent component copy consistently. Not all copy should be displayed—or changed—in the same way. Some copy represents fixed, actual labels, such as a header's navigation options or fields in a login form ("Username" and "Password"). Other copy may depend on the component's context of use, format decisions, or available space.

Dan Brown summarized the various techniques to represent copy in design assets in his "Representing Data in Wireframes" poster presented at the IA Summit in Montreal, Canada, in March 2005. In the poster, he introduces different types, risks, and misrepresentations of data in wireframes. He also defines five approaches, which are an excellent framework for you to decide how to represent copy within library components (**Figure 10.10**).

1. **Actual:** Displays the copy as intentionally fixed, unchanging, how it will look in the final interface. Actual data is often used for fixed header and footer navigation, form labels (such as "First Name"), section headers, and other values that shouldn't change. Additionally, this approach uses actual values for fixed items, such as addresses and phone numbers, although this may distract a stakeholder evaluating the interface.

2. **Dummy:** For dynamic values, consider inventing dummy data to appear like actual data but which intentionally and implicitly communicates that the values aren't real. Values like Homer Simpson, Mickey Mouse, and John Doe are dummy values, and are often used in displays, such as profiles, lists (search results, for example), and tables. However, stakeholders may misunderstand the data's meaning relative to the design's purpose, which in this case is to include a first and last name.

3. **Symbolic:** Displays copy as a series of repeated characters to communicate field length or type. While XXXXXX is distracting, use symbolic values to communicate price ($###.##), date (MM/DD/YYYY), time (HH:MM pm), and other common data formats.

❶ **Actual Data**

Contact EightShapes
Corporate Headquarters 8818 Sunset Drive Arlington, VA 22445 Phone: (703) 555-1212

❷ **Dummy Data**

Contact Acme Co.
Corporate Headquarters 123 Main Street Anytown, NY 11111 Phone: (111) 555-1111

❸ **Symbolic Data**

Contact XXXXXXXXX
XXXXXXXXXX XXXXXX ### XXXX XX, XXXXX XXXX XXXXXXXXXX, XX ##### Phone: (###) ###-####

❹ **Lorem Ipsum**

Contact Lorem Ipsum
Evellabores aut hillabo ritatio restet vollo qui, simos 12345 Phone: (123) 123-1234

❺ **Labeled Data**

Contact [Company]
[Office Location Name] [Address] [City], [State] [ZIP Code] Phone: ([###]) [###]-[####]

Figure 10.10 Content represented as actual, dummy, symbolic, lorem ipsum, and labeled data.

4. **Lorem Ipsum:** Creates or replaces copy with placeholder Latin text (usually beginning with "Lorem ipsum dolor..." thus the name lorem ipsum) to replicate random but realistic text otherwise absent of structure. Lorem ipsum is valuable when representing a long paragraph passage, or even random header values across sections. However, the structure lacks labels and length that contribute to understanding the potential content at a deeper level.

5. **Labeled:** Encloses a variable name in brackets, such as [], <>, or {} (depending on your convention). For example, you could display a name as [First Name]. Labeled values are very effective when documenting each interface element and mapping variable content to a content management system or feed.

   If a value (such as article body copy) is much longer than a labeled name, append lorem ipsum *after* the labeled name within the brackets, for example, "[Article body copy lorem ipsum im aut omnia saessi conempel id et quia es]." However, if the value is shorter than the name (as in a state abbreviation), you may be stuck choosing a misleading longer label ([State Abbr]) or an ambiguous abbreviation ([SA]).

   Labeled data is most effective and helpful for developers and quality assurance analysts implementing and testing a design, but it may seem foreign and odd to less literate stakeholders reviewing a design for the first time. Labeled data is completely inappropriate for designs used in usability testing, since participants won't understand such attribute-based displays. Therefore, data is often transformed from actual to labeled values as the design solution matures and moves toward specifications.

Predefined components often blend two or more of the five approaches, such as the book commerce component depicted in **Figure 10.11**. The approach you choose depends on how well stakeholders (and designers using the library) understand and interpret each type. For a component library, balance actual data with labeled values and avoid dummy data that can feel arbitrary and specific to one designer's personality.

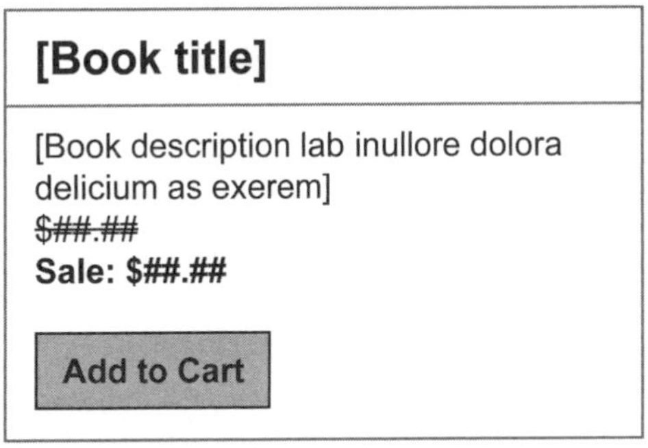

> ## [Book title]
>
> [Book description lab inullore dolora delicium as exerem]
> $##.##
> **Sale: $##.##**
>
> [**Add to Cart**]

Figure 10.11 A wireframe component that blends four data representations: labeled ([Book title]), symbolic ($##.##), actual (Add to Cart), and lorem ipsum ("lab inullore dolora...").

Avoid one common pitfall: embedding guidelines in textual copy, such as the guidelines shown in **Figure 10.12**.

Although it may be tempting to reveal editorial guidelines or data requirements inside the artwork, the approach is not scalable and causes a confusing blend of screen design and annotation. It may seem convenient to embed editorial guidelines inside a wireframe list of "Key Benefits" of a product. But what happens if your list allows for up to three bullets, but has four or more guidelines? Or, what if nice bulleted lists don't represent other chunks of your interface but also have guidelines? The approach breaks down quickly.

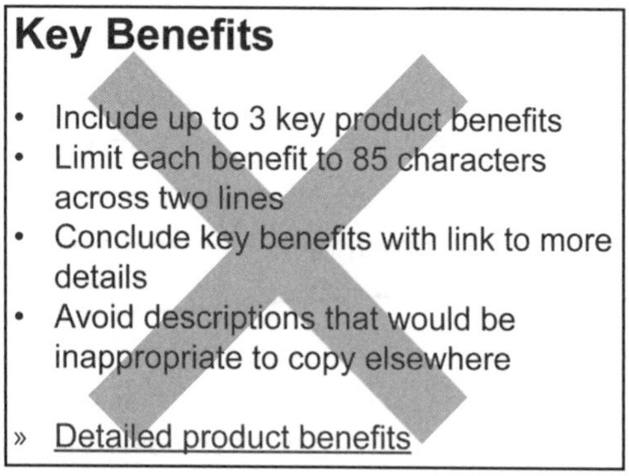

Figure 10.12 A portion of a wireframe that embeds guidelines into the screen design.

11

BUILD

You've identified all the components. You've organized them into categories, prioritized what needs to be built first, assigned names and IDs. You've got templates created, conventions established, and designers at the ready. Now it's time to build the library!

The process of building a component library includes the following:

- ▶ Clarifying contributor roles
- ▶ Transforming templates into build file(s) suitable for building and maintaining components
- ▶ Assigning, building, reviewing, and refining each component
- ▶ Assembling collections of predefined pages and elements
- ▶ Packaging templates, components, pages, and element libraries for distribution

Roles

Building a component library requires a standard set of roles to ensure that you know who is producing, reviewing, and integrating each item. For a small library, a single person can assemble the entire collection. This has many advantages, including consistency of the following:

▶ Production and visual appearance

▶ Style names and definitions across artifacts, including wireframe and comp templates to CSS within HTML markup

▶ File structure, including pages, layers, and objects

▶ Names of and keywords associated with individual component items

More than one person may need to contribute to libraries that are larger or need to be produced faster. In that case, identify a leader (usually, the librarian) to assign, monitor, and aggregate assets built by other contributors. Typically, such contributions begin after a lead has crafted a mature baseline of templates with grids and styles.

The lead is responsible for ensuring consistency of all assets, and may "smooth out" differences in artwork produced by others. Periodic reviews enable contributors to compare progress, artwork consistency, personal style, and key decisions. Such reviews enable contributors to synchronize tactics in real time, avoiding the costly process of smoothing inconsistent production as the process draws to a close.

For teams creating components across more than one asset type (wireframes, comps, and/or HTML/CSS markup), align efforts to ensure both visual and naming consistency. If a team has leads for each discipline (such as a lead interaction designer for wireframes and a lead visual designer for comps), identify one lead responsible for the catalog and monitoring consistency across the work of each discipline. For a deeper discussion of roles, including that of the librarian, refer to Chapter 12, "Administer."

Not every stakeholder—not even every designer—may be involved in building components. However, engage designers and stakeholders to solicit feedback, identify potential champions, and promote the library before it's officially packaged and distributed. Their comments will improve the process, refine the library's organization, and empower others to influence the library's direction.

Build Files

A template is great for creating page designs, but may not be suitable for building and storing all of the actual components in a library. When building a large number of items, you'll likely author similar components, variations, and examples together: headers and footers on one page, sidebar components on another, and modal panels together. This layout doesn't resemble a page design whatsoever, but instead resembles an organized layout of reusable assets as illustrated in **Figure 11.1**. We refer to such a document as a build file. A build file is a document used to create and maintain many components in a single file, and serves as the source from which to package each individual item.

By centralizing the entire library (or, at least, a considerable portion of a library) in a single file, you can synchronize styles, aggregate items from other contributors, smooth out differences, and manage changes—all in one place.

Figure 11.1 A portion of a build file containing many different components.

Setting Up a Build File

Many aspects of a build file are exactly the same as your template: styles, layers, grids, and more. However, the build file should have a larger canvas that is oriented toward a common printer paper size (such as tabloid or legal). Do not feel constrained to fit components within a standard page layout. The larger size will provide you with more space to build, organize, and manage items.

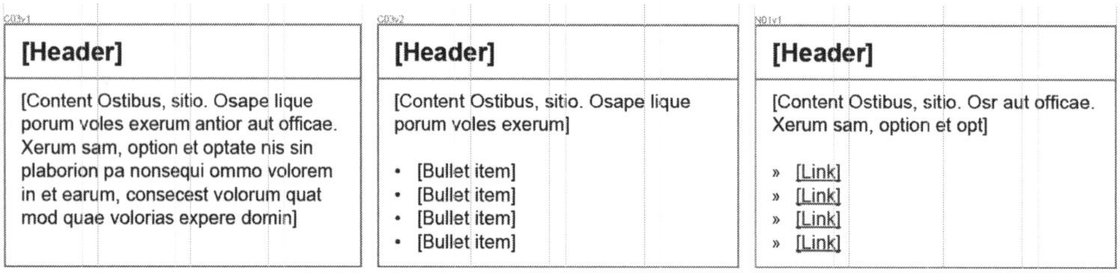

[Header]

[Content Ostibus, sitio. Osape lique porum voles exerum antior aut officae. Xerum sam, option et optate nis sin plaborion pa nonsequi ommo volorem in et earum, consecest volorum quat mod quae volorias expere domin]

[Header]

[Content Ostibus, sitio. Osape lique porum voles exerum]

- [Bullet item]
- [Bullet item]
- [Bullet item]
- [Bullet item]

[Header]

[Content Ostibus, sitio. Osr aut officae. Xerum sam, option et opt]

- » [Link]
- » [Link]
- » [Link]
- » [Link]

Figure 11.2 Components in a build file, grouped within a grid as variations adjacent to one another as opposed to within page layouts.

It is very common to evolve style names and definitions in the build file during the process of building components. Just be sure to synchronize style changes with the template before packaging the library.

Also, you can create different grids of guidelines based on common column sizes in your overall grid, repeating these mini-grids across the build file's page. For example, even though the page template has just one sidebar of 180px, create a background that repeats a 180px column three times across the build file layout (**Figure 11.2**). This is useful for creating many component variations common to a region of the page layout within one page of your build file.

Organizing a Build File

Components are usually ordered and grouped within the build file based on the component library's taxonomy. Each component is laid out in order within each category: by component, variation, and example. If a build file is well organized, then it is much easier to find, update, move, and export each item over time as the library evolves.

Also consider having a separate page for the variations and examples of each component. While this may result in almost empty pages for some components (such as a page title), the extra space serves as a cue for the librarian to know what goes where and have space to add items over time.

Multiple Build Files

As component libraries grow and change, you may need to set up more than one build file. Common rationales for creating two or more build files include the following:

Retired components should be kept separate from the active component library so that there's no confusion as to what components are active. Don't throw away retired components!

Multiple collections or design systems should be kept separate from one another, such as for different publishing platforms, sets of grids, site sections, or other distinguishing criteria.

Pilot and/or in-development components should be kept separate from the active library.

The Build File as a Reference Document, Too!

With a bit more work, you can also extend a build file to be a handy visual reference for a library. Tighten the layout and add additional annotation adjacent to categories, components, and variations. Then print the build file as a more usable reference document (**Figure 11.3**) so that it can be referred to during design projects, meetings, and other instances when designers must browse the catalog to find a component of interest.

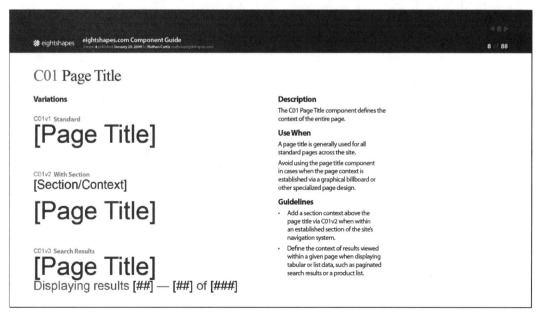

Figure 11.3 Source artwork of components (in this case, page title variations) placed in a reference document that includes annotations.

In effect, the build file transforms into a photo gallery that designers use to systematically display many components on a single page for cataloging, identification, and selection.

To formalize the build file as a reference document, include the following additional content:

▶ Title page clarifying the context of the build file and its content

▶ Table of contents, ordered by component categories and/or IDs assigned to each item of the library

▶ Component codes and names emphasized throughout if a team adopts a more formal organizational system

▶ Descriptive document information, including title, author, version, date, page number, and overall page count repeated on every page

Time to Build!

Now comes the fun part: actually building out each individual item in the library. When creating each component, consider the steps illustrated in **Figure 11.4**.

Figure 11.4 Steps for building each component.

1. **Assign:** If the component library is built by more than one person, then the group should meet early on and assign subsets of the library to each individual. Assign different component types (for example, all video players and interactive media) or categories (for example, all header, footer, and navigation components) to the same person rather than randomly assigning each library item to each person. This will ensure that smaller sets are more consistent from the outset, and that designers can focus on a small, related batch.

2. **Draft:** Each item is rendered in whatever asset type(s) (wireframe vs. comp vs. HTML/CSS markup) will be included in the library.

3. **Review:** Whether one or more persons are involved in assembling the library, it's vital to review assets with other designers and/or stakeholders before publishing an item in

the library. Reviews are critical for eliciting feedback, synchronizing design work, and involving stakeholders in the process.

4. **Revise:** If an item requires changes, revise the component before submitting the final version to the librarian for inclusion in the build file.

5. **Smooth:** Even if the library is built entirely by one person, review the entire collection from a higher level to ensure consistency. For projects with many team members, synchronize items as contributors submit finalized artwork. In effect, "smooth out" the differences in construction, organization (including styles), and visual appearance that arise from different contributors, such as the proliferation of unaligned objects of a designer versus the clean and aligned version (both shown in **Figure 11.5**). This usually requires the librarian to review and revise each asset as it is integrated into the library. Sometimes it's as easy as pushing a few shapes around. But this can be much more painful if the team hasn't adopted a baseline of templates, styles, and conventions early on and evolved them together during the process.

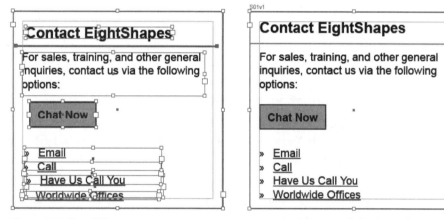

Figure 11.5 Two different component constructions: on the left, a poorly built wireframe component with too many poorly aligned objects; and on the right, a smoothed, polished version within a single, styled frame.

6. **Complete:** Once an item is reviewed, revised, and synchronized, it can be considered complete and ready to be packaged.

Wires to Reality

AUTHOR: **Andrew Payne**

ROLE: **Design Technologist, Sun.com**

When it comes time to build out components into HTML, there are often a few things that need to be sorted out first. Even complete wireframes and graphic designs can lack a total description of what needs to be translated into the code version.

Fallbacks?

A common hole in designs and wireframes is lack of coverage for fallback behavior. What happens to users without JavaScript, users without mouse access, or blind users? Even fallbacks for things like shorter or longer text blocks need to be considered when coding the HTML. Communicating these types of issues early on can help reduce open issues remaining at the end of the design phase. If possible, include developers early in your process and press them to consider these types of issues quickly so that fallbacks and alternatives can be built into the design.

Too Much Information!

Sometimes wireframes and designs are packed with a ton of examples for a component. While this helps everyone understand what is possible with a given component, sometimes it can be a burden when building out the HTML. A challenge of creating components is distilling a design down to essential HTML elements.

You may have designs illustrating nine different combinations of paragraphs, lists, images, and headings, but in the end they can all be the same type of content block. Amid your plethora of variations, include one variation with all the possible elements and use other examples omitting optional parts to illustrate how to mix and match optional elements.

Keeping the Downstream Happy

If you're an engineer building HTML and CSS and your work will get passed off to other engineers to build applications or directly to publishers to build pages, then review it with them before designating your work as complete. They may request changes that are minor for you but a dramatic time saver for them. Also be mindful of your code's complexity. You may be able to make compromises to your pure, ideal code in order to deliver assets that are easier for them to combine and maintain.

Your goal should always be to produce components that others can consistently implement and correctly use. Beyond simply providing a consistent experience for your users (isn't that everyone's goal?), good components will also keep your code base tidy, agile, and easily controlled by the CSS.

Pages and Elements

Sets of fully assembled page types and more atomic design elements complement a library of components as helpful collections of items that are often reused.

Page Types

Designers significantly benefit from browsing and utilizing page types. A page type is a complete, predefined page layout that consists of an assembled set of components, such as the one shown in **Figure 11.6**. Creating a library of page types can clarify the use of a component by showing it in context.

A page type is also valuable as one or more of the following:

▶ A starting point to update that page for a future project

▶ A standard layout that organizes components in a meaningful way

▶ A full-page example assembled via components to reinforce the approach to designers and stakeholders

▶ A supporting artifact for writing guidelines for components and pages

A team may choose to create a few representative page types, such as a home page, a search results page, or a product page, or may use a component and page type library to catalog and evolve a much more extensive collection of page types across projects and efforts.

Managing a page type library also brings the additional task of synchronizing component and page types whenever a library is updated. Since page types are built from components, if a component changes, then every page type that uses that component must be updated.

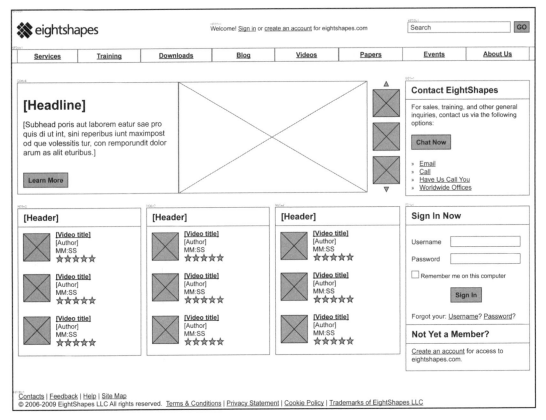

Figure 11.6 A page type.

Just as components are built, consider aggregating page types in a build file. That way, page types are sourced from the same place (including styles and layers), synchronized easily with evolving components, and presented as a handy visual reference if exported as a PDF document.

Element Libraries

Just as teams augment a component library with assembled page types, designers also benefit from organized collections of individual, atomic design elements, such as the form controls shown in **Figure 11.7**.

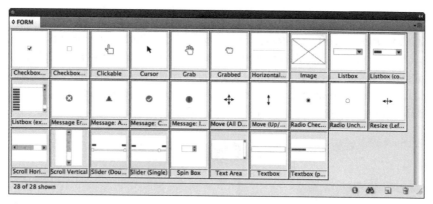

Figure 11.7 An element library used to rapidly create wireframe form layouts.

Popular collections of reusable design elements include the following:

▸ Form controls, such as a checkbox, radio button, textbox, text area, list box, drop-down menu, scroll bars, cursor variations (such as a pointer and hand), and more

▸ Interactive icons, such as messaging icons, interactive cues (collapse / expand, previous / next), close window, and more

▸ Navigation and buttons

▸ Advertisements, including standard IAB sizes, such as leaderboard, tower, and medium rectangle

▸ Frequently used snippets of text

Elements are commonly made available via library panels (also referred to as a stencil, symbol panel, or object library) in a tool's workspace, although some tools may lack this capability.

Packaging

Once component artwork is final, package it so that designers can obtain, unpack, and get started easily. How you package components depends on what software tool you choose. However, you generally choose one or both of the following options: distributed in a library panel within the workspace, or distributed as separate files.

Components in a Library Panel

For many popular software design tools, you can distribute components as a set of reusable library items displayed as a panel or window (**Figures 11.8** and **11.9**) within the tool's workspace. Depending on the tool, this panel may be referred to as a stencil (Microsoft Visio and OmniGraffle), common library (Adobe Fireworks), symbol library (Adobe Illustrator), or object library (Adobe InDesign).

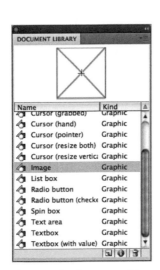

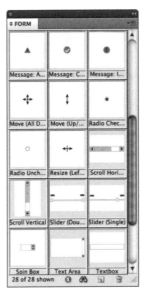

Figure 11.8 Library panel in Adobe Fireworks.

Figure 11.9 Object library panel in Adobe InDesign.

Create the library, add components one by one from the build file to the library, and then distribute the library with the broader system. Refer to your software tool's Help for information on how to create, manage, and distribute components using a library panel.

When creating a library panel, the following considerations apply:

Avoid document-specific libraries: Don't embed a library within a document template, but instead as a library that's reusable across and distinct from any one document. This will reduce document template file size; optionally enable you to create multiple, categorized libraries if necessary; and modularly manage templates separate from components themselves.

Importing libraries from document to document: Many tools enable you to import a collection of components from one library to another library or into a document. This can be helpful for quick tasks, but it also runs the risk of creating multiple instances of the component library that can lead to out-of-date components being used or retained in unpredictable places.

Discourage designers from changing panels: Warn designers that they should not update or add to distributed libraries, since a librarian will update and release future versions that would overwrite older versions.

Advantages

Library panels (such as a Microsoft Visio stencil) are very familiar to all but beginning users of each particular software tool. Using this approach comes with the following advantages:

Efficiency: Dragging and dropping a component from panel to document is incredibly fast. Leaving a tool's workspace can be cumbersome, so browsing, selecting, and adding components from a collection of thumbnails feels the most productive.

Consolidation: A library panel organizes the components in one place, particularly if a panel includes components from one category. Therefore, opening and using panels implicitly informs a designer about the library's organization.

Disadvantages

However, when adapting to a large component library, such panels have drawbacks like the following:

Weaker metadata: Most software tools limit the amount of descriptive information you can add for each item. Typically, this information is limited to a name and thumbnail but may also include type (such as graphic versus animation) and description (a longer field to aid retrieval via in-panel search). In general, finding items within a larger collection can be challenging.

Insufficient thumbnail size: Panels in workspace are already small enough, so the thumbnail display of a specific item within that panel is even smaller. If you have a complex component—or a thin shape, such as a wide but short header—then the panel limits your ability to distinguish between similar items.

Collective distribution: Whenever one item in a library changes, you have to distribute the entire library. Quick distribution via email becomes cumbersome since a library's file size can increase significantly when it contains many complex components. You could distribute an item in a separate document with instructions for users to add it to their library from there, but that's cumbersome.

Components as Individual Files

Depending on your software tool choice, you may have the option—or be required—to distribute individual components as separate files. In this case, a component is placed individually via a file dialog or dragged and dropped from a file residing in a folder on your operating system.

The Place command is common for tools in the Adobe Creative Suite, including Adobe Photoshop (placing a separate PSD file into the open PSD file, resulting in a smart object), Adobe Fireworks (placing a separate PNG file into the current PNG file, resulting in embedded artwork), and Adobe InDesign (placing a snippet like those shown in **Figure 11.10** into a document, resulting in embedded artwork).

When you use components as individual files, each item is exported from a build file one by one, with appropriate file names and subsequent metadata added after the export. Refer to your software tool's Help for information on how to create and manage components as smart objects, snippets, or another type of file.

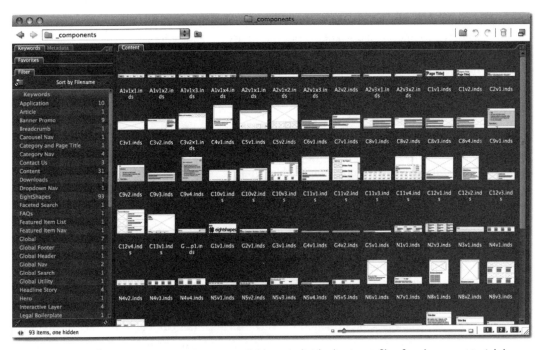

Figure 11.10 Wireframe components that are available as individual snippet files for placement in Adobe InDesign (browsed here via the content and filter panels of Adobe Bridge).

Advantages

Although using a separate dialog to place artwork can feel cumbersome at first, nearly every component library that we've built uses this approach.

This approach has numerous advantages that include the following:

Discrete item management: You can manage, version, and distribute each item in the library separately rather than within a library file.

More file content: Instead of relying on a simple object for the component itself, you can include more information in the file's content, such as specific layers, annotations, and other facets that would be inappropriate for a component added from a library panel.

Advanced metadata: Adobe Creative Suite enables you to add additional metadata to each file. By tagging each file with numerous keywords, you provide much richer experience for filtering and retrieving components within tools like Adobe Bridge, which lets you organize, browse, and locate the components you need and then drag them into your document of interest.

Disadvantages

This approach also has some disadvantages:

Outside the workspace: Users can feel less productive when they have to leave the workspace to add a component, whether via a dialog to navigate their file system to find the component or by switching to a different application from which to drag and drop.

Feeling overwhelmed: For larger component libraries of more than 200 items, seeing each component as a different file may lead some users to feeling overwhelmed with too many options. Even though metadata enables filtering to smaller sets, the initial perception of a vast library can be intimidating. For whatever reason, this feeling is not as acute when using library panels inside the workspace itself.

Preparing Each Component

The packaging process from build file to library panel(s) or individual files includes the following considerations:

Naming: Whether you choose to package items in a library panel, as an individual file, or both, name the item using a combination of both the code and name. If a component's name is "Search Bar," its code is "G04v1," and this is the default variation, label the item as "G04v1.SearchBar.Default." If the item were stored as a separate file (such as a Photoshop PSD file), then the filename would be "G04v1.SearchBar.Default.psd."

Grouping: If your library has more than 20 to 30 items (most libraries have over 100), then consider organizing items into multiple panels (if using library panels) or folders (if using separate files) for each category.

Tagging: Once in a library or separate file, tag the component with keywords to improve retrieval, particularly if your software tool enables dynamic filtering or search.

Distribution

Once all components have been assembled as libraries and/or files, you're almost ready to distribute the package! All that remains is organizing the numerous asset types—components, page types, templates, and element libraries—into a single package for distribution.

Figure 11.11 illustrates a well-organized folder hierarchy that contains all files, appropriately organized by type. Since templates serve as a design's starting point, consider putting them in the root directory. If directories contain numerous files, consider subdirectories for deeper organization. Ultimately, organize the files in a way that balances how to easily use and maintain assets.

Files are commonly distributed via an archived ZIP file that compresses what may be a file collection of immense size. Zipping up files also enables you to (a) distribute the entire set as one file and (b) name that file according to a release or date number to distinguish this version from other subsequent or preceding versions.

Once distributed, the library is out in the open. Teams will start to use it, and will need help on how to best adopt the tools, techniques, and standards. At the same time, librarians will shift from leading a period of building into administering, documenting, and promoting the library over time.

Figure 11.11 A sample organization of InDesign library asset files, including templates (.indt), component snippets (.inds), element libraries (.indl), and page types (.inds).

12

ADMINISTER

A component library simply cannot happen without a librarian, who administers the component collection through times of discovery, build, and maintenance. But that's not all. The librarian also acts as a primary point of contact and advocate for the standards and practices that the library advances.

This chapter explores the role of the librarian and key activities involved in administering a component library, including the following:

- ▶ Being an effective advocate and "go-to" authority
- ▶ Defining the librarian within an organization
- ▶ Tracking a component's life cycle and how to limit use through release status
- ▶ Updating the library through three key activities: managing the catalog, creating design assets, and authoring guidelines
- ▶ Publishing library assets and notifying stakeholders
- ▶ Empowering feedback and participation through discussions and ratings

The Librarian

At a minimum, a librarian must portray a certain confidence, since taking on the role of librarian demands that you advocate standards in a way that others can follow. You must love the library. You must believe. Actually, you can't *just* believe. You must evangelize, too.

Faith Sharing

Evangelism can be a dirty word. It conjures up images of some so-called authority at a pulpit, raging against design excess that crushes an organization. Nah, the librarian's role isn't to bully designers into submission. You can't be a blowhard trying to curtail a design organization into a controlled regime of robots. Nothing turns off designers more than someone putting them in a box.

Instead, evangelizing means sharing your faith in the library. You'll be a leading face of the library, standing on stage, presenting the library, and defending it to a wide audience. It's an important, visible role where you put yourself on the line. You must be ready to answer questions large and small, and respond to queries and challenges you cannot anticipate. You are a public witness of why the library exists, what it means to you and the organization, and how it leads to the salvation of all designers. OK, maybe that's laying it on a bit thick, but you get the idea.

But just as (or more) important, you can share your faith through smaller, more personal interactions. When you see an emerging design solution pop up in your email inbox, you must wear your librarian hat as you reply. When you are participating in design and code reviews, you must communicate library impacts. When new people join the team, you must take a moment to share benefits of the standardized approach. And when management is talking process and procedures—and management does that a lot—it's you who must find a way to embed the library in the conversation.

The "Go-To" Authority

A librarian is more knowledgeable about the entire library than anyone else. You'll be looked to as an educator, teaching the pros and cons of design decisions and how they reflect the holistic perspective you possess. The library can become a rich, deep repository of standards, techniques, and design decisions recorded over a long period of time. Everyone else will expect you to know the details and share the history and rationale of why things are the way they are.

Librarian, Curator, Champion, Detective

AUTHOR: **Christian Crumlish**

ROLE: **Curator, Yahoo! Design Pattern Library**

My business card says "curator," the HR department calls me an "interaction designer," my profile on Yahoo!'s Backyard intranet says my role is "pattern recognizer" but sometimes I call myself a pattern detective.

Why "detective"? Well, there's an element of investigation and sleuthing involved in capturing and nailing the patterns emerging from all the design work we're doing at Yahoo! Sure, the occasional enthusiastic designer will come to me to propose patterns. I love it when that happens, but I can't rely on this as my sole source of leads.

If you're a designer with your head down in a design project, it takes an extra effort and commitment to step back and think about whether you have stumbled onto a pattern that you could document for the benefit of your design community.

More often, it's up to me to notice, hear about, or discover emerging or converging design patterns and to elicit them from the designers in the trenches, sometimes by literally interviewing them, debriefing them if you will, to figure out what the contours of the pattern might be.

I'm not the pattern police. We encourage but don't force people at Yahoo! to design with patterns. Instead, I do a lot of formal and informal consulting internally to help leverage the patterns and to make sure we are reusing modular components wherever possible.

When I hang up my detective hat, I'm still the curator of the library and much of my work involves shepherding patterns. This includes both the general-purpose interaction patterns and a new set of Yahoo! network standard components we call ONE, for One Network Experience.

I try to do this shepherding as collaboratively as possible and I try to be the primary author on as few patterns as possible. I provide templates with starter questions, I review drafts to offer feedback and ask for revisions, I set up brainstorming sessions with whiteboards to talk through stickier points. Sometimes we open up a general discussion about a user interface element (most recently, accordions) and I try to synthesize all the examples, and suggestions and controversies, seeking a volunteer to write the draft whenever possible.

As an internal evangelist, it's also up to me to promote the existence and importance of the pattern collections and to train designers both in how to use the patterns as design-aid references and how to contribute to the library by giving feedback, suggesting missing patterns, or helping in the writing or revision of a pattern.

I give talks to smaller design teams, travel to various Yahoo! offices, use internal social interfaces to make connections and follow trails, and do my best to know as much as possible about what every design team at Yahoo! is working on. Recently, I've also been trying to reach out to our researchers, who are not classified by HR as designers but who often sit on incredibly valuable hoards of user experience insights.

My tenure as library curator has passed the two-year mark (longer now than either of my two illustrious predecessors, Matt Leacock and Bill Scott) but we do not have a formal succession plan. I don't anticipate any trouble recruiting a successor for the day when I want to return to the trenches, but in the past there have been gaps between curators during which the library would drift. It behooves me to keep an eye out for promising up-and-coming designers with the gift of seeing the patterns (or perhaps of caring that they see them).

Teachable moments abound, not just for designers who have something to learn from the library but for the librarian, too. Shifting design conditions provide opportunities to acknowledge change and recognize how a library may not meet current needs. Effective librarians challenge standards baked into a library just as much as designers do. That doesn't mean that you should accommodate any and every designer's whim. But you can't be a brick wall either, shutting out alternative perspectives or a better solution. This openness can improve the library's credibility and assure designers that the library is a reflection of the best design, as opposed to all design being a limited vision of past work and a librarian's inflexibility.

You must also be conscientious of the operational details of building and sustaining a component collection. Recall the library taxonomy in Chapter 9, "Organize"? It is the librarian's responsibility to assign component codes and answer where and why everything belongs where it does. It's up to the librarian to own that taxonomy, and watch out for others who mistakenly misuse component reference codes because they don't know any better.

You'll also take on the role of taskmaster, knowledgeable of what's published, what's being worked on, and what's on the horizon. As a manager of the component catalog, it's up to you to manage author contributions, make sure everything fits together, and respond to requests to change or extend the library.

But you can't do it alone. Effective librarians solicit help and delegate tasks that integrate the perspectives and contributions of other designers and stakeholders. Distributing responsibilities is critical. You don't just share the load because you don't have the time and energy to do everything yourself, but also to heighten participation and acceptance. You can manage assignments, progress, and communications, but others can help complete a considerable amount of work under your tutelage.

Defining a Role

Someone has to keep the library's lights on. It's a good idea to concretely define early on who will play the role of librarian. Leadership and momentum may shift to one or a few individuals who really seem to get it and drive the effort. But a component library is not born until someone is assigned to curate the collection over time. Allocating a resource— even if only dedicated part time—goes a long way to legitimize the library and give it the minimum care it requires. A librarian must have enough time and focus to attend to the details. There can be many components, changes, requests, and enhancements active at the same time, and someone must keep an eye on all the moving parts.

In most organizations, it's not just a few designers who are affected by a component library. Instead, component influence can (and hopefully will) spread far and wide. Even within a design team, multiple disciplines may be involved: from information architects and interaction designers to visual designers and even content strategists. What role is ideal for a librarian?

In most cases, the librarian works within the group funding the work, and it's rare that the group funding the effort will want someone outside the organization to lead the way. Beyond ownership considerations, the person best suited for the librarian role depends not just on personality, commitment, and skills. It also depends on who will be affected most by the library, such as those who do the following:

- ▶ Rely on the library the most in their day-to-day workflow
- ▶ Need to access the library often and unpredictably (as opposed to only during formal design reviews and structured collaboration)
- ▶ Contribute content in the form of guidelines, design assets, and other inputs that become the library's foundation

When a librarian is organizationally separated from those most affected by the library, many challenges—and even questions of legitimacy—arise. Designers trust standards authored by their own team, as opposed to some faceless lead who isn't in the trenches with them. It truly is the "standards police" when a nondesigner swoops in to tell designers what they can and can't do.

One team faced such organizational separation just as a library was getting off the ground. As the component library project began, the core team included individuals who were jazzed about the project, believed in standards, and were ready to effect positive change. The excitement of these individuals was palpable. They were obvious candidates for the role of librarian, and their spirit was unswervingly gung-ho.

Then BOOM! A corporate reorganization tore the team apart, with the enthusiastic individuals allocated to disparate groups across the enterprise. During the upheaval, distractions were plentiful, and not surprisingly the library work slowed. As the dust settled, a strategy team was formed to own long-term design vision as well as standards that included the burgeoning library. The first problem was that the strategy team didn't include any of those early, enthusiastic library advocates; instead, they were allocated elsewhere and now knee-deep in design projects. Even worse, the strategy team didn't participate in the day-to-day design work that directly influenced—and was influenced by—the library.

Ultimately, the library activity stopped. It wasn't that those gung-ho individuals no longer believed in standards or a library, far from it. But their new responsibilities and organizational distance from the strategy team hindered progress and communication. The strategy team admitted the library was the "right thing to do," but it lacked evangelists, commitment, and momentum. Organizational change and disruption notwithstanding, the enterprise would have been better off to identify a librarian closer to or within the design team. Unfortunately, sometimes such arrangements are impossible.

Multiple Librarians and Boards

Many roles can influence a component library: information architects, interaction designers, visual designers, engineers, and more. Each can have a different perspective, different needs, and different goals. All voices should be heard, and encouraging active participation from multiple disciplines makes your library stronger.

One team chose to have two librarians: an interaction designer paired with a visual designer. Both knew their complementary roles and had a common vision for the library's purpose. Sure, it made sense to identify who was responsible for what operationally, and the interaction designer took charge of the taxonomy. Their close collaboration inspired two teams to adopt a common system. As a result, collaboration across disciplines increased substantially.

Multiple librarians and significant participation across your organization can ensure that your library survives unanticipated change. What if your librarian quits and starts a new job somewhere else? Sure, you can plug that hole with a different person, but domain knowledge and library credibility may have just walked out the door. Make sure the library's future is bigger than any one individual by supporting and encouraging active participation from as many team members as possible.

Teams can create opportunities for participation and influence by creating review boards and working groups that span disciplines, teams, or organizational silos. If cross-functional teams are sharing the library, they can jointly address critical issues like how the library is organized, or even day-to-day considerations of whether a new component is worth adding. These teams raise credibility and expose the library to more potential adopters. That said, you still need a librarian to monitor requests, assign responsibilities, maintain the catalog, and publish assets. Must it be one person? Perhaps not, but as a cross-functional team includes more and more participants, the "go-to authority" could become ambiguous. Therefore, work hard to clearly define roles and responsibilities.

A Component's Life

Components can rise in a furious period of excitement, and fall quietly out of favor. Many components live a meager, quiet existence, lingering in the library forever. A component's life cycle can be represented by the many phases of its existence (**Figure 12.1**). Understanding the life cycle can help you more effectively identify what's valuable and cull out what should be removed.

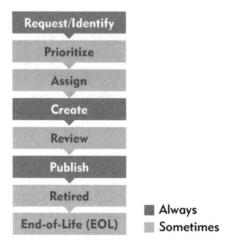

Figure 12.1 The phases of a component's life cycle.

A component transitions through a series of steps, from identification to its end-of-life. The following steps enable you to track and communicate component status:

1. **Identified.** Every component begins its life by being identified, whether during a discovery exercise, design project, analysis, or even some executive screaming, "We need it, now!" A library requires a systematic approach to take requests, identify new items, and add them to a catalog.

   The front door for making requests and identifying new candidates should include some kind of triage. One team used the librarian for an initial decision: Add to the library, dismiss immediately, or defer a decision to a larger group (**Figure 12.2**), such as a review board that discusses requests periodically (such as week to week).

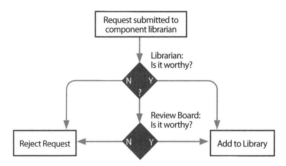

Figure 12.2 A basic triage process where a librarian makes clear decisions to include or dismiss candidates for new components, and can defer to a larger group in cases that are less clear.

   Rome wasn't built in a day, and neither is a component library. Stakeholders declare (or should be asked) how important an item is, how soon it'll launch, how soon guidelines are needed. Therefore, create a priority scale (such as high, medium, and low) to manage component priority for items that aren't addressed immediately.

2. **Assigned (optional).** If component artwork or documentation is created by someone other than the librarian, then at some point you'll assign it. Even better, track the assignment in the catalog, identify milestones hard or soft, and keep an eye on how the assignment is progressing.

3. **Created (also referred to as Drafted).** Component design assets and guidelines are created and prepared for review by peers and other stakeholders.

4. **Reviewed (also referred to as or inclusive of Tested).** Very basic components flow right through the process, not requiring oversight before making their way in. But

most—and certainly the most significant—warrant peer review, feedback, and even testing with authoring tools. Once reviewed, a component may need to be revised or is ready to publish.

5. **Published (also referred to as Active or Released).** Once a component is available to the organization, it is considered published.

   Components can change over time, due to improvements, fixes, and other adjustments. If the change is nontrivial, it may warrant a new variation and phasing out or even ending the life of older variations.

6. **Retired (also referred to as Deprecated).** Components fall out of favor, but can live on in design documentation as well as a live experience. Page designs often include retired components that aren't ideal but haven't been replaced. Therefore, a design library should retain and support retired components.

7. **End-of-Life.** Ending a component's life has significant impacts. Once ended, support is no longer available from design teams, just as engineers will cease code support (such as removing CSS rules from style sheets). This process requires effort and proper communication across groups, but is a necessity to minimize maintenance costs and limit inappropriate use.

Release Status

Just because a component has been published and even used doesn't mean it's available for anyone to use anywhere. You can communicate limited availability with a release status.

Design and engineering teams alike have scenarios where they want to try out a component—even in a live, production environment—but also communicate that it's not ready for wide adoption.

The most common release statuses are the following:

Test. Teams may want to see how a component performs "in the wild" before approving it for general use. Such trials, for activities like A/B tests or usability tests, may be short-lived, but once others see the component, they may start clamoring to use it, so use test status to communicate the special conditions around its use.

Pilot (also referred to as Beta). You may feel confident about a component's success but not want it proliferating widely across an experience. Therefore, designate it as a pilot component. Honestly, some components remain in pilot mode forever, because either they never catch on or librarians never promote them to active. On the other hand, some items undergo a pilot period to work out the kinks and then transition into general availability afterwards.

Active (also referred to as General Availability, or GA). At this point, all aspects of component development have been completed: it's in a production environment; it's available for anyone to use (appropriately); and relevant documentation, metrics, accessibility, and other details have been fully integrated.

Not every team takes component releases this seriously. Some teams use components simply to improve design consistency and production efficiency. The last things on their mind are code releases and formal software development processes; instead, they just want to produce better design faster, and that's just fine. But for teams embedding components more deeply into design and development, release status enables you to communicate precisely how and when a component can be used across an enterprise.

Updating the Library

The components are coming! The components are coming!

You've received an email in your component request inbox, just reviewed a project's design documentation, or recognized a gap in the library. Components must be added or updated. What do you do?

The nuts-and-bolts activities to add to and update the library boil down to three key activities:

Manage the catalog to capture requests, coordinate activities, and evolve the taxonomy.

Create design assets, such as snippets, stencil items, separate files, or other formats as required by your software tool.

Write guidelines to educate users and govern use of each item.

Catalog

The component catalog enables you to manage each item coming into, existing in, or retiring from a component library. When you need to track a new component, add a record to the catalog and record its status (such as identified or assigned), priority, and even a potential name and category.

You should create a unique identifier to refer to each item. If your library taxonomy already exists (see Chapter 9, "Organize") and you know where the new item fits, then assign the component code immediately. Engineering and QA teams may be keenly interested in component codes to include in markup and write test cases, respectively. So don't be a bottleneck because you want the codes to be perfect.

On the other hand, if you haven't yet created a formal taxonomy or if the candidate's place in the taxonomy is unclear, then avoid assigning a formal component code. Instead, wait until the taxonomy—and the new component's place in that taxonomy—is clear, and use a temporary ID number until the formal code is defined.

During the remaining workflow, you can use the catalog to monitor assignments for creating design assets and guidelines.

Assets

Designers need reusable design assets (the artwork) so they can repeatedly and quickly produce viable design solutions. But being a librarian doesn't mean that every component added to the library requires pixel-perfect artwork.

For comp assets, try to obtain artwork created by designers for specific projects, so you aren't saddled with an untenable backlog of artwork to create. Stable, final comps should be a precise rendering of the final design, so comp artwork is very time-consuming to create, subject to high standards and a formal review process. Therefore, a librarian's mantra should be: "I don't do comps. Give me the pixel-perfect art, and I'll integrate it into the library."

The story is quite different for wireframes. For projects, wireframes are imperfect, lower-fidelity renderings, and designers (including myself) may take shortcuts to get a wireframe completed. Wireframes are *always* accompanied by disclaimers like "this isn't pixel-perfect" when presented to less knowledgeable stakeholders.

But a wireframe library is held to a higher standard, even if the artwork is still not pixel-perfect. Across more than ten wireframe libraries that I've created and helped manage, I've never reused wireframe artwork provided by designers. Instead, wireframe artwork is created from scratch. It's just as fast—if not faster—to produce wireframes from scratch as to source, copy, and integrate wireframes from other designers. Additionally, the wireframe starting points you publish are more consistent since they are based on the styles, layers, and grids already embedded in the library. Maybe that consistency can even empower designers to confidently learn and adopt similar practices, too.

For both comps and wireframes, artwork should still be reviewed and synchronized to ensure that styles, layers, grid guidelines, labels, and other characteristics are consistent with library conventions. In addition, copy and imagery should be generalized or supported with sufficient variations and examples to communicate component flexibility and context.

Ultimately, the artwork must be integrated into the distributed library. For wireframes, that means adding it to the build file and exporting as an object for a panel or as a separate file. For comps, that usually means creating a unique file for each component (or even variation and example, depending on your practice).

Guidelines

Design assets are meaningless, if not downright destructive, if applied in a haphazard, uninformed way. Each component belongs to the library because it serves a purpose, solving a specific design problem in a way the team anticipates will need to be applied again. How do you know what problem it solves? How do you instruct the masses on how it should be applied? You can communicate proper use through good documentation, primarily in the form of guidelines.

The librarian should be relatively well-versed on the production of effective guidelines. Chapter 13, "Guide," provides a deeper description of how to author relevant guidelines for a component library. However, first things first: A librarian shouldn't approach guideline composition as a one-man show. It's not up to the librarian to author everything, and librarians should go to great lengths to make sure other team members author guidelines.

However, a librarian should be prepared to facilitate the production of guidelines by involving smart, qualified designers and other capable authors. By empowering other authors to participate in the library, you raise awareness, lighten your own load, and generate more buy-in from them and others who see the broader contributions.

When documenting a new component, the first author you consider should be the very designer who created the solution. That person is likely mindful of design details and has grappled with the constraints, dead ends, and boundaries that came up when creating the component. But the designer does not necessarily need to be the author. You can find good guideline authors among publishers, content strategists, managers, or really anyone involved in the design process. Any author who has a good understanding of the solution is a reasonable choice to consider as a contributor to the library's documentation.

It is usually up to a librarian to assign, track, and aggregate guidelines from authors. However, the authoring process may take on a life of its own and warrant separate documentation.

One team created a "Guidelines Dashboard" (**Figure 12.3**) to track guideline composition across many steps. The dashboard included each component—or even an individual variation—as a separate row, and columns were used to record the name, author, each step of the authoring process (from research to review to publishing), and more.

Priority 1=Now 2=Next 3=Later	Topic	Author	Reviewers	(1) Obtained Source Material?	(2) Drafted?	(3) Reviewed by peer (in UX)?	(4) Approved by key stakeholder(s)?	(5) Copy Final?	(6) Published?	Notes
1	Tabs	JB	JD, KW, KR	Done	Done	Done	Done	In Progress		
3	Personalization	JB	JD, KW, KR	Done	Done	Done	In Progress			
1*	Contact Us	JB	JD, KW, JBa	Done	Done	Awaiting Review				
2	Ratings	NC	JD, CP	Done	Done	Awaiting Review				
1	Category Navigation	NC	JD, KW, KR	Done	Done	Awaiting Review			Draft Published	
2	Comments	NC	JD, KW, KR	Done	Done	Awaiting Review				
2	Utility Header	JB	JD, KW, KR	Done	Done	Awaiting Review				
1	Video Player	NC	JD, CP	Done	Done	Awaiting Review			Draft Published	
3	Video Search Results	JB	JD, KW, KR	Done	In Progress					
3	Breadcrumbs	JB	JD, KW, KR	Done	In Progress	In Progress				
2	Bookmarks	JB	JD, KW, KR	In Progress	In Progress					
1	Share	JB	JD, CP	In Progress						
2	Popin	JB	JD, CP	In Progress						
3	Media List	JB	JD, KW, KR	In Progress						
1	Search Filters	NC	JD, CP	In Progress						
2	Search Results	NC	JD, KW, KR	Not yet started						
3	Advanced Search	NC	JD, KW, KR	Not yet started						
3	Progress Indicator	NC	JD, KW, KR	Not yet started						

Figure 12.3 The "Guidelines Dashboard" that enabled a small team to identify, prioritize, and track completeness of numerous components in the library.

Notice how each column represents a different phase, and the librarian used cell background color to indicate when each step was complete. This created an interesting visual effect: The more complete the authoring process, the farther the bar extends to the right, like a bar graph. Color and other formatting were used for the most notable aspect: communicating when an item was stalled due to lack of peer or stakeholder review and feedback. The librarian and teammates could share the dashboard with management, who in turn could stoke the fire underneath delinquent stakeholders to get the process moving again.

Publishing

No library has ever been published in a single stroke, never to change again. In fact, in a rush to get out useful materials to designers, a library may be published before its first version is even comprehensive. The librarian administers the publishing process, controlling what design assets and guidelines are visible to an organization.

"Where's the Latest?"

Designers are often on the lookout for new assets, frequently querying a librarian with questions like "Where can I get the latest templates?" and "Is my version the most recent?" Everyone will wonder if the documentation they see is up to date, and "When will the new components be available?" In fact, to most stakeholders, availability is neither when the component is used in the live site nor when it's allowed to be used on a project. Rather, it's when the component is published (guidelines and design assets alike) to the team and publicly visible as a standard.

The librarian communicates what's available and how designers and other stakeholders can learn from and use the library. In many libraries—particularly immature or burgeoning ones—the publishing process can be unpredictable. As long as designers are going to the right place to get the assets, it's up to you to just make sure that what's there is up to date.

In other cases, publishing may be somewhat haphazard. For example, smaller portions can be published ahead to a design team that needs components and is working against a tight deadline. Delivering codes and polished artwork to a design team efficiently can be critical to project success in the short run *and* to successfully integrating components into the design and development process over time.

Predictable Publishing Cycles

Mature libraries benefit from—and even depend on—stricter, predictable publishing cycles. With a schedule in place, you can set expectations on how often new items are published, when stakeholders can anticipate the next set, and when you can and cannot deliver updates. To stakeholders, a response like "We'll be sure to include these components in our next release, due in three weeks" is far more palatable than "We'll include these components whenever we get around to publishing."

One team established an easy-to-remember four-week cycle for releasing components. The team reviewed project work and clarified requirements during the first two weeks, built components during the third week, and published updates and notified stakeholders during the final week (**Figure 12.4**). With that baseline, the librarian could plan accordingly, and stakeholders had a clear sense of how the library operated.

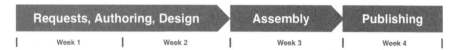

Figure 12.4 A month-long publishing cycle that defined expectations on when interested stakeholders could anticipate active participation and newly published assets and guidelines.

A predictable process enables you to set realistic expectations for your constituents. Without it, stakeholders feel more justified in making individual demands and requesting immediate delivery. Sure, a publishing timeline doesn't mean that you always can prevent such demands from becoming reality. But the process is a basis for challenging unrealistic requests and educating stakeholders about the cross-enterprise benefits of the library.

Distribution

As described in Chapter 11, "Build," you can distribute the library in something as simple as a ZIP file of templates, libraries, and useful documentation. However, you don't want to have to field countless requests to send the library to each person who sends you an assets request. Instead, set up a common location where everyone can download the collection.

There are many different options, some dependent on what environments you have available:

Email. Unless your file size is just too large, you can distribute the system via email. However, email saddles you with distribution on demand, and you'll get annoyed with the repeated requests just as much as stakeholders will get annoyed waiting for you to respond. Avoid email if possible, except for cases when you must immediately distribute critical portions to design teams.

Download from a Collaboration Tool. Many organizations use project management or collaboration software (such as Microsoft Sharepoint or Basecamp from 37signals) that enables file uploads and downloads. If your team uses such a tool, offering assets here may be the path of least resistance. Just set up a persistent project or folder (such as "Component System") and provide access to each interested person. Drawbacks include administering access permissions and using a collaboration system that, while ideal for distributing files, may not be fine-tuned for administering a library in conjunction with guidelines and other materials.

Download from a Library Site. As described in Chapter 13, "Guide," many teams create a custom Web-based destination for the component library. If that's the case, then enabling download of design assets and documentation from that location is an obvious and optimal solution.

Copy from a Shared Drive. Some teams collaborate via a shared drive, from which you can enable download from a folder. That said, do not store library source material at that location, for others could copy—or worse, delete—files on the shared drive. Instead, store the master copy in a more secure location and copy a publishable version to the location from which others can download it.

Download from a Private URL. Most teams big enough to warrant building a component library have access to sufficient infrastructure (like the options listed above). That said, in some cases the download rests behind a firewall that vendors cannot access. In that case, you could make the download available outside the firewall via a private URL that you distribute to vendors. However, make sure there are no incoming links to the location, and that such a solution doesn't violate IT standards of your organization.

Providing access to a ZIP file doesn't answer the question "OK, I've got the design assets, but now what?" It's helpful to supplement the download with basic and easy-to-access materials to help users get started. These materials should describe what's included, how to extract and begin using the system, and where to find helpful documentation. Clear pointers to a getting started guide—or even a quick video that orients users on the system basics—can go a long way to reduce frequently asked questions. These materials are a core aspect of teaching people how to use the library, which is described in Chapter 14, "Adopt."

Notifications

Placing a file on a server for download raises the question: How are people going to know that the system is available if you don't notify them? Therefore, look to establish a consistent and accessible way to communicate changes to the component library. Email subscriptions and/or a blog with RSS subscriptions can do the trick.

In addition to announcing that a new version of the library has been released, you'll also want to communicate other library developments, like emerging components, guidelines that are coming soon, what designers have been assigned to author what pieces, and new requests recently added to the queue.

Notifications benefit from a consistent, scannable structure. Interested readers will not want to spend hours reading your laundry list of details, but they will want to scan the notification for items of interest. **Figure 12.5** shows an email template for one team's periodic notification.

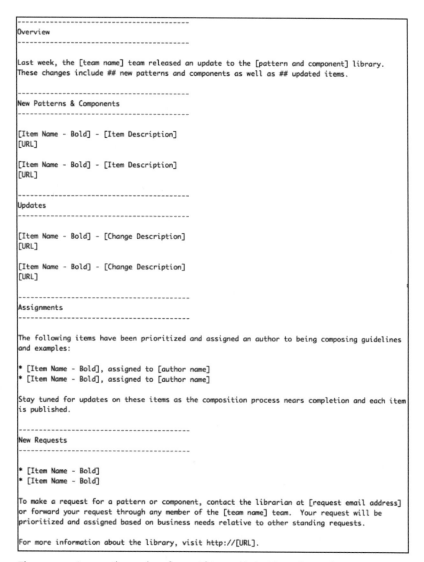

Figure 12.5 An email template for notifying stakeholders about changes to a component library.

In this particular example, the primary audience is the interaction design team. The librarian wanted to keep designers informed in order to reduce design duplication and raise awareness of emerging standards. The email includes clear section headers (New Items, Updated Items, Assignments, and New Requests) that the librarian can use to communicate details.

Inputs and Feedback

The librarian doesn't own the library; the organization does. The librarian must act as facilitator to ensure that the library remains a healthy, vibrant part of the organization's culture and process. With that in mind, it's often the librarian (or designated partner) who fields requests, inputs, and feedback from the organization.

Whether the library is in use by a small team of user experience designers or adopted far and wide across an organization, there must be a clear front door where designers can submit requests and ask for advice. Common methods for submitting component requests are an email alias (such as components@yourcompanyname.com) or Web-based request forms that capture requests and other important criteria.

Discussions

Discussions can foster a shared vision of the library's role, direction, and growth. Ideally, many of those discussions happen in real time as designers work with stakeholders during a project. The library provides a baseline for making design decisions during planning sessions, brainstorming, design reviews, test planning, and a slew of other team interactions. Such discussions also reveal candidates for new components and enhancements.

Obviously, a librarian cannot attend every single design review—that's preposterous to even consider. Instead, a librarian can help designers represent the library, know how to apply components, and explain how components are changed or extended.

Online discussions are also valuable. Dedicated forums and comments can capture feedback in a Web-based medium that perpetually records and exposes different perspectives across the team. Online discussions can guide the library's course and suggest new components and areas of emphasis.

Not every component-specific discussion needs to happen out in the open. In some cases, it may make sense to convene a smaller group of experts or library champions to plan library activities, discuss big decisions, and establish best practices. Closed discussions are warranted for reviewing assets and guidelines, too. Providing access to only a small team is preferred to opening up discussions to an entire group before a component is ready for enterprise-wide consumption.

13

GUIDE

Library users must understand what's in the library, why it exists, and how to use it. Library documentation shows your team how to use your valuable investment.

This chapter will teach you how to do the following:

- ▶ Use Web site documentation as a hub for library activity and knowledge.
- ▶ Publish component references and getting-started documents that go beyond your typical style guide.
- ▶ Embed instructions and details into component artwork.
- ▶ Use design patterns as a foundation for writing about components.
- ▶ Devise a set of components attributes that works best for you.
- ▶ Know when to author—and *not* author—visual specs.

Documenting a Library

The library's reach and effectiveness can be extended significantly by the quality of its documentation. You can't rely on hallway conversations, project collaboration, and training sessions to embed a library into the psyche of your organization. You have to provide persistent access to the library to guide your organization. The three primary venues for publishing component documentation are Web sites, documents, and embedded annotation inside artwork itself.

Web Sites

Sure, a Web-based solution should provide an easy-to-navigate collection of standards and reference material. But since it's a Web site, you expand the site's purpose to document how your team will do the following:

- ▶ Document component standards and implementations.
- ▶ Distribute library versions.
- ▶ Notify interested users about updates via blog posts, RSS feeds, and mailing lists.
- ▶ Teach concepts including design system basics, standards, software tools, and process.
- ▶ Discuss component use via moderated comments and forums.
- ▶ Blog about updates and new ideas.
- ▶ Collaborate on draft guidelines during authoring processes.

Be clear as to what voices and points of view the library represents. Is it a publication of your design team? Or does the site promote a unified perspective of the library across your organization? How does your site fit into other online documentation your team publishes, such as wikis, blogs, and project management software? Who will use the site the most, and what content do they need most?

For example, if the site is used first as a component lookup to find tips and code, then architect the site to promote findability (through component names, codes, and thumbnails) and emphasize code snippets. Alternatively, if the site's primary goal is basic education of new design staff, then orient high-level pages to establish broad understanding and expose component details on deeper pages.

If design and development teams end up building separate sites for their respective assets (such as design standards versus code), then work hard to map the two experiences together during upfront planning and smart links back and forth. One organization realized this early on: It became clear that both teams wanted publishing control and were constrained to separate systems. By meeting often as the two sites emerged, they built a blended experience with helpful links at levels both high (such as the homepage) and low (by linking from component design standards to code and back again).

Another organization couldn't see the forest for the trees. Two distinct sites emerged: Developers built a site strictly supporting code reuse, and the design team organized a site around design patterns with entries that often overlapped with reusable code. While the two teams worked together at a strategic level, the two sites represented disparate experiences with few connecting links, conflicts in nomenclature and organization, and an intentional separation since the librarians never agreed on a vision for a shared catalog. Fortunately, designers and engineers muddled through both libraries. The company reaped significant benefits and cost savings from reuse, but I wonder if they could have realized even greater cost savings and wider adoption had the teams driven harder to coordinate a blended library.

Implementation

The goals of your Web-based destination may be fulfilled or tempered by the solution you can build. Some teams have unfettered access and funds to build the optimal solution for their needs. But most teams find themselves making compromises in functionality due to limited time, funding, or freedom within a constrained IT environment. Common implementation options include the following:

Home-grown systems. This is expensive and time-consuming, but ultimately the most advanced and tailored solution for an organization. Yahoo has written (on boxesandarrows.com) and subsequently spoken extensively about the challenges and roadmap they've traversed. **Figure 13.1** displays the landing page of Yahoo's public pattern library, although the team uses and manages a much more robust and collaborative Web-based solution internally.

Sun Microsystems also built a custom Web site as the cornerstone of their efforts. Lucky for us, they expose it to the community, too, at Sun.com/webdesign/ (**Figure 13.2**). The site is an authoritative look into each and every piece that publishers use to build Sun.com pages, including usage guidelines, technical notes, graphical examples, and especially the code itself. Why is it public? The internal team wanted no barriers for vendors to access and use the library (such as a long approval process to access the private Sun network). Such efficiencies trumped the need to keep the site confidential, although the team does manage proprietary information behind a firewall.

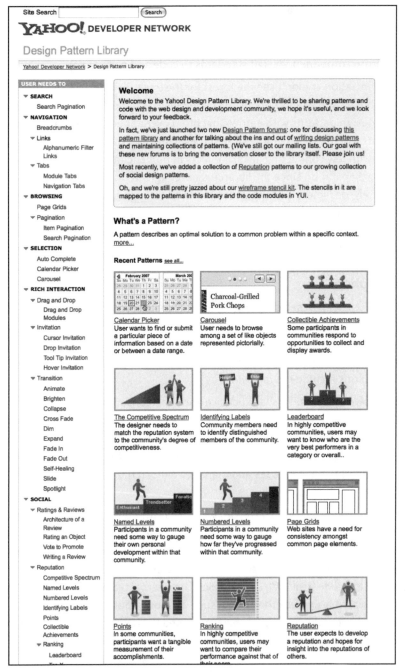

Figure 13.1 Yahoo's public design pattern library, which shares a vast collection of patterns with the public at large. (*Courtesy of Yahoo! Inc.*)

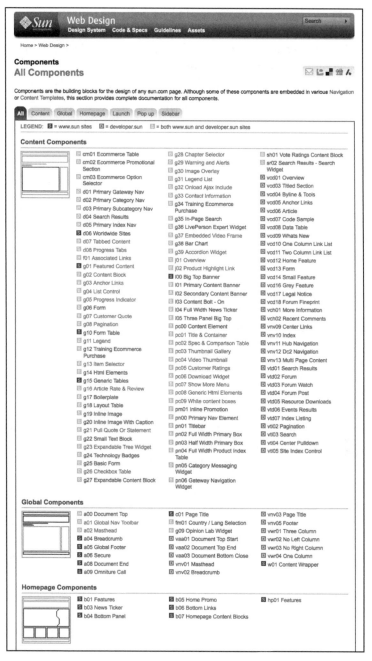

Figure 13.2 Sun.com's component library, available at http://www.sun.com/
webdesign/, features every single component used to publish Sun.com pages.
(*Courtesy of Sun Microsystems*)

Collaboration tools. One team effectively used Jive Software's Clearspace tool that includes a well-suited three-prong feature set: wiki (with articles per pattern and component, including editing permissions for team and individual, commenting and ratings), discussion boards (for new requests and general discussions), and blog (to publish ongoing notifications and articles about the overall library).

Wikis. Other teams have set up wikis to publish component documentation. This may be a good short-term fix, but isn't really a tenable long-term solution unless you customize collaboration, assign permissions, and govern document structure to ensure a consistent experience. Wiki solutions are typically available as free, open source software, but require you to install, configure, and administer the solution.

Blogs. You can also use open source software like Wordpress to publish pages and blog entries relevant to your library. Blogs enable discussions via comments, enable RSS subscriptions, and if you go with a common platform like Wordpress, enable relatively simple extensions and customization via plugins.

Rolling Out the Repository

AUTHOR: Jennifer Bohmbach

ROLE: **Information Architect, Gumption**

Getting a documentation system in place was only the beginning. We still had to educate designers and others about how to use the components and the overall system correctly. My story is about how we worked to make that happen.

Background

Before the library, our team was not creating unified documentation. We had situations when team members were on vacation, documents needed to be altered, and we had to wait until the person who made the document returned. Not an efficient way to work. Everyone was doing their best; we just had not taken the time to get our documentation approach in order. We had already built a code library; we wanted to be able to put those same components into documentation. In addition to the components, we needed uniform templates to present the information to stakeholders, developers, and collaborators.

Benefits

Getting the documentation library in place really helped us, because it created a unifying language to communicate our ideas through templates for our deliverables, training materials, and a library of reusable components. This meant that any one of us could alter another team member's documents, if necessary. It also meant that collaboration was accelerated, because we were playing in the same sandbox with the same set of pieces and parts. Our stakeholders began to see similar documentation and grew smarter about how to read it. The documentation system itself also pushed us together to solve problems or questions as we learned how to use the system as a team and helped each other understand and evolve the tool set.

Roll Out and Adoption

Not everyone was an immediate fan. There is a learning curve to adopting a new tool set; therefore, training on the new system was required to set the team up for success. People had all grown accustomed to using our own approaches. It's challenging to let go of that because it takes time to become efficient with new tools. I needed to show my team that once they had gotten through the initial learning curve, there were great rewards on the other side. I reminded team members that we had team goals that led us to creating and agreeing to use this system. We had decided as a team we wanted to work in a more uniform manner. The system was our solution.

These building blocks freed us up to spend more time thinking about actual solutions instead of spending time with project-specific documentation. Once we had a basic understanding of usage of the system in place, we continued to identify opportunities to extend the system to support our work. A few things we did:

- ▶ Authored and executed a communication plan about the system, including blogs, email aliases, and expected release cycles for the system
- ▶ Trained vendors we were working with to use our system to add value and extensibility to their documentation
- ▶ Created training materials for the system in such a manner that they would be reusable
- ▶ Practiced accessibility for questions and support. I personally made that a top priority, especially during the initial year of roll out.

> ▶ Created a single repository where the parts of the system could be accessed
>
> ▶ Continued to TALK about what was working and what needed to be enhanced, added, or altered
>
> The system is a living entity. It is a tool set that continues to evolve over time based on what the team using it needs it to do. Team members needed a way to gain access to the latest updates and to contribute and share ideas for improvement or extension of the system.

Documents

Unfortunately, some teams can't build a Web-based destination for their component documentation. A team can lack any combination of resources, time, money, technical skill, or even an approved IT environment in which to build a site. Such limitations are commonplace. Out of ten large user experience design teams, only four could build a Web-based destination to centralize documentation. The remaining six teams had to depend on one or more useful documents that could be printed, shared, and evolved over time.

Beyond a Style Guide

When the topic of library documents begins, the team's initial response is invariably, "Well, we have a style guide already." Usually, the admission is followed by a description of a meager document that includes a color palette, a page on typography, and—if you are lucky—perhaps a visualized page grid or two. In fact, I was astonished to find that a Fortune 500 company with a years-old site design distributed its style guide as a solitary JPG image attached to an email! Sure, this is a helpful starting point for visual designers, grounding them in fundamentals, but such a guide is nowhere near a comprehensive description of experience design standards.

In some cases, a style guide is actually a far more serious collection of standards. Basic typographic foundations (such as font family and size) are coupled with sufficient examples, variations, and context. Expanded color descriptions include gradients, examples, and even relationships with typography. Grid variations identify how to apply layout decisions to numerous page types. Beyond those basics, the guide expands on visual standards of iconography, illustration, photography, and more. Even better, visual practices can be coupled with editorial guidance, tone, and branding fundamentals.

The style guide's growing content base can blur lines of scope and ownership. Often-times, a style guide is owned and produced by a visual design team and led by a creative director or art director. A moderate amount of collaboration with editors and content strategists can raise document value by incorporating editorial guidelines. But even then, who owns what and what is the workflow to publish updates? The lines blur further as interactive guidelines—like states, behaviors, and structure—blend in, too.

If nothing else, now's the time to start questioning the document's title, because "Style Guide" narrows expectations. Instead, perhaps the team refers to a "User Experience Guide" or "UX Standards." Explicitly, readers may then appreciate the document's broader appeal. Just as importantly, team members across disciplines will feel more empowered to contribute to and influence content that they care about most. **Figure 13.3** shows the table of contents of a user experience guide that involved multiple authors and sought to communicate standards to a wide, diverse audience. Notice, however, what's missing: components themselves.

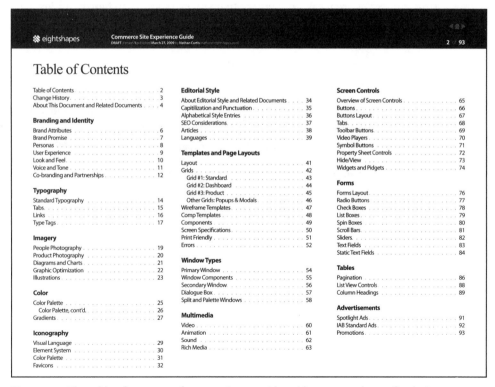

Figure 13.3 The table of contents of an experience guide, with content relevant for design teams and stakeholders alike: visual style, editorial style, interaction guidelines, branding, research, template layouts, and more.

Some teams take the guide document concept a bit too far, however, adopting an "everything but the kitchen sink" approach. Their mantra? If it's a standard, then throw it in the style guide! Suddenly, a document intended to include basic tenets of visual style has ballooned into a repository of best practices (such as "When to Use Flash"), accessibility requirements, code best practices, and more.

Avoid this approach, or your document could result in a hodgepodge of decreasingly organized standards. Instead, establish well-defined boundaries for what your experience guide contains, such as visual style, editorial style, and branding. You could even include interaction guidelines for common elements and components, such as form controls, popup windows, and other generic behaviors.

But stay away from documenting each and every component in a style guide or experience guide. Instead, create a component reference.

Component Reference

A component reference is a document that serves as a comprehensive index of standards and visualizations, component by component. Your library's component reference should remain independent of a style guide since these guidelines do the following:

▶ Include contributions by many authors

▶ Change frequently and likely not at the same time as core standards

▶ Require their own component-by-component organization and labels, including categories, codes, variations, and examples, which is much different than style guide content of color, grids, typography, and other general topics

A component reference document contains one or more pages per component, often organized into chapters based on categories, and front matter like a table of contents, change history, and other supporting material. At a minimum, information on each component should include the following:

▶ Name (such as Page Title)

▶ Category (such as Content)

▶ Code (such as C01V1)

▶ Visualization (such as a wireframe, comp, or screenshot)

If the component has more than one variation or is augmented by examples, then present each one visually, and include a list of variations and examples for quick reference.

Figure 13.4 shows a component reference guide, which actually resulted from formatting and printing the build file (see Chapter 11, "Build") with minimal additional details like component name.

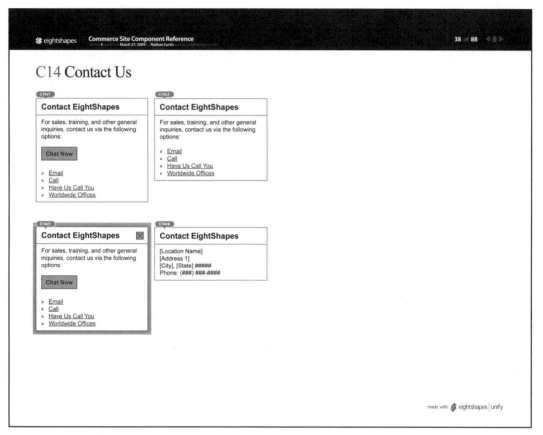

Figure 13.4 A component reference guide printed from a build file, with page titles indicating the component name and code.

For teams looking to record much deeper component details as described later in this chapter, create standard layouts that position component pictures adjacent to attributes like overview, use when, guidelines, and other considerations. You can even overlay redlines (lines that define padding, gutters, and other sizes) on top of components and mark each element of the component one by one to connect artwork with annotations to the right (**Figure 13.5**).

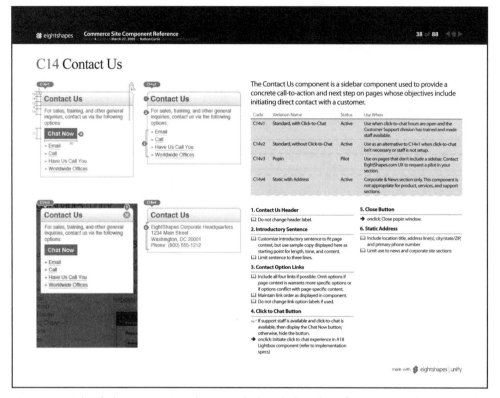

Figure 13.5 A detailed component guide page, which includes a list of variations and examples, marked elements (1, 2, 3, ...), redlines, and detailed interactive specifications.

Users Guide

Not every designer immediately understands how to use your system's tool of choice, add components to page layouts effectively, or request changes to your library. So in addition to—or as a part of—your component reference guide, consider creating a Component Library Users Guide.

A Users Guide aims to help designers and others adapt to using components in their own workflow. Also referred to as a Getting Started Guide, a users guide can get individuals off on the right foot more quickly and confidently. Consider a users guide for teams that need a consolidated place to get answers to questions like the following:

- ▶ What is the component library, and why does our team use components?
- ▶ Where do I download the system from?
- ▶ What software and hardware do I need?
- ▶ How do I create a page based on components?

▶ Which page layout or grid should I use?

▶ What are some effective shortcuts and best practices for designing with components?

▶ What are the best ways to validate that I've used components correctly?

▶ How are my designs reviewed during the design and development cycle?

▶ How do new components from my project get added to and updated in the library?

▶ What is our internal process and workflow for managing the library?

The amount of software-specific content can vary based on how much your team needs to be trained and how proficient they are at using help found within the tool itself. Ideally, scenarios like "Open template, add components, arrange components…" are explained conceptually so that designers are quickly productive (**Figure 13.6**). But repeating or building on software help can become burdensome if the team can't be taught what features are most important and where to find more details.

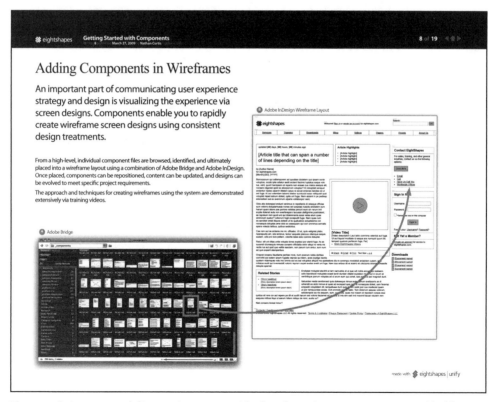

Figure 13.6 A conceptual diagram in a users guide that shows how components are added from a library (in Adobe Bridge) into a wireframe (in Adobe InDesign).

Documentation in Assets

Don't forget to try and maximize the documentation embedded in your design assets themselves. Designers spend most of their time in authoring tools such as Adobe Photoshop, Microsoft Visio, programming tools, and even text editors!

Earlier chapters described the benefits of marking components with reference codes that tie chunks of the experience to the standards they represent. Beyond that, also consider how you can embed information into assets through the following:

Layer names. Some visual design teams choose to organize comp component variations within the same Photoshop or Fireworks file. In that case, it's important to identify each variation precisely based on what layer it appears on.

Hidden layers. A librarian can embed documentation like usage tips, redlines, and alternate styles and copy on layers that are hidden by default. This annotation increases file size and requires maintenance. However, it may be the only—or most easily accessible—type of documentation for a designer to use.

Object and file names. Teams vary on their inclusion of component names, component codes, or both in the name of a component object (in a panel) or file. Choose what works best for your team. However, including both may improve retrieval and precision when teams are looking for just the right one.

File metadata. Adobe Creative Suite files (such as a Photoshop PSD or InDesign INDD or IDMS file) support an extensible metadata platform (XMP) whereby you can add metadata to a file, embed guidelines, and improve your team's workflow and asset retrieval. For more information on XMP, refer to http://www.adobe.com/products/xmp/.

Standardizing Components

Documenting a component within a library isn't the same as creating project-specific documentation. When in the depths of a specific project, you are likely discussing tradeoffs, quickly communicating back and forth with engineers, and making design decisions amid an ongoing collaboration that all interested parties participate in.

When using a library, much of that context and fluidity is absent. Instead, readers independently work on different projects, and each needs the library for his own reasons. Therefore, a more diverse audience will rely on component documentation with the following characteristics:

▶ Formal, and precisely reflects a standardized, vetted view on component usage

▶ Well written

- ▶ Structured consistently across all components in the library
- ▶ Generalized to cover all appropriate reuse
- ▶ Organized and written for multiple audiences (such as product owners, publishers, and engineers)
- ▶ Inclusive of perspectives beyond just the author or designer on the project

Learning from Design Patterns

When documenting a component library, you can learn from and borrow many pattern-based techniques, and also diverge from that set for pattern attributes that are not appropriate in a more prescriptive component-based environment.

When documenting patterns, authors employ standard attributes that are easy to understand and write. The attributes most commonly used to describe a pattern are displayed in **Table 13.1**.

Table 13.1 Standard Attributes Used to Document a Design Pattern

Attribute	Purpose	
Title	Label the pattern with an unambiguous name, which is also used as a reference from other patterns and documentation.	Required
Problem statement	Describe the problem a user encounters in user-centered terms.	Required
Sensitizing example	Depict pattern visually in a picture that is worth 1,000 words. The visual example is particularly vital if your audience is often not going to read your words anyway.	Required
Use when	Define when to appropriately apply a pattern.	Required
Solution	Connect the problem statement to a set of guiding principles for using the pattern in the context of your design solution.	Required
Rationale	Describe the forces that led to the pattern solution.	Required
Special cases	Identify where a designer can justifiably diverge from a solution.	Optional
Examples	Put the pattern into context via real-life examples.	Optional
Open questions	Track issues and questions that arise over the life of the pattern.	Optional
Related publications	Formally list publications that served as inspiration, reference, or related works.	Optional

Attribute	Purpose	
Related patterns	Connect the pattern with other patterns that may be siblings, parents, or children within a pattern taxonomy.	Optional
Related research	Create connections between the pattern and ongoing and historical research.	Optional
Future research	Catalog suggestions for future research that could mature and extend the pattern.	Optional
Accessibility	Capture tips and concerns for coding a pattern solution.	Optional

For example, the Yahoo Design Pattern Library defines core attributes of an Item Navigation pattern with clear, well-written statements (**Table 13.2**). (Refer to http://developer.yahoo.com/ypatterns/ for more information).

Table 13.2 The Item Pagination Pattern from the Yahoo Design Pattern Library

Attribute	Description
Title	Item Pagination
Problem statement	The user needs to view data items from a potentially large set of sorted data that will not be easy to display within a single page.
Sensitizing example	See **Figure 13.7**
Use when	There is more information than can comfortably fit within one screen. The items of interest can usually be found on the first few pages. If the data needs to be explored deeply, consider displaying the content in a scrolled area instead.
Solution	Break the list of items into a sequence of pages. Provide links to access the previous and next pages of information. Provide links to jump to the first and last pages in the set. Provide information about what type of object the user is browsing. Provide information about the set of objects the user is currently viewing. Present links in the following order: First, Previous, Next, Last. Use graphical arrows to increase the target size of the links. Show the displayed states of controls when they are unavailable.
Rationale	Displaying arrow graphics helps differentiate the links and provides larger click targets. Unlike in Search Pagination, the controls are visible at all times during paging (even when disabled). This prevents distraction to the user that would occur when removing unavailable controls during paging.

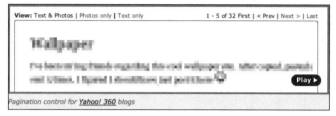

View: Text & Photos | Photos only | Text only   1 - 5 of 32 First | < Prev | Next > | Last

Wallpaper

Play ▶

Pagination control for **Yahoo! 360** *blogs*

Figure 13.7 Sensitizing example for a Yahoo pattern, playable as a movie but with text blurred.

By using a standard set of attributes to describe a pattern, authors consistently compose a large collection of definitions in a format readers can learn and become accustomed to.

Component Attributes

You can use similar attributes for a component library, but the documentation will have a different tone. Components are more prescriptive, fixed design solutions that leave less room for interpretation. Therefore, component documentation often does not include a deep rationale and justification for their use; instead, readers are encouraged to apply the standard. The mentality is "Use the component *this* way," although designers should also extend existing components as needs and budget permit.

If your library is based on a more formal taxonomy, the concept of variations, examples, and related components can take on a more formal role. Gone are less formal examples suggesting what may work, replaced instead with formal examples with finished visual design, recommended content, and associated code snippets to drop into your Web page designs.

That said, it's up to you and your team to define what types of component documentation work best for your organization. Use the organized set of attributes defined in **Table 13.3** as a starting point for how you will document components.

Table 13.3 Component Attributes as Starting Points to Document Your Component Library

Attribute	Purpose	
Title	Label the component, variation, or example with an unambiguous title.	Required
ID & Taxonomy	Define a reference code (such as HF04v1) that uniquely refers to the item, or even establish a deeper taxonomy to organize your items.	Required
Picture	Similar to a pattern's sensitizing example, you can set the tone with a powerful picture.	Required

Attribute	Purpose	
Overview	Introduce the component with a two- to three-sentence summary.	Required
Status	Identify if the component is active, pilot, test, or retired (refer to Chapter 12, "Administer," for stages of a component's life cycle).	Recommended
Use when	Define when to appropriately use a component in your design solution. Include additional subheads such as "Don't Use When," "Page Regions," and "Page Types" to more concretely define appropriate use.	Required
Guidelines	Specify the appropriate states, behaviors, data formats, and editorial guidelines relevant for a component to be published appropriately.	Required
Visual style	Illustrate visual standards such as layout, padding, margins, typography, and color.	Recommended
HTML & CSS Code	If available, publish code snippets so that developers and publishers can easily grab relevant code and include it in their pages.	Recommended
Technical notes	Provide detailed instructions on how to properly use code snippets, including relevant style sheets, platforms, and markup nuances.	Recommended
Design assets	Distribute design assets such as wireframe stencils, wireframe snippets, and comp files directly from the documentation, if relevant and not a maintenance burden relative to the consolidated distribution of the entire asset library.	Optional
Open questions	Track issues and questions that arise over the life of the pattern.	Optional
Related components	Connect the components with other components that may be siblings, parents, or children within the library.	Optional
Accessibility	Capture requirements for implementing an accessible component.	Optional
Metrics	Codify approaches for integrated metrics and analysis into component implementations.	Optional

Picturing Each Variation

A component picture should convey both its appearance and its context of use. You want to make the component feel as real as possible, but you also don't want to mistakenly narrow a component's use by illustrating it with a picture that creates too many assumptions about position, size, copy, or other facets.

Since a component can have multiple variations, try to align the most relevant or frequently used variation as the first of a set. That way, when readers first encounter a component's set of variations, they'll see the representative archetype as the first of the bunch.

Consider the alternatives outlined in **Table 13.4** when illustrating a component in your documentation.

Table 13.4 Pros and Cons of Alternatives for Each Type of Picture You Can Use in Your Component Guidelines

Picture Type	Pros	Cons
Wireframes	• Easy to produce if the library contains wireframe design assets • Generalizes context to focus readers on structure and behaviors rather than a single, visual instance	• Lacks context to make judgments in context of real use • Appears less polished, thus less standardized
Comp	• Easy to produce if the library contains comp design assets • Enables engineers and publishers to use artwork for creating code if code doesn't exist	• May limit interpretation of flexibility • More costly to maintain across a library of many assets, relative to wireframes and automated HTML displays • Feels contrived if not rendered with actual copy and images (often the case when sourced from project work prior to publication)
HTML rendering	• Automate from a code library (such as Sun.com/webdesign/) to reinforce connection to code • Shows actual component rendering in a browser—nothing is more real than that	• Only possible for Web-based documentation; not relevant for documents • Many component libraries include only design assets, thus code isn't available
Screenshot of actual use	• Feels real given that it's from the live site • Readers can apply context to make judgments	• Not connected to assets used by designers to create screen design • Static capture of live instance may unduly narrow context of use

Picture Type	Pros	Cons
Video	• Demonstrates component use as a prototype • Can include multiple examples to heighten understanding • Can include a voiceover that instructs users in real time	• More costly to produce • Likely infeasible for all items in the library, thus resulting in inconsistent pictures across items
Link to live site	• Numerous links can convey flexibility of use and reinforce "Use When" • Strengthen credibility by illustrating success stories	• Pages in production may make tradeoffs or presentations that contradict • Links that aren't closely watched can break over time as page URLs change or are retired

A Concrete "Use When"

Components are more prescriptive than patterns. Your description of when to use a component must be concise and precise. Components aren't meant to be randomly used anywhere, anytime. Therefore, consider describing some or all of the following details, when appropriate, to communicate when to use a component:

Page types. Components can be tied to particular page types, such as a site section, transactional flow, or even a single page design.

Page regions. Components are almost always tied to a particular area of a page layout. For example, the header can't be placed at the bottom of the page, a sidebar component shouldn't be reused in the body content, and local navigation often has a fixed location. If you define your grid(s) with simple areas, you can identify a page region with a simple reference to the area's name.

Use with. If a component is often used with or even requires the use of another component, establish those relationships concretely.

Publishing platforms. Component implementations may be tied to a particular subset of publishing platforms depending on available markup/CSS or suitability to a particular portion of the experience, or to limit use to a particular team.

Don't use when. Sometimes the best descriptions are those that create boundaries and catalog attempts to use the component inappropriately.

Anti-components. Components fall in and out of favor, and you can describe cases that—while once appropriate—are no longer recommended and may even produce bad results when employed. Ideally, identify the preferred alternative. This may also take the form of references to deprecated components that have been replaced.

Visual Style

Components eventually include a refined, polished visual design. Given all that hard work to get there, you'll want designers, engineers, and publishers to easily emulate the design. A component's visual style can be standardized with the following:

Redlines. Prescribe your layout assumptions by overlaying lined annotations to define size, spacing, and margins of each element. Such annotations are often referred to as "redlines" since designers overlay red lines above a comp, along with numbers that define the pixel size of each annotation.

Type tables. Document typographic standards for headers, titles, paragraphs, lists, and more via a table, where each instance is a row, and columns describe style, size, weight, decoration, and color of each typeface.

Color palettes. Although a site's color palette is ideally documented apart from any single component, specialized color and gradient values for a component can be helpful.

If your organization isn't devouring visual style standards, then don't go overboard. Documenting visual standards is time-consuming, takes up a lot of space within component libraries, and can distract readers from important fundamentals.

Additionally, if your team is creating a tandem code library, your best bet may be to avoid visual style guidelines altogether. Instead, strongly encourage engineers and publishers to adopt code that accurately implements the visual system. By using the code, they can stop using guidelines to reinvent code from scratch, which risks visual degradation and inconsistency.

HTML and CSS Code

Not every team has the authority, funding, or wherewithal to create a code library that complements the standardized design assets you've produced. However, large organizations that assembled combined design and code libraries have gotten much closer to reuse nirvana.

Ideally, design assets, standards, and code repositories are documented in a blended, Web-based experience. Internal customers—product managers, engineers, designers, really everyone—ascribe more credibility to a component-based approach that spans disciplines and organizational silos. Therefore, making HTML markup and CSS available alongside standards and design assets can be a big win.

Tips for documenting component code include the following:

Easy Cut and Paste. Enable engineers to easily extract code snippets to include in their own work.

Toggled Displays. Show the code alongside sample displays, or enable readers to toggle between a code and display view to relate the two.

Technical Notes. Not all code is self-evident. Augment code snippets with implementation instructions, to whatever level of detail is necessary.

Comments. Include comments in your code to assist implementation. In particular, recall that each component is a page chunk, so demark the starting and ending points of each component chunk with comments that refer to at least the component ID.

Code snippets are often useless without the broader code framework of page template starting points, cascading style sheets, and associated JavaScript libraries. Therefore, connect code snippets with a clear path to acquire the entire framework.

Writing Process

Most of the time, one person cannot document an entire component library alone. This is especially true if documentation spans disciplines like strategy, visual design, and technical code. Instead, a librarian must shepherd contributors to assist. Refer to Chapter 12, "Administer," for tips on how to solicit authors and track progress through the writing process.

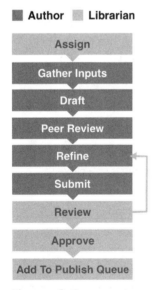

Once one or more authors have been identified, composing guidelines follows a pretty standard writing process, as shown in **Figure 13.8**.

Authoring component guidelines can occur during, at the end of, or sometime after the end of a project cycle when the team has the bandwidth to iterate and publish the material. Refer to Chapter 15, "Integrate," on how component guideline authoring can integrate into your project's workflow.

Gathering Inputs

Designers can struggle when they stare at an intimidating blank canvas. Obviously, this entire book is about starting points so that you can populate that blank canvas when starting a new project. But the challenge of a blank canvas is even more acute when a designer is asked to write guidelines.

Figure 13.8 Common steps for librarians and authors working together to create and publish component guidelines.

The two responses we hear most often are "I don't like to write" and "I don't know where to start." Sure, writing takes practice, but it also takes inspiration. The best way to be inspired is by gathering inputs from a range of sources. Point authors to existing component guidelines—as well as a template of expected component attributes like Use When—to give them a sense of what is expected. With that structure, designers will see that this can be more "fill in the blanks" than they anticipated.

Encourage authors to cast their net wide when looking for inputs. The following list includes many different content types that could influence the guidelines:

▶ Project documentation, including specs and prototypes

▶ Interviews with project participants

▶ Public pattern libraries like developer.yahoo.com/ypatterns/, welie.com, ui-patterns.com, uipatternfactory.com, and designinginterfaces.com

▶ Online publications like alistapart.com, boxesandarrows.com, and useit.com

▶ Research, including usability tests and other internal efforts

▶ Brainstorming with the librarian and other teammates

▶ Feedback on existing components

▶ Live, implemented experiences

▶ Site analytics

▶ Books, conference papers, and white papers

▶ Competitive analyses

Project documentation is a great resource. Hopefully designers have recorded some thoughts or examples of how to use a component during their project work. If detailed project specs are not available, perhaps a prototype, design drafts, or even notes from a collaborative design session could help inspire guidelines. Be careful, however, not to mash project specs into the guidelines template. Specs are often written for a tight, familiar audience working within project constraints instead of a broad audience reusing an item flexibly across an experience.

Projects also involve a range of participants, so encourage the author to reach out to or even interview participants to incorporate more perspectives, and who knows—even dig up more artifacts! The guidelines template can serve as a great framework to structure the interview, too.

Reviewing with Peers

Writing should not be a solitary exercise. Instead, improve your outputs by reviewing your work with peers. Start with the librarian, who sees all the content flowing in and can help inspire, direct, and synchronize the tone of an author's contribution. But components often span disciplines, and an author can get valuable feedback from engineers, testers, product managers, and others who will benefit from—and be held accountable to—their guidelines.

Diverse viewpoints will point out where guidelines are too strict, too loose, or too ambiguous to fit the needs of an organization, resulting in better documentation. Implicitly, their participation increases your credibility in two ways:

▶ First, you'll have incorporated feedback from those whose buy-in you need the most—and who may even evangelize on your behalf!

▶ Second, you can demonstrate to everyone else that many perspectives are represented.

Sharing and Collaborating

Getting a component "out there" to an organization is often a high priority. Design and development teams can create classifications (such as "pilot") to communicate how widely to use a component, but sometimes it's important to simply publish even rough documentation so an organization can learn, use, and adopt a new approach.

When putting a component into the wild—particularly through published documentation—you'll want to create opportunities for readers to participate and contribute their own perspectives. Maybe it's feedback via an open comment form associated with each Web page of documentation. Or, perhaps you refer to library guidelines during a collaborative session or design review and implicitly open it up for critical feedback. Regardless, find mechanisms to incorporate the guidelines into the fluid discourse that accompanies each project moving forward. That reference, as well as your ability to teach the library to others and integrate the approach into your workflow and culture, will make or break the library in the long term.

14

ADOPT

You can't roll out a vast collection of components and expect everyone to instantly get it. Instead, the rollout must be coupled with a planned program of training and materials that teach designers and other stakeholders how, why, and when to use components.

A coordinated program of activities and reference materials to foster adoption of the component library can combine the following:

- ▶ Pilot period(s) that test processes in narrow, contained settings to work out the kinks
- ▶ Live face-to-face training sessions that start with the basics and follow up with specialized topics
- ▶ Coaching
- ▶ Online discussions, blogs, and email notifications
- ▶ Video-based training

Planning

The most common way to improve adoption is through training activities where you teach your team about the process, design assets, and other aspects of the library.

Therefore, plan a program that prepares design, engineering, and other groups to adopt new techniques and adapt to the component library you've built. It's not as simple as putting together a slide deck you can cover in an hour. Instead, plan a rollout that covers key periods—before, during, and after you launch the library—that can take the form of a pilot phase, basic training, and follow-up activities, respectively. In fact, your plan could cover activities through one month (basic training), three months (reiterating basics, addressing growth, and adjusting based on feedback), and even six months out (assessment of progress and success).

The adoption phase should not be the first time that your organization catches on to an emerging component library. Ideally, you have exposed interested parties to your program through activities like a component discovery workshop (see Chapter 8, "Discover"), guideline reviews, proof-of-concept demonstrations, and even pilot project participation.

By the time you reach the adoption phase, you should have a very strong understanding of what the library is and how it fits into your design and development process. And you should be ready to clearly communicate that strategy to your teams, along with what path they'll take to adopt the new techniques.

Pacing

As you consider the rollout, define a pace of adoption that best suits your team's personality, opportunities, and maximum likelihood of success. As a launch or pilot approaches (even a month in advance), you must have a strategy for teaching the library to others and defining expectations for how fast, and how comprehensively, they'll need to adopt new practices.

Trial by Fire

One team adopted a component-based approach to design and documentation via trial by fire. The director of user experience had recently built a team from the ground up in months to include over 20 interaction and visual designers. His company's start-up setting was tumultuous, and project priorities shifted constantly. But the organization had yet to settle into "business as usual"—including expectations and process for creating and documenting design.

The director saw an opportunity, and he took it. His message was clear and unyielding: Learn this system now, use it on all projects, and communicate design consistently as a team.

So what happened? The designers knew their mission, learned core system principles and tool techniques, and produced consistent design and deliverables within weeks. The director wasn't misguided; instead, he knew that he'd hired a seasoned staff that could adapt quickly without too much fuss. Make no mistake, there was a learning curve and designers felt pain during the rapid transition. But they ascended the learning curve quickly, perhaps because they had no other choice. A lone, loud voice resisted amid declarations of tool and technique autonomy, but that voice was drowned out by the team's broad success.

Admittedly, the system didn't last forever, and the start-up's shifting processes, design standards, and staff drifted the team away from the component library over 12 to 18 months. But the (relatively) small investment in a component and template library yielded unmistakable returns: quicker delivery times, improved consistency across in-house and vendor staff, and increased credibility.

Gradual Acclimation

Demanding that every individual adopt a new set of standards, assets, and methods—all the while learning a new software tool—can be a daunting and maybe even insurmountable task. Some teams may simply revolt if not given the proper time and nurturing to adapt to new practices.

An interaction design team manager was shepherding ten designers in adopting their new component library. However, the team was migrating from multiple different applications to a shared software tool, team proficiency and experience varied from senior practitioners to entry-level, and all sorts of projects were under way or starting up. With that in mind, the manager softened adoption expectations early on, preferring a gradual period in which individuals could acclimate to new tools and libraries. Such flexibility was no more apparent than in the team's willingness to use existing tools and familiar (if much rougher) libraries to build out over 100 wireframes for a new project over the next month. The new component-based system would have been ideal, except the team wasn't ready to dive in headfirst given the risk around tight project delivery dates and an uncertain learning curve.

That's why most managers choose to gradually acclimate their teams to new practices over time. In this case, you can be somewhat forgiving if designers stick to old habits, tools, and templates to complete projects in the early stages of adoption, such as in the weeks following a basic training session. But such early forgiveness can't distract from the long-term goal of adopting a common baseline of the library.

If your adoption will take place more gradually, clearly define expectations that your design staff must convert to the new practices. One way to ease concerns is to concretely define a date after which all new projects will use the collection of components and templates. Before that date, if you've already started creating designs and deliverables, stick with what you've got and don't worry about retrofitting your work to the new templates. But once that date passes, any new deliverables would be bound to the set of standards that you launch.

Pilots

You can precede the official launch of your system by testing it during one or more pilot periods. During a pilot, you try out a near-final system version amid real or simulated project conditions. In essence, a pilot is a moderated trial period in which a small group can try out the system, test its viability, correct glitches, and adjust assets and documentation before it's distributed to a wider audience. Pilot periods also offer you the opportunity to test how you'll teach the approach and refine your communications.

When planning your pilot period, work to do the following:

- ▶ Prove the concept in a project-based setting, demonstrating that the techniques lead to greater efficiencies, consistency, and reuse.

- ▶ Teach the library, assets, and approach to a limited group to ensure that you can effectively communicate system value and use.

- ▶ Confirm and adjust the library's organization and nomenclature.

- ▶ Establish credibility with a successful case study.

- ▶ Spread involvement progressively beyond the system's authors before widely publishing the solution.

- ▶ Identify and fill gaps in design assets and documentation.

- ▶ Determine the key breaking points in adoption, process, and tool use, so that you can focus training sessions.

Pilot periods are most effective when design assets, documentation, and new processes can be applied to real projects. Piloting the system against real projects forces designers to use it in real conditions against real deadlines, which leads you to expose and correct real problems. Ideally, pilot projects are self-contained, won't impact other efforts, and are deep enough to sufficiently stress test your approach. You can limit your exposure by choosing projects of smaller scale and less visibility, at least at first. If you have time, roll out a system across multiple pilot phases in projects of increasing scale, complexity, and participation.

Piloting the system in real projects isn't a must, and designers can alternatively work on designs and deliverables in the background if necessary, whether for a "fake" project or by recreating old deliverables using new assets. However, if a project isn't real, then it's certainly not a priority. Pilot participants lose focus when "playing with" a system in the background when project deadlines loom. In addition to higher priority distractions, such simulations lack the urgency and inspiration of real projects, which can skew and reduce the value of informal trials.

During pilot periods, encourage participation from many disciplines if possible. If your system will impact the creation of wireframes, prototypes, comps, and HTML and CSS markup, then choose a pilot project that includes those deliverables, even if on a small scale. That way, you can test cross-disciplinary impacts and also build consensus and momentum across teams.

Set Clear Expectations for the Pilot

A pilot phase benefits from limited participation, visibility, and expectations. One large user experience team intended to precede a wide rollout with a small, contained pilot phase. Over the years, they'd evolved a culture of loosely defined roles, tool indepen-dence, and individual autonomy amid a flexible design process. Some designers yearned for greater structure, and the prospects of using components to produce wireframes and comps promised efficiencies, consistency, and increased collaboration with engineer-ing. But others were sensitive to standard practices and stricter expectations of how to design with specific tools to produce specific outputs. So project leads set out to test the approach with a few select designers in the context of a few small projects.

Well, at least that's what they intended to do. But planners failed to identify specific projects. And once word spread, nobody wanted to be left out. For political, cultural, and historical reasons, teams feared the pilot would solidify a mandated approach without their influence. The sponsor's response was to invite more and more participants to the pilot kickoff work-shop. A single day of informal demos, open discussions, and pilot planning transformed into a formal two-day lecture to over 40 staff members from across many teams.

The pilot training session was a disaster. The library's assets were rough, and its organiz-ing principles untested. Documentation was sparse. And the procedural impacts—to be explored via pilot projects—were not yet defined. In the end, the training sessions were not a total waste of time. Attendees learned new methods, tips, and techniques. But they asked probing questions and expected answers to reveal a mature, solid strategy. Definitive answers didn't exist, at least not yet. So most team members were confused, directionless, or worse, dismissive. The endeavor was fatally damaged. Poor pilot phase execution contributed to a missed opportunity to transform a culture and integrate components into design.

Therefore, when planning a pilot, keep in mind these lessons learned:

Define participants, activities, and objectives. You must have a plan for who's going to participate, what you want them to try to accomplish, and what you hope to learn.

Limit participation. Sure, no one wants to be left out, and others may fear that new standards may emerge without their influence. But to include everyone transforms a pilot into a full-blown launch. So, communicate your approach, encourage suggestions, but still limit participation in your pilot activities.

Finalize process from a pilot, not for a pilot. Use the pilot period as a testing ground to see what activities, deliverables, timelines, and communications work best for your team. Once complete, use your findings to recommend a process for your wider team. Plus, during a pilot, communicate that your workflow is not yet set in stone, and that participants should suggest alternatives if something seems broken.

Save long, formal training for launch. Pilots should get you valuable feedback more quickly for lower costs. Therefore, instead of formal, drawn-out training and lectures, prep pilot participants with the essentials that they need, and provide open forums and paths to request more details.

Live Training

Once you are ready, consider launching your system with a "basic training" session to communicate changes and teach essential techniques. During the session, you can introduce new concepts, introduce the library, demonstrate how to use tools and assets, and facilitate discussions to ensure that everyone understands the approach. At the conclusion of the training session, designers should be able to answer basic questions such as the following:

► What are components, why do I care, and how does this impact my day-to-day work?

► Where do I get the system, and what do I need to set up to start using it?

► How do I create basic designs?

► How do I reuse design assets in my projects? How do I share components and collaborate with others?

► How do I communicate designs within *our* process?

- How does this system make me a better designer within my organization's broader mission?

- What is the library, how do I use it, how does it change, and where do I go when I have questions?

- How do I use this new tool, and for things I don't know and when I want to learn more, where do I go?

Getting people together in the same room to learn together is a great way to communicate and create discussions around core principles, techniques, and process. Keep in mind, however, that getting everyone together in a room is also difficult and expensive. Your basic training event—whether two hours, a half day, a full day, or even multiple days—must be worth it to participants, so plan well and prepare good demos. Don't wait until just days before the training takes place to nail down the day and time, and make sure you iterate with key project stakeholders to brainstorm, detail, and even publish a well-defined agenda beforehand.

Focus on Fundamentals

Your system may be gloriously comprehensive from your point of view. Hopefully you've ironed out all the details before launching it in your group. That said, breadth and formality could overwhelm an audience seeing the system for the first time.

As you prepare your agenda and demonstrations, focus on key concepts and primary tasks so that attendees leave feeling equipped with the knowledge and confidence that they can do it themselves. As a facilitator, ask yourself, "Is this topic absolutely essential for them to be successful?" If you burden beginners with too much, they can become frustrated or lose focus. Instead, demonstrate fundamental processes like creating a screen design and communicating it through a deliverable, such as a set of drafts, deeper specifications, interactive prototypes, or whatever is most important to them.

If you've run a pilot period prior to your training session, enlist pilot participants to prepare and present common deliverables they produced. Over the course of a long day of training, pilot participants can add a refreshing voice and support the core training of the lead facilitator. You can allot 10 to 15 minutes for each presenter to share what he produced, how he produced it, how the artifact fit into the process, and how well it worked. By having peers present their work, you can build credibility and trust with your audience. In addition, the presentations reinforce real deliverables that the audience will produce and can establish—or trigger discussions about—expectations for level of detail and format. What a great forum to openly share the challenges and successes your team experienced during the pilot!

You may be tempted to fill that training session with countless nuggets of helpful tips and tricks. Avoid drowning your team with too many details! If something seems slightly detailed or specific to you, it is likely way too detailed for everyone else to absorb on a first pass. Instead, track those deeper details (via slide footnotes, in a list, or other means) separately from the fundamentals. Such topics may even be great candidates for deeper dives in subsequent, specialized sessions.

Finally, beware that a presenter with deep experience and knowledge runs the risk of moving too fast for an audience. Slow down your presentation if necessary, and avoid software shortcuts and personal tricks that are lost on a crowd that's seeing concepts for the first time. In fact, consider turning off ALL keyboard shortcuts when demonstrating software, which will force you to walk step by step, menu by menu through each task. Beginners learn far better by the slower, sequential demonstration, and more proficient tool users can catalog which techniques they can simplify via their own shortcuts. For example, you can custom-fit a screenshot in a rectangular frame manually with a sophisticated sequence of actions, or fit it to a default (but sometimes less optimal) size using a shortcut. I'll perform the action manually step by step once, twice, or even three times, but mention the shortcut each time and even start using it later on.

Encourage Feedback

A component system may be a big change for some attendees, overlaying significant rigor and formality (such as component reference codes like G07v4) that designers may not be used to. Be sensitive to this transition, but also clearly communicate that some aspects require designers to adjust their understanding and approach for creating designs.

As you teach new topics and techniques, be open to—and even pause and overtly call for—feedback from attendees. Feedback is critical, for it's *their* system just as much as it's yours. If you are lecturing and demoing for an entire day, create an environment that encourages open discussion within the constraints of time and material you must cover. Set that tone early in the day and reserve time at key points throughout training for organic discussions to evolve. Give individuals an open forum to learn, question, and improve upon the baseline established by the library. While you can open the discussion with a brief set of slides or even an interactive demo, you can then facilitate a two-way conversation with learners to identify what's working and what's not. Some may not be comfortable challenging ideas in the open, so identify other opportunities for feedback, too: through moderated forums, through their manager, or best via personal conversation with library advocates.

In addition, lean on your participants to help identify and prioritize what they need to learn. During basic training, communicate what topics won't be covered, encourage attendees to suggest other topics, and even track topics of interest in the list as ideas occur. The list is a great takeaway so you can plan subsequent training, reinforce that you are responsive to their needs, and communicate that adoption occurs over time rather than during one training day.

Address Diverse Audiences

Encourage attendance at key training sessions from the many audiences that will be affected by the new system: from designers to engineers, QA to product managers, project managers to leaders of each organization.

For one team, we planned an agenda that fostered joint learning across disciplines when appropriate, focused on discipline-specific techniques and deliverables separately, and enabled executive participation (that was, not surprisingly, constrained to a brief visit). The training was divided into four segments over two days:

1. **Day 1, Morning: Introduction, Business & Team Objectives, and Library Review.** This first section was a high-level overview and demonstration, targeted at executives as well as designers and engineers. Everyone attended, and executives defined clear team objectives. Nothing beats executive sponsors espousing the virtues of reuse, collaboration, and the benefits of your team's investment in components. Their voice carries more gravitas and influence than that of a librarian.

2. **Day 1, Afternoon: Process, Deliverables, and Standard Documents.** After the executives left, all remaining team members focused on creating consistent documentation for strategy, design concepts, prototypes, and design specifications.

3. **Day 2, Morning: Wireframes**. Interaction designers dove deep into efficient techniques for creating wireframes, with light participation and attendance from visual designers looking to collaborate.

4. **Day 2, Afternoon: Comps.** Similarly, visual designers had a focused session on creating high-fidelity screen designs and documenting detailed typography, color, and more. Interaction design leads collaborated as well.

This plan enabled us to provide general training applicable to all stakeholders, but also dig into specialties that were the library's focus. For example, visual designers explored advanced features (such as Photoshop's layer comps) more deeply without boring or confusing other people like product managers and content strategists.

In general, limit demonstrations of complex techniques that are peripheral to the core tasks everyone performs. Sure, more proficient people appreciate keyboard shortcuts, time-saving techniques, and whiz-bang features that prove that the adopted tools are sufficiently powerful. Maybe you flavor your demos with hints of those tips. But do so in moderation, so as not to alienate or bore beginners. Keep the focus on necessary basics so that everyone walks away with a shared appreciation for the fundamentals.

Create Teachable Moments

Your training sessions should include useful and realistic demonstrations that attendees can easily map to their own practice and experiences. However, be ready for—or even plan out—opportunities for powerful, focused "teachable moments." Such moments may be an area of focus for a segment of training, such as how you can reuse a component (like a header) across pages and deliverables. Or perhaps it's a more conceptual segment that expands on core component-based benefits like consistency, collaboration, and reuse.

For teams managing larger sites, the site's homepage makes a good example to demonstrate how to think more broadly about reuse. A site's homepage is almost always the page that warrants the most focus and investment for a business. No page has more traffic, visibility, executive attention, and formal process built around maintenance, publishing, and controlling brand identity.

It's not surprising, then, that a homepage design is unique, different than every other page in a site's experience. A homepage often contains a unique collection of components that cannot be reused on any other page type. The layout is fixed, tightly governed, and so hard to change that it requires nearly herculean efforts across many teams to design, test, agree on, build, and launch a new version.

Take a look at Cisco.com's homepage in **Figure 14.1**. Beyond the header and footer shared with the rest of the site, the remaining components are specific to the Cisco.com homepage: an interactive billboard users can expand to reveal a "mini-site" of content, and a few tiles underneath that highlight audiences and promotions. These are designs that aren't reused elsewhere, so avoid adding these components to your library, right?

Actually, maybe the homepage is a *great* example of how to think differently about reuse. Depending on your site, here are some reasons you might want to consider including homepages in your component and page type libraries:

> **Internationalization.** Large corporations commonly deploy a new homepage design first in their home country, but then other "country site" owners look to emulate the design in the context of their country. Instead of a one-off page, now you could have upwards of 70 homepages, each managed by a different team!

Publishing. Homepages are subject to periodic publishing cycles, whether monthly, weekly, daily, hourly, or by the minute. By having reusable assets, publishers, producers, site strategists and other nondesigners can mock up a version to communicate requirements or content without engaging with the design or engineering team.

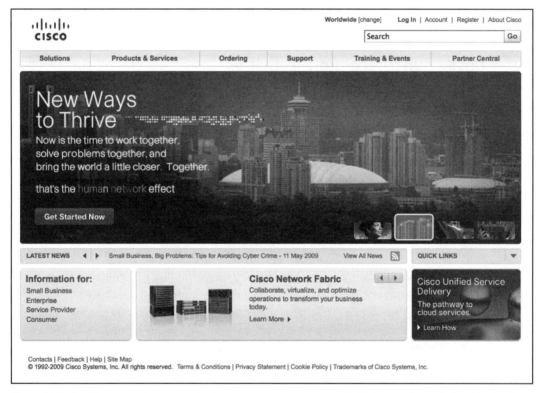

Figure 14.1 The Cisco.com homepage includes numerous components that are not—and should not—be used elsewhere in the Cisco.com experience.

Attention. The homepage gets a lot of attention. By componentizing it, you provide an example for your library that everyone is familiar with and can learn from.

Design Context. Designers themselves may want to illustrate a broad experience that includes the homepage as an integral part. While the homepage isn't subject to change, it may include critical links that are a starting point for a flow, section, or other area that is the subject of a design project. Therefore, having customizable homepage assets can be quite handy for storyboards, wireflows, and other design communications.

Remember, the purpose of talking about the homepage isn't to convince your team that the first page to componentize is the homepage. Far from it, actually. Instead, use the homepage as a way to reinforce that reuse can benefit in unexpected ways. There may be some great opportunities in your organization to use components to improve collaboration, spread of standards, and consistency—not just how to reuse a chunk across different types of pages.

Post-Launch Training Activities

Training sessions are powerful venues for teaching a large group about your component library. However, if you rely solely on a large training session as your only teaching opportunity, your library could drift into obscurity. Follow your training session with additional activities and reference materials to sustain, expand, and assess the library's success.

Publishing Tips and Techniques

Just as Chapter 12, "Administer," described how to periodically publish the library's design assets, you can also publish helpful tips, techniques, and case studies to interested stakeholders.

Email notifications of new components, training tips, and other new content about your library can be sufficient, if permitted within your organization and distributed to a wide audience. Blogs are another effective way for stakeholders to subscribe to content that reinforces how and why the library is a great resource, and online discussion forums can provide a permanent repository of challenges—and solutions—your team encounters, as described in Chapter 13, "Guide."

Coaching

Librarians and other experts on how to use the library should also reserve time in their schedule to provide individualized coaching to team members over time. New designers will need to be introduced to the principles, standards, and expectations of how to produce a design. While good documentation can enable them to learn the system on their own, one-on-one conversations with an expert can significantly enrich their understanding, too.

Maybe more importantly, a librarian should be on the lookout for opportunities to teach existing designers how to best use the system. Perhaps it's during a design review, or maybe it's during a collaborative design discussion. No matter what, advocates can educate peers about the library in the context of creating an optimal design solution.

If you rely on designers to seek out coaching, you'll be disappointed by the lack of interest. In many organizations where coaching was funded, advertised, and even emphasized, designers generally did not take advantage of the service. Maybe they were intimidated, or didn't see the value. But more likely, coaching is not at top of mind when a designer is deep in a project. If you find that your team lacks interest in coaching, try some structured techniques like office hours or a segment in a status meeting (ideally at the beginning but limited to ten minutes) to see if that helps. One team even scheduled monthly two-hour sessions built around reteaching core concepts, but intentionally left agendas more open to discussion and tangents that attendees could take to address their own challenges.

Selling Softly Through Audits

AUTHOR: **Robert Fabricant**

ROLE: **Vice President Creative, Frog Design**

Design systems are more about cultural change than creative practice. Owning a design system is not the same as using one. For internal design teams it can be a challenge to kick-start this process. You spend a lot of time talking about how great it would be to have a system to capture and distribute common patterns and components. But how do you get started, particularly when the initial investment of time and effort is not going to result in any new products, services, or revenue for your company?

As much as you would like to think that consistency and integrity are sufficient goals for investing in a modular design system, that is just not enough for most stakeholders. Business and particularly marketing managers are generally aware that there are inconsistencies in the way different features have been implemented across their site or online application. But addressing those inconsistencies is not at the top of their list of concerns. We have often found that there is a considerable difference between being aware that you have a problem and actually coming face to face with all the vivid details. Often, you can increase their motivation by showing them exactly how these inconsistencies are playing out in front of their customers.

UI audits of common features, like search or login, can be eye-opening—particularly to senior managers with broad responsibilities across the product portfolio. We worked with a client whose business consisted of a Web application that helped lawyers file documents in multiple state and local jurisdictions. One of the most important features of this application was a "Jurisdiction Picker"—a complex, faceted search mechanism for checking filing requirements in many different states at once. You might think they would have developed something this complex only once. But they had four or five different implementations within the same Web application. We did a UI audit and component prioritization workshop and insisted that senior managers attend to highlight these issues.

An audit will usually reveal some quick wins, such as nomenclature, for proving the value of a systematic approach and building your credibility. This is not the most creative work. And you may need to conduct this audit on your own time, which can be difficult if you are already loaded with design tasks. But it always pays off. Confronted with specific (and often absurd) examples, it becomes much harder for business managers to dispute the overall need for a design system.

If this isn't enough (or even if it is) you should also gather some anecdotal evidence from customers/consumers. This can be as simple as reaching out to family and friends and walking them through the site to get their feedback. It never ceases to amaze me how much management, especially senior executives, will be moved if they hear about these issues from a user instead of their design team. If your Web site or application serves a more specialized audience, there may be ways that you can gather feedback from sales or customer support people to provide you with similar evidence. Produce a simple report combining these anecdotes with your top line audit. Then figure out a way to circulate it to key influencers and you should see a change in attitude. Make sure to include specific quotes, images, and video of users whenever possible. Empathy is a surprisingly powerful force in business decisions when used effectively.

Additional Live Training and Workshops

You can also consider follow-up sessions on advanced topics after the team has used the system for a while. For example, you can follow basic training with deep dives into topics like prototyping, sketching, modular wireframes, or other topics that could relate to using components. One manager used the basic training session as a springboard for subsequent training on annotating wireframes and writing patterns. While the subsequent training didn't focus on components per se, the session's content, exercises, and objectives were very consistent with lessons learned during basic training.

Additional activities afford you an opportunity to gauge the pulse of how well your team is adopting a component-based mindset. Prior to the follow-up session on annotating wireframes, each attendee had to complete a homework assignment: Prepare one to two pages of annotations based on component artwork provided by the manager. The exercise was revealing. The good news: There were many similarities across submissions and the staff demonstrated clear growth since basic training. The bad news: Inconsistencies in style, tone, and structure abounded. Fortunately for everyone, the submissions created a platform for discussion, improvement, and shared empathy for engineers who consume deliverables that the team produced.

Video-based Training

Seeing is believing. While designers respond that a live training session is the best way to learn fundamentals, they also admit video-based training in the form of screen recordings is also very effective. Videos are a great way to do the following:

- ▶ Capture instruction and insight in a permanent, retrievable way.
- ▶ Watch training at your own pace, alongside your work.
- ▶ Augment essential topics taught during live training with special topics.
- ▶ Respond quickly to emerging, project-specific needs and other "how to" requests.
- ▶ Sharpen software tool skills in a way that you can replay as many times as you need to.
- ▶ Demonstrate tool features and tasks in a manner far more succinct than typing sequential instructions.
- ▶ Archive live training demos, which can be improved by tagging portions or chunking longer sessions into meaningful segments.

Videos are valuable not just as a reference for those who attend live training, but also as a viable first step for those who were unable to attend or joined the team after the training was conducted.

Figure 14.2 captures a frame from an EightShapes instructional video that demonstrates how to quickly create wireframe prototypes. Notice how the timeline includes tagged keyframes (such as Export to SWF & HTML), enabling a viewer to find topics of interest fast.

Figure 14.2 An EightShapes instructional video on how to create a clickable prototype using wireframe page designs. *(Courtesy of http://unify.eightshapes.com/)*

Starting a Collection

Include as many lessons from basic training as you can, and add special topics that you—or other participants—have identified. A getting-started series has proven invaluable for getting new designers up to speed on the library. Such a series could include videos that can be watched in less than a half hour, like the following:

1. **Getting Started:** Download the assets, explore the templates, and learn about basic reference materials.

2. **Browse the Library:** Visually explore, filter, and use available component design assets.

3. **Create a Wireframe from a Page Type:** Start by opening a template and placing a complete, component-based page type as a starting point.

4. **Create a Wireframe from Components:** Learn how to create a wireframe from scratch, one component chunk after another.

5. **Create a Wireframe Form from Scratch:** Use standard design elements like a checkbox and text field to build a form from the ground up.

6. **Create and Reuse Component Variations:** Create new variations of existing components or even a new component from scratch, and reuse it across numerous page designs.

7. **Build a Prototype:** Thread together numerous page designs and behaviors in building an interactive, clickable prototype.

8. **Publish a Deliverable Document:** Lay out and annotate page and component designs in a document, and publish the file as a PDF.

Tips for creating an effective library of video-based training include the following:

Keep it short and sweet. Users appreciate bite-size chunks that comprehensively address a topic but don't meander on and on about details that aren't as important. Most effective videos I've produced run no more than five minutes, and some may be even less than a minute.

Maximize access. Unfortunately, most companies don't have robust applications for you to publish videos internally. As an alternative, you can look to sites like youtube.com or viddler.com to create channels for your video-based training. If you need to broaden distribution but limit access to people in your company, you can share secret URLs to each video so you can limit training to only those requiring access.

Plan your demonstration. In live demos, audiences can forgive you for meandering from time to time. Not so in video-based training: You've got to be specific, clear, and on message when recording a piece. Plan what you'll cover before hitting the record button (such as via an outline of key points and prepared assets), practice, and reshoot until you get it right.

Produce and edit. Some video topics may not be as popular or watched as frequently, and therefore don't warrant more than a single take. But for essential topics—such as getting started, create a wireframe, or create a prototype—consider recording separate clips, editing them together, adding titles and subtitles, and even recording a voiceover separately.

Publish what you've got. You can't produce and edit a large collection all at once, so communicate to stakeholders what videos are available now, and which are coming soon, and enable them to make requests, too.

The assets you build, the sessions you conduct, the training materials you prepare, and the guidelines you write all aim to maximize the adoption of component-based techniques by your organization. No one, from designers to engineers to stakeholders, will learn everything there is to know about a component library in one sitting. Therefore, a variety of options will foster more engagement at all levels, both corporate and personal. Ultimately, prepare your team to embed component-based techniques into the design and development of a user experience. Integrating these techniques into your process is the subject of the next, and final, chapter.

15

INTEGRATE

You can't just build a library, distribute it to everyone, and expect that they'll use it effectively. Communicating how components are created and change over time is fundamental to the success of your library.

This chapter dives into how components can impact process, including how you do the following:

- ▶ Plan how the library impacts you and your process.
- ▶ Distinguish between projects that reuse existing design versus those that require new, customized work.
- ▶ Ensure that you can start projects quickly and independently.
- ▶ Design, document, and develop solutions using components.
- ▶ Review proposed designs and code in the context of the library.
- ▶ Choose when, how, and for whom to standardize.

Plan

Designers will be more likely to buy in to using the library if they understand exactly how it impacts them. They'll need to adapt to a new process, and you'll need to communicate how much freedom they'll have to solve their design problems. When I've interviewed designers, they've consistently expressed concern over the independence and freedom they want to sustain and how that affects the quality of their work.

When discussing how your component library affects your team's workflow, answer questions like these:

▶ How does this fit in my process for designing (or engineering, publishing, ...)?

▶ Where do I get the library, and how do I come up to speed quickly?

▶ Must my design only use library components, or can I create my own?

▶ How much will the library speed me up—or slow me down?

▶ Do I need to coordinate with more people to get my work done?

▶ Who owns the library? How much influence do I have in changing it?

A Spectrum of Creativity

A component library can impact projects in simple or sophisticated ways. Consider the simple case: Designers use a library of reusable assets to more quickly create better designs. That may be as simple as downloading a library, learning how to use the tools and assets, and producing new screen designs. Producing designs faster? Great, goal achieved, end of story. For some teams, that's the end of the line.

On the other hand, most organizations investing in a component library plan for deeper impacts to their process. With a component library at your disposal, you can begin to transform how designs are created and experiences are standardized. One useful way to distinguish projects that use components is along a spectrum of reuse versus invention: those that use packaged, prefabricated components and page types ("template" or "turnkey" efforts) versus those that require significant new, custom design work.

Design Templates

Sometimes your goal is to create and package a design as a prefabricated collection of page and component templates that other designers and teams can use again and again. Teams refer to these packages by a variety of names, like "template-based" or "turnkey" solutions. Design templates are built by engineers, but also used by publishers, producers, strategists, writers, and design production staff (producing artwork over and over) to repeatedly publish content once the design is deployed.

Consider a Web design team at a big company with a large, diverse product catalog. In order to simplify publishing content about new and updated products, they invested significant effort to create product page templates, components, and guidelines. For each launch, they wanted to empower a producer to choose the right page template, work with stakeholders and writers to compose content, and publish the solution independently.

These templates used components from the library. Page types were based entirely on components for billboards, videos, feature lists, data tables, sidebar promos, contact widgets, and more. Designers worked hard to define and document both pages *and* components, and layered editorial instruction page by page using guidelines on how to employ each component in context.

With templates in hand, each launch required far less participation from design staff. Surely, they remained available for questions and quick reviews of proposed implementations. However, the templates eliminated the need to deeply involve designers throughout content production and deployment. Plus, since page types were based on library components, templates evolved in lockstep with the design system in a fluid, predictable way.

You're Soaking in It… Relax

AUTHOR: **Chris Haaga**

ROLE: **Director of Web Experience Design, Sun.com**

There's always room for extension and evolution of the component library. Design or publishing teams will discover a content or functional requirement for which we don't have an existing solution and we have to jump in and investigate the problem. To ensure compatibility, we develop new designs with an eye on our existing conventions. We also look ahead to anticipate the implications of a new design. How flexible does it need to be? How might it break? Does this design represent a leap that should impact how we think about designing and building things?

We currently have about 150 core components in use. Most of them have two to three versions to accommodate variation in content or function. All are essentially interoperable, with each component having been designed with consideration to relative scale, weight, color, behavior, and compatibility with other components, as well as broader architecture and design principles.

While this component-level action is thoroughly interesting to the Web development team, our partners on the business side can't really relate. Components are parts and they want something more complete. They need page designs. So, back to the reason we have components: to build pages.

The Sun.com design team operates with the notion that approximately 80 percent of the site can be highly templated and successfully meet everyone's needs, from the business to experience design and publishing teams to our customers. The other 20 percent is referred to as "custom" and consists of unique page designs supporting specialized content and/or functional needs, such as the homepage. "Custom" is also used to characterize new page designs that are in a trial state. New designs are often tested on the live site and refined before being documented and propagated as a formal template.

There's a spiraling aspect to the template work; as we close in on the 80 percent, it begins to look as if 90 percent might be attainable. Meanwhile, cracks are forming on the older templates and we need to upgrade or overhaul those page designs to improve performance, meet new requirements, or just get them feeling fresh again.

Speaking of fresh, we're also invited from time to time to apply Executive Centered Design principles to a project. Such projects usually begin with a pronouncement that our bag of tricks doesn't contain enough magic to meet the needs of a new product/program/initiative. Time is usually tight and expectations are high. But that's OK, because we have our wits and our components. That's right, we still go to the bag. And we're usually successful at rapidly developing something new and cool by relying on our components as foundation and conjuring up one or two smartly con-ceived, well-placed elements that provide a wow factor without having to abandon our system. We end up getting points for letting go and breaking rules. And when we get back to the shop, we document the new things and drop them in the bag.

When more typical requests come in that have to do with creating a new page, among the first things we want to know is, do we have a solution ready that meets that need? If the answer is yes, we jump into a workflow we refer to as "turnkey." In that mode we keep the team small and we operate with a production-oriented attitude. If we don't have a ready-made solution, we initiate a custom design proj-ect and go through a fairly typical Web development workflow. The system is never complete. The business changes, the Web evolves, customers react, and our under-standing grows. Components provide a way of thinking and a particularly useful vocabulary in our ongoing design discussion.

Custom Designs

Not every project results in the predictable reuse of existing components. Instead, many projects—and most of a design team's efforts—involve custom work to extend a design system. Custom design work means new components. Usually, the bigger the project, the more new components you should plan for.

Hold on a second. Didn't you create a component library so you don't have to design, document, and build new components with each project? Absolutely. But the library only accounts for problems you've solved already.

Therefore, it's important to be willing to embrace new designs. During project planning and design discovery activities, library advocates must be aware of emerging design needs. At that point, high-level brainstorming begins to suggest existing components just as much as needs for new variations and even components overall. During those early formative stages, the team should recognize, prioritize, and plan for new components.

In fact, I need look no further than a design technologist I work with who manages the component library I depend on for my own design work. He recently joked that I'm "the guy that's writing a book on modular components who comes up with new components with every project." We work together often, and early in a project I'll point out likely new components and later on will concretely list proposed components and variations.

The reality is that to solve new problems, you often need new components. So conversations must acknowledge the need for custom designs. Our solution to a given problem balances many factors: possible reuse, complexity, competing project priorities, available time and deadlines, and so much more.

The most important point: We communicate. Our instant messages are fast and furious, opinionated at times, but always recognizing the role of the library. In that context, I'm the designer and he's the librarian *and* design technologist building code. Our fluid communication and level of mutual comfort may not be typical of most designers using a component library for the first, second, or even third project.

In another situation, a director of user experience was very cognizant of the distributed teams that used the common component library, and the limited access to (or even knowledge of how to access) the librarian prevented that kind of constant, familiar exchange. Therefore, he and his team worked hard to integrate component activities and reviews into existing steps of their experience design and development process, as shown in **Figure 15.1**.

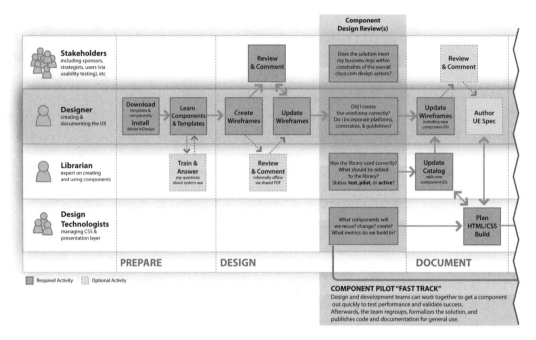

Figure 15.1 A design and development process from a component point of view. The diagram doesn't seek to illustrate the vast complexities, iterations, tasks, and milestones of a thorough, large-scale project plan.

Integrating component activities into your process involves a number of activities from the start to finish of a project, including the following:

Prepare. Make sure your design staff is set up to understand and apply components, acquire the standardized templates and library assets, and learn how to use the system.

Design and Document. Component libraries can strongly influence how you construct and detail an experience design, and use the library as a platform for further innovation to create new solutions with new components.

Develop. Engineering and testing teams can use components as a basis for planning, architecting, building, and deploying their work.

Standardize. Once new components emerge, teams must work together to organize and publish design assets, guidelines, and code libraries.

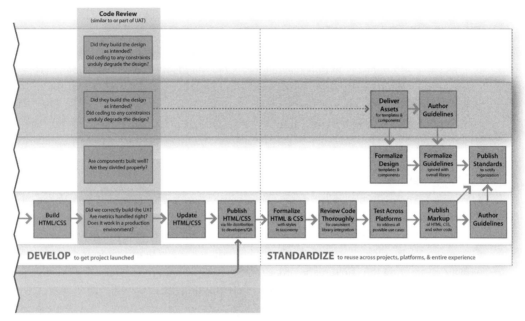

Instead, it illustrates some of the basic impacts and important activities involved in integrating a component library into your process. (*Created with the Cisco.com User Experience Team. Used with permission.*)

The remainder of this chapter drills deeper into some of these key activities to help you consider possible impacts to your process. With these activities in mind, you can plan how to communicate similar methods and activities to your teams as you roll out your own library.

Prepare

You can't create a component library and expect all designers to simply pick up the assets and run with them. Additionally, even if you set aside time to facilitate formal training, not everyone will be able to come and new designers are sure to come aboard after the training anyway.

Therefore, you'll need to equip designers with the tools, assets, and knowledge they need to learn the system fast, and acclimate to using the system fast, too. A startup process should empower designers to prepare independently as much as possible. Key questions they always ask include the following:

What is this stuff?

First and foremost, you'll need to have a quick, effective story about what the library is. This can't be a deep set of only partially readable Microsoft PowerPoint slides that you used for a big training session. Instead, you need that set of defining materials that a designer can review independently to understand components, your library, your templates and asset libraries, and the fundamentals of how to apply them during design activities.

How do I get it?

Materials are going to be available somehow, somewhere, optimally via a Web-based download or shared drive. You'll want to have a consistent, easy-to-remember path for everyone to retrieve whatever materials you have, as explained in the Publishing section of Chapter 12, "Administer." Hopefully it's not just you but many teammates and advocates who are promoting the convenient URL or folder to download the system. On the flip side, it's sometimes good to have a central person distributing the library assets to interested parties. That way, you can be aware of new teams adopting the system and new projects to which it's being applied, before designers jump in head first without background they might need.

How does it work?

If your design assets are distributed as a ZIP file, you'll need to have some useful training materials and documentation so that designers can learn about the system. Chapter 14, "Adopt," covers many of these alternatives, so you'll want to clearly outline the basics on how to get started with the following:

- ▶ Getting Started and Users Guide materials, whether Web- or document-based
- ▶ Workflow descriptions that define expectations and process at a high level, and prepare designers for component-specific impacts and reviews
- ▶ Sample deliverables that communicate depth, style, fidelity, and dos and don'ts based on past projects and anticipated use
- ▶ Video-based training, such as a series of videos that demonstrate enough of the basics so that designers can feel confident and be productive
- ▶ Librarian-facilitated training, whether via formal sessions, informal conversations, or even quick questions via email or instant message

Design and Document

During design projects, components are very effective starting points for assembling known—and unchanging—portions of page designs. They enable a designer to consistently and quickly frame a solution into which they create their custom design work.

To be successful, a designer should be familiar with the common page layouts, grids, basic styles and page hierarchy, and other aspects of a design system, whether the system is supported by a component library or not. However, if designers understand the design system and basics of the component library, then set them loose. Encourage and empower them to come up with creative but realistic solutions.

Equipped with a library of reusable assets, designers need help finding the right components. An iterative design process may yield teachable moments where a librarian can quickly review designs and gently nudge the designer toward established solutions in the library.

However, librarians and other experts shouldn't constantly "look over the shoulder" of designers during their iterative design process, pointing out all the "mistakes" the designer is making. Instead, that's what a component design review is for.

The Component Design Review

In many projects, designers propose new components whether they know it or not. Some new component candidates are entirely viable and necessary. Others may be duplicates of—or very similar to—components that already exist.

A component design review is a great way to take a look at a design solution from the perspective of components, modular thinking, reuse, and impacts to the library. The review usually occurs near the end of a design cycle once a solution is starting to gel. The discussion may be an explicit meeting (as with some teams that have it as a formal milestone) or an implicit part of how designers formalize their work with feedback from engineers, the component librarian, and other team members.

Before the Review

As a project nears the component review, the team should ensure that the design has stabilized considerably. As you begin to nail down your design and prepare for the review, you should do the following:

▶ Schedule the component review with enough lead time to ensure participation from key engineers and the librarian.

- Reconcile emerging designs with the component library, replacing proposed elements with existing components when new designs aren't justified.

- Annotate designs (wireframes or comps) with component markers.

- Highlight and clearly list all new components across page designs so that engineers and the librarian can quickly scan designs and assess changes.

During the Review

The component design review is where you review designs, discuss alternatives, and prioritize components to build and add to the library. During the meeting, the design team must do the following:

- Communicate the solution across page types, demonstrating how components fit and vary.

- Define components and assess their value based on scale of reuse, sophistication, and other themes outlined in Chapter 8, "Discover."

- Align components with metrics, accessibility, and other team standards.

- Identify known gaps that remain.

After the Review

Based on review outcomes, designers, engineers, and the component librarian should reach a consensus on design decisions, tradeoffs, and the direction of the project. This can spawn activities like the following:

- Designers revising their work as necessary, with updated documentation and relevant component-specific annotations

- Librarians adding new components, variations, and examples to the component catalog, assigning reference codes (such as G01v1) if you use them, and distributing library impacts to project participants

---

 TIP   Create a handy visual reference for engineers and designers by augmenting your component library summary with component variations screenshots, using the component code as the file name. You may even use these screenshots to create wireframe component assets later.

- Librarians identifying artwork contributors and guideline authors

- Engineers and design technologists launching technical analysis, planning, and even prototyping

What Happens to Visual Design?

Creating a component library often means solidifying and even codifying a design system: typography, grids, layouts, color palettes, and more. Therefore, when your process leverages a component library, you can use wireframes and other lower-fidelity deliverables to communicate design to engineers, and rely on established visual style instead of creating pixel-perfect comps.

Therefore, take advantage of potential efficiencies and avoid recreating full-page comps and detailed, annotated redlines for where you've got established components and visual conventions. Teach your team to depend on CSS, comps in the library, and other visual standards instead. Not only will you stop wasting time unnecessarily recreating comps, but you'll also avoid subtle inconsistencies that arise when, invariably, designers start nudging elements in ways that drift from the visual system and degrade consistency—with little or no incremental business value.

Does that mean that you can now remove a visual designer from your project team? Hardly. You should always involve graphic design experts with a deep, authoritative knowledge of color, grids, layout, typography, and other aspects of the design system. They are an important—maybe the most important—reviewer of wireframes and other lower fidelity designs to ensure that proposed solutions align with system principles. Trust them. They've got a trained eye to see if a proposed use of existing components and elements (such as a long header label, lengthy paragraph, or assortment of widgets) requires more thought to ensure that the design works.

Comps are vital for custom work and new component designs. However, the more systematic your design system, the more you'll be able to make the visual design process smoother and quicker for template-based efforts. For some projects, the visual design step can transform from a rigorous process of creating detailed comps to more of a thoughtful review. This will enable your visual designers to focus on where their expertise matters most: custom design work that'll "move the needle" and push the boundaries and vitality of the overall design system.

Develop

Following a period of collaboration between designers and engineers, the engineering team will begin to build their solution out. At some point, early drafts will give way to more functional and precise versions that are mature enough for team members—designers and stakeholders alike—to review how the solution is emerging.

The Component Code Review

Analogous to the component design review described earlier, the engineering team can facilitate a component-centric code review to obtain feedback and final inputs before completing their work.

Before the Meeting

The component code review should occur after some period of building the necessary markup, styles, and behaviors of the solution. Therefore, engineers should prepare a collection of built page layouts or even prefabricated scenarios to succinctly walk through. They should also be prepared to highlight specific implementation details (accessibility, metrics, and more) as well.

During the Meeting

Engineers will typically facilitate a walkthrough of screens they've produced, whether they are static HTML prototypes that reflect the visual design or functional systems that include more sophisticated behaviors and states.

The review provides a platform for different roles to ensure that the work is nearing a solution that meets their needs. **Table 15.1** reflects common questions asked by different roles.

Table 15.1. Common Questions Asked During a Component Code Review

Role	Questions for a Code Review
Stakeholders	Does the design still meet my business needs? Did the build process result in any constraints or tradeoffs that degrade functionality and hamper business objectives? Does the build integrate metrics correctly?
Designers	Does the design still meet my business objectives? Did I consider all necessary component variations? Are there variations I need to document, render, or ask them to adjust?
Engineers	Does the build realize the design solution as expected? Have we accounted for all necessary variations? Is the build flexible enough to be reused elsewhere? Do the components meet accessibility and code standards?
Librarian	Are the components built in a way that aligns how we chunked them earlier? Will we be able to reuse these parts for other projects? Does the implementation shift how we write guidelines and deploy reusable assets?

Role	Questions for a Code Review
Publisher	Can I reuse these designs and/or code chunks effectively on subsequent projects?
	Does the build handle content variations in copy, images, and messaging, including internationalization concerns?

Code reviews can often degenerate into detailed pixel pushing in which designers home in on imprecise layouts and identify specific changes. Make no mistake—this is the time to do just that, and ensure that an accurate design is implemented. However, if the group is larger and the pixel pushing is extensive, then offload those discussions to smaller, even paired, discussions between designers and engineers.

After the Meeting

Depending on the scale of changes and additional design work necessary, the team may reconvene for another code review or two. However, once the engineering and testing teams have enough to finish and deploy the experience, the librarians and designers can begin focusing on how to get relevant components into the library as standard, generalized solutions.

Standardize

Adding a component to a library takes time. To standardize a component could mean adding it to a catalog, giving it a reference code, creating design assets like a wireframe symbol or comp sample, writing guidelines, and building and validating HTML and CSS markup.

When do you standardize something? When your organization is going to benefit from having reference numbers, design symbols, guidelines, or code at its disposal. Not a moment before.

The degree and breadth to which you standardize something depends on your library's base of users. If your team is going to value design assets but won't take the time to read guidelines, then don't author guidelines. If your organization thirsts for instructions on how to apply a component in their strategy and publishing, but your designers won't use the components in future designs, then author guidelines and skip building design assets.

Make the library fit into the way you want to reuse solved design problems. Once aspects of a designed and engineered experience stabilize, you can initiate activities to standardize it. Sometimes, it's near the end of a design cycle. Other times, as a project nears launch.

Maybe it's not even until the components have been live for some time. It really depends on the stability of the assets and your interest in teaching others and proliferating assets throughout your organization.

Therefore, structure post-project activities to standardize what you need, including the following:

Create Design Assets. As described in Chapter 11, "Build," incorporate new component designs into your library of design assets once the design has stabilized.

Write Guidelines. Chapter 13, "Guide," describes guidelines that you and your team can compose to promote consistent usage of components over time.

Formalize Code. As you work to get the code just right for the release, go the extra mile to incorporate HTML, CSS, JavaScript, and image assets into your generalized library.

Pilot, then Generalize. Temper initial investments in building code and guidelines by piloting a solution more quickly. Once the solution proves effective, then circle back to formalize code across platforms, distribute design assets, and compose guidelines for standard application.

Chapter 12, "Administer," describes aspects of publishing and notifying the team about component library updates. Be sure to consider how to best blend that with ongoing project workflows and resource allocations.

Components are a platform for incorporating reusable, standard design solutions across a range of design, development, and publishing projects. The standards you create should be a library of the people, by the people, and for the people. Those people may be the design or engineering teams, seeking to incorporate efficiencies and standards into their own, internal team practices.

Or the library's influence may be meant to spread across disciplines, from content strategists to product managers, from publishers and writers to testers and even more distant brand, marketing, and executive groups. As the library spreads, it transforms from a design or code resource into a baseline and culture that transcends thinking about "standards" and becomes more a way to do business. While administration may remain the purview of librarians on a design or development team, the value, focus, and library design widens to accommodate many teams, practices, and business objectives.

In the end, components present an opportunity for you to create a more consistent, predictable, and learnable user experience. Standard component treatments help you reapply solved, effective design solutions over and over. As a result, things like consistency and usability increase. And, perhaps, so does customer satisfaction and brand loyalty. Ultimately, it's those most important people—the actual users of your site—that the library can benefit the most.

Index

B

Unified Modeling Language: Systems Analysis, Design and Development Issues

Keng Siau
University of Nebraska-Lincoln, USA

Terry Halpin
Microsoft Corporation, USA

IDEA GROUP PUBLISHING
Hershey • London • Melbourne • Singapore

Acquisition Editor:	Mehdi Khosrowpour
Managing Editor:	Jan Travers
Development Editor:	Michele Rossi
Copy Editor:	Maria Boyer
Typesetter:	Tamara Gillis
Cover Design:	Deb Andree
Printed at:	Sheridan Books

Published in the United States of America by
    Idea Group Publishing
    1331 E. Chocolate Avenue
    Hershey PA 17033-1117
    Tel: 717-533-8845
    Fax: 717-533-8661
    E-mail: cust@idea-group.com
    Web site: http://www.idea-group.com

and in the United Kingdom by
    Idea Group Publishing
    3 Henrietta Street
    Covent Garden
    London WC2E 8LU
    Tel: 44 20 7240 0856
    Fax: 44 20 7379 3313
    Web site: http://www.eurospan.co.uk

Library of Congress Cataloging-in-Publication Data

Siau, Keng, 1964-
    Unified modeling language : systems analysis, design and development issues / Keng Siau, Terry Halpin.
      p. cm.
    ISBN 1-930708-05-X (pbk.)
     1. Object-oriented methods (Computer science) 2. Computer software--Development. 3. UML (Computer science) I. Halpin, T.A. II. Title

QA76.9.O35 S54 2001
005.1'17--dc21
                                                     00-066955

British Cataloguing in Publication Data
A Cataloguing in Publication record for this book is available from the British Library.